HERITAGE STUDIES 5

Third Edition

bju press®

Greenville, South Carolina

NOTE: The fact that materials produced by other publishers may be referred to in this volume does not constitute an endorsement of the content or theological position of materials produced by such publishers. Any references and ancillary materials are listed as an aid to the student or the teacher and in an attempt to maintain the accepted academic standards of the publishing industry.

HERITAGE STUDIES 5
Third Edition

Coordinating Author
Peggy S. Alier

Authors
James R. Davis
Annittia Jackson
Lori Weir
Debra White

Second Edition Authors
Eileen M. Berry
Dawn L. Watkins

Project Editor
Maria Soria

Project Manager
Donald Simmons

Consultants
Dennis Bollinger
Dennis Peterson
Jamie Swingle
Sherri Vick

Bible Integration
Bryan Smith

Page Layout
Bonnijean Marley
Northstar Creative

Cover Design
Cathryn Pratt

Designers
Duane Nichols
Cathryn Pratt
Dan VanLeeuwen

Photo Acquisition
Carla Thomas

Illustrators
John Cunningham
Courtney Godbey
Preston Gravely
Jennifer Lowry
Duane Nichols
Dave Schuppert

Produced in cooperation with the Bob Jones University School of Education and Bob Jones Elementary School.

Photo credits appear on pages 343–46.

"Exposure" by Wilfred Owen, from THE COLLECTED POEMS OF WILFRED OWEN, copyright ©1963 by Chatto & Windus, Ltd. Reprinted by permission of New Directions Publishing Corp. (p. 55)

"Their Finest Hour" by Winston Churchill. Reproduced with permission of Curtis Brown Ltd, London on behalf of the Estate of Winston Churchill. Copyright © Winston S. Churchill. (p. 205)

© 2010 BJU Press
Greenville, South Carolina 29614
First Edition © 1985 BJU Press
Second Edition © 1998, 1999 BJU Press

Printed in the United States of America

ISBN 978-1-59166-570-0

15   14   13   12   11   10   9   8   7   6   5

Our Commitment. Your Confidence.

Creative
Updated look. Colorful, interesting pages.

Credible
Thorough research. Solid content.

Christian
Nothing to conflict with Truth. Everything to support it.

Contents

Themes of *Heritage Studies 5*

 Geography—The study of the earth's surface and how it is used

 American History—The study of America's past

 Government—The political system for ruling a country

 Economics—The study of how people use resources to meet their needs

 World History—The study of the past of the countries of the world

 Culture—The way of life of a group of people

Chapter 1

Fences Seen and Unseen

In Proverbs 3:19 we read, "The Lord by wisdom hath founded the earth; by understanding hath he established the heavens." Bible verses such as this one remind us that God created our world. Every mountain and valley is exactly where God wanted it to be. Our planet did not "just happen." As we look at the earth's amazing design and provisions for life, our hearts should praise the Creator.

The Bible tells us that God made the earth to be our home. He supplied it with abundant resources for us to use and to enjoy. Every day we are learning more about the earth and its resources. We use this knowledge to help us provide for our physical needs and to build great civilizations. Our challenge is to use the earth's resources wisely and in a way that honors the Creator.

"For thus saith the Lord that created the heavens; God himself that formed the earth and made it; he hath established it, he created it not in vain, he formed it to be inhabited: I am the Lord; and there is none else."

Isaiah 45:18

What Is Geography?

History and geography both help us understand the world around us. History is the study of *the past*. **Geography** is the study of *place*. Geography helps us learn not only where places are but also how they differ and why.

The word *geography* comes from two words. *Geo-* means "earth" and *-graphy* means "written descriptions." A basic tool in studying geography is a map. Maps represent places on earth. Maps are what men "write" to show what they know about the earth. The art of making maps is called **cartography**. In this word, *carto-* means "map," and *-graphy* means "writing." A mapmaker is called a **cartographer**.

geo · graphy
"earth" · "written descriptions"

carto · graphy
"map" · "writing"

3

A **geographer** is a scientist who studies the earth. Geographers who do not believe that God is the Creator can still discover the wonders of the earth. However, they will miss the wonderful testimony of God in nature. They may also draw some incorrect conclusions. One such conclusion may be that evolution is a fact. If a geographer believes this, then his estimation of time will be off by millions of years. How much better it is to say with the psalmist, "I will speak of the glorious honour of thy majesty, and of thy wondrous works" (Psalm 145:5). God's creation testifies of His existence.

Studying the Earth

Grab your pencil! Let's join Gus and learn about globes and maps.

Early mapmakers made maps for kings. The kings used maps to plan wars, open trade routes, and build new cities. The earliest map that we have is on a clay tablet and shows rivers and mountains.

Globes

The first geographer was a Greek mathematician named Eratosthenes (ER uh TAHS thuh NEEZ). At a time when most scientists believed the world was flat, Eratosthenes believed the world was a sphere. Look at the old map made by Eratosthenes. What do you know about the world that he did not?

Before spacecraft could take pictures of the earth, people discovered land shapes by sailing around them. Many explorers helped add to our knowledge of the world's shape. Some sailed around the tip of Africa. Some sailed to the New World. And some sailed around South America.

Since the earth is a sphere, a globe represents the earth most correctly. One of the first globes ever made was the handiwork of Martin

Behaim of Germany in 1492. Globes have been made in many different sizes. In 1999, one particular globe called Eartha was added to the *Guinness Book of World Records*. The book's editors named Eartha as the world's largest rotating globe. It measures 41.5 feet in diameter and fills a three-story room in Yarmouth, Maine.

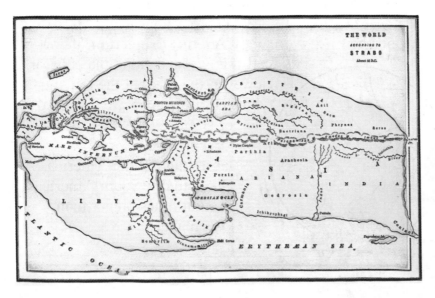

This map shows how Eratosthenes thought the world looked.

Flat Maps

Have you ever taken a ball or an orange peel and flattened it? What happens to the sphere shape when you press on it? The same problem happens when you flatten the sphere shape of the earth. Many areas on a flat map appear to be a different shape or size than they really are. These areas are **distortions** and do not accurately show the earth as it really is. It is impossible to take information from a sphere and make a flat map from it without cutting or stretching the original shape. Cartographers have been struggling with this problem for centuries.

A flat map may not represent the earth's shape or surface as accurately as a globe does. But flat maps can show more details. Imagine how large a globe would have to be to show all the

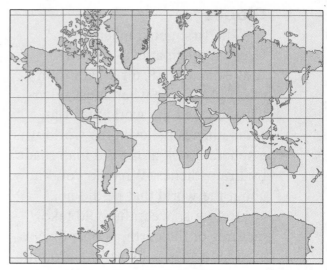

Mercator Projection

streets in your state. Flat maps are also easy to carry and store.

Map Projections

Any method that cartographers use to show the earth's round surface on a flat map is called a **map projection**. Each map projection has distortions. One of the most common projections is the **Mercator** (MUR KAY tur) **Projection**. It correctly shows land along the equator. However, the areas at the top and bottom of the map are distorted or stretched. On this map, Greenland appears to be larger than South America. But actually, South America is eight times bigger than Greenland.

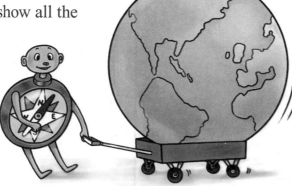

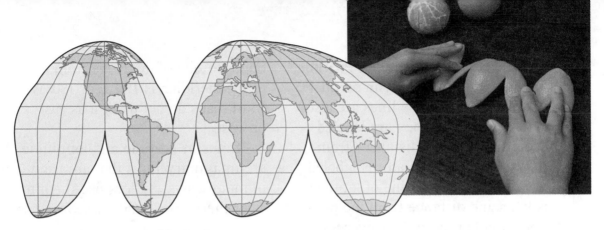

Goode's Interrupted Projection

Another common projection is **Goode's Interrupted Projection**. This projection cuts and flattens the earth like an orange peel. The map remains in one piece, but the earth is "interrupted" with gaps or cuts. The shapes and sizes of landmasses are fairly accurate. But this projection distorts distances and all north to south directions.

Latitude and Longitude

Imagine one child asking another, "What's the difference between a globe and the earth?"

"I don't know," the other replies. "What?"

"Well," says the first child, "the real earth isn't labeled!"

A globe shows you what the earth's shape and surface are like. But there are some things on a globe that are not on the real earth. The earth does not have actual lines on it the way a globe does. Nor does the earth have dots and stars showing cities, or lines dividing countries.

Such marks help us read maps and globes more efficiently. These marks also help people everywhere read maps in the same ways, whether they speak Chinese, English, or Spanish. Knowing how to read a map or a globe is sometimes as important as knowing how to read a book.

A century after Eratosthenes drew his map, a Greek philosopher named Hipparchus (hih PAHR kus) made it easier to locate places on a map. He added lines in an even pattern to his map. We still use these lines today. The center line wraps around the widest part of the earth. It is like a great belt that divides the earth into top and bottom halves. This belt is an imaginary line called the **equator**. The halves it forms are called the Northern Hemisphere and the Southern Hemisphere.

The equator is a **line of latitude**. Other lines of latitude run parallel to the equator. These lines are also called *parallels*. They are labeled according to their distances from the equator. The equator is labeled at 0° latitude. Each line of latitude is the same distance from the next line. None of these lines ever touch each other. Parallels that are north of the equator are in the Northern Hemisphere and are labeled *N*. Parallels that are south of the equator are in the Southern Hemisphere and are labeled *S*. Look at the map. The lines of latitude going through the United States are 45°N and 30°N.

Lines also run north and south on maps. A line that circles a globe north to south is called a **line of longitude** or a *meridian*. These lines are not parallel. They are far apart at the equator but touch at the North and South Poles.

The meridian labeled 0° longitude is the **prime meridian**. It divides the Eastern and Western Hemispheres. Meridians east of the prime meridian are in the Eastern Hemisphere and are labeled *E*. Meridians west of the prime meridian are in the Western Hemisphere and are labeled *W*. The meridian on the opposite side of the globe from the prime meridian is 180°E or 180°W. Most maps do not mark it as east or west.

Lines of latitude and longitude are imaginary lines that are used in many ways. Sailors use them to steer their ships, and surveyors use

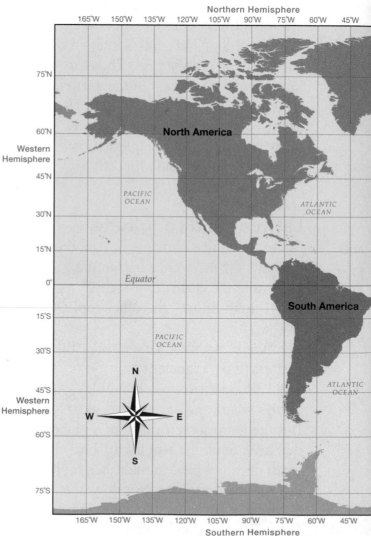

8

them to find and set boundaries for land properties.

Dividing the Earth

The earth can be divided in different ways. These divisions help geographers study and compare the earth's resources and its people.

Continents and Oceans

Perhaps the most obvious division of the earth's surface is by its landmasses and oceans. Most geographers refer to the seven large landmasses as **continents**. The largest is Asia. It is connected to Europe. Some geographers combine these two into one large continent called Eurasia. The other continents are North America, South America, Africa, Australia, and Antarctica.

A world map also shows four **oceans** or large bodies of water. They are the Atlantic, Arctic, Indian, and Pacific Oceans.

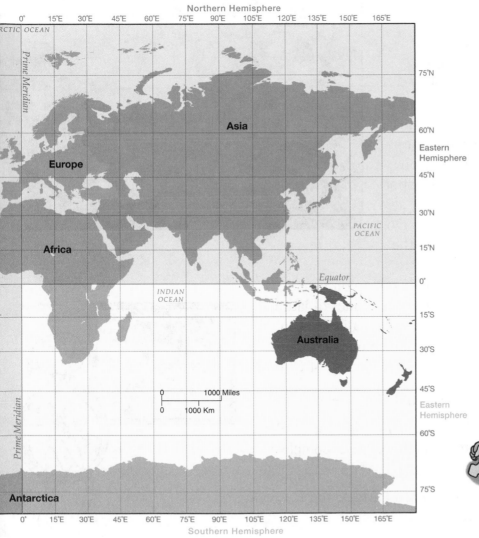

Measuring with Latitude and Longitude

The lines of longitude and latitude form a **grid**. A grid helps you use the lines of longitude and latitude to locate any place on a map or globe. Reading a grid on a map is much like reading a graph.

Look at the *World: Physical* map on pages 316 to 317. Find the equator and the prime meridian. Put one finger on each line. Follow the lines to the spot where they meet. They meet at 0° latitude and 0° longitude. Do the lines meet on land or in the ocean?

Look at the *World: Political* map on pages 316 to 317. Put a finger on each of these lines of latitude and longitude: 30°N, 120°E. Follow the lines to the spot where they meet. In which country do these lines intersect? Did you find the country of China?

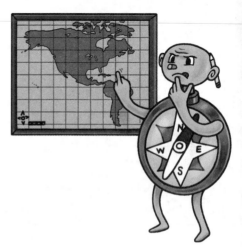

1. Get your Activity Manual and a pencil.

2. Using maps in the Student Text and your knowledge of latitude and longitude, complete the Activity Manual page.

3. After you have completed Parts A and B, work with a partner to complete Section C.

Political Boundaries

A **political map** shows the man-made boundaries around countries. Borders between the countries are called **political boundaries**. These boundaries show the land belonging to the government of each country.

A country's borders can change rapidly or stay the same for hundreds of years. Different events can cause a boundary to change. A war or treaty

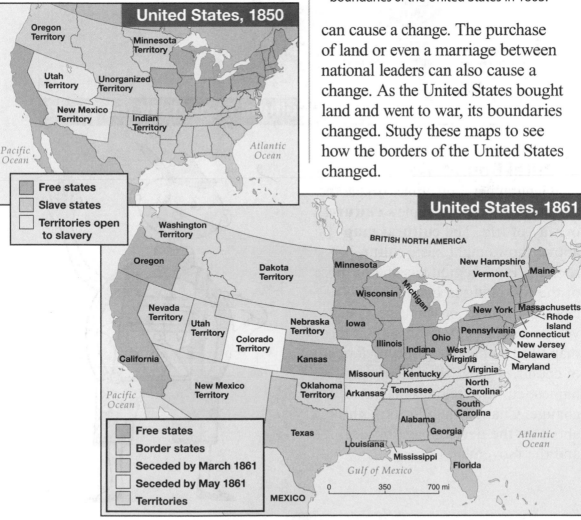

United States, 1803

The purchase of land changed the political boundaries of the United States in 1803.

can cause a change. The purchase of land or even a marriage between national leaders can also cause a change. As the United States bought land and went to war, its boundaries changed. Study these maps to see how the borders of the United States changed.

United States, 1850

- Free states
- Slave states
- Territories open to slavery

Oregon Territory, Minnesota Territory, Utah Territory, Unorganized Territory, New Mexico Territory, Indian Territory

Pacific Ocean, Atlantic Ocean

United States, 1861

Washington Territory, Oregon, Nevada Territory, Utah Territory, California, New Mexico Territory, Dakota Territory, Colorado Territory, Nebraska Territory, Kansas, Oklahoma Territory, Texas, Minnesota, Wisconsin, Michigan, Iowa, Illinois, Indiana, Ohio, Missouri, Kentucky, Arkansas, Tennessee, Louisiana, Mississippi, Alabama, Georgia, Florida, New Hampshire, Vermont, Maine, New York, Massachusetts, Rhode Island, Connecticut, Pennsylvania, New Jersey, Delaware, West Virginia, Virginia, Maryland, North Carolina, South Carolina

BRITISH NORTH AMERICA

Pacific Ocean, Atlantic Ocean, Gulf of Mexico, MEXICO

- Free states
- Border states
- Seceded by March 1861
- Seceded by May 1861
- Territories

0 350 700 mi

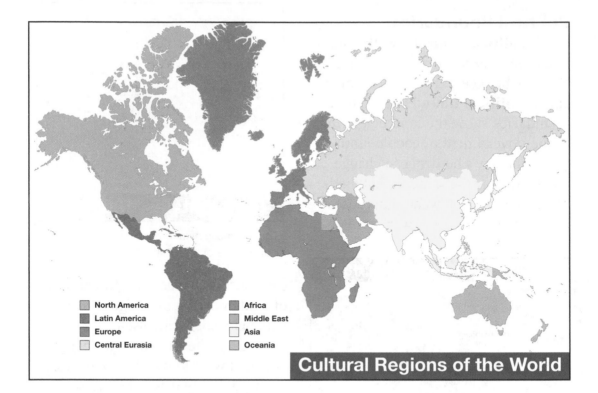

Cultural Regions of the World

North America
Latin America
Europe
Central Eurasia
Africa
Middle East
Asia
Oceania

Cultural Boundaries

Geographers sometimes divide the earth according to people's **culture**, or way of life. The **cultural map** above shows eight basic cultural regions. Each region has one or more of the following in common: customs, beliefs, or language. Can you name the regions shown on the map? Just as the physical boundaries of countries grow, shrink, or change names, cultural regions may also change. Changes may be brought about by the development of ideas and the movement of people.

Mississippi River

Natural Boundaries

Geographers can also define the boundaries of regions according to land features. Some rivers, mountain ranges, lakes, and seas form borders. These borders are called natural boundaries.

Help Gus decide what natural features form the state borders on the map.

Look at the Geogloss on pages 322 to 323. There you can find the definitions of the natural features.

How many states border the Mississippi River? What other natural feature borders Tennessee?

What natural features surround the borders of Asia?

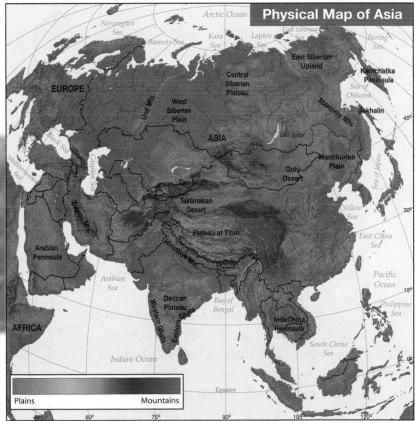
Physical Map of Asia

Time Zones

Another way of dividing the earth is by time zones. A **time zone** is a region that shares the same time.

In the past, people mainly used the sun to tell time. When the sun was at its highest, people knew it was noon. But since the earth rotates on its axis, not all places have the sun at the same time. When the sun rises in New York, it is still dark in California.

Using the sun to tell time made it difficult for people traveling by railroad in the 1800s. Times varied from city to city. As a result, people agreed to divide the country into regions. These regions had different bands of time known as time zones. As modern transportation developed, time zones were added around the world.

Finding the time in areas other than your own involves addition or subtraction based on the directions of east and west. For every zone you move to the east, you must add one hour to the time in your own time zone. For every zone you move to the west, you must subtract one hour from your own time zone. Find your own time zone on the map. Then name a place that would show a time two hours earlier than your own.

The **International Date Line** marks where the date changes. It is an imaginary line in the Pacific Ocean at about 180° longitude. A person who travels west across the date line loses one day. A person traveling east over the date line gains one day.

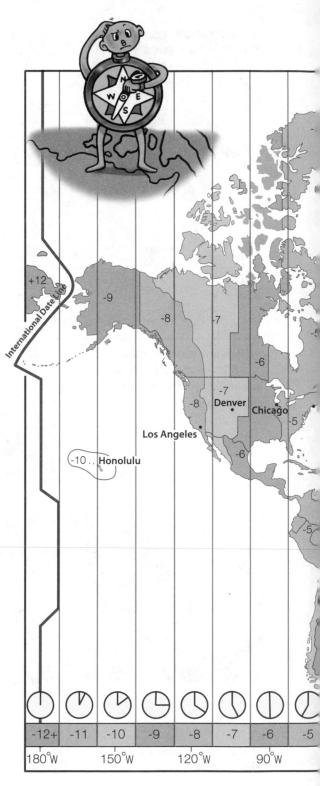

14

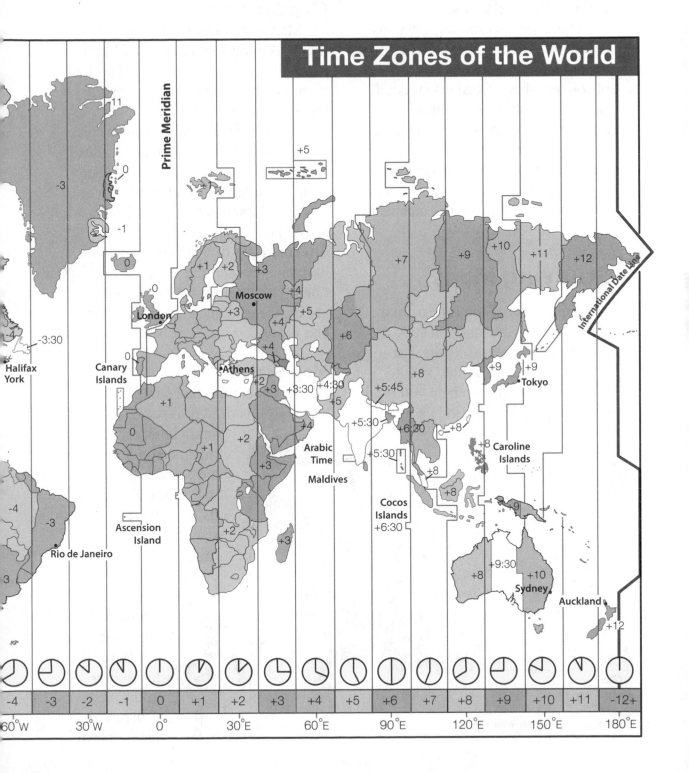

Time Zones of the World

Other Boundaries

There are also specialized maps that show the earth divided by climate, population, kinds of vegetation, kinds of soil, or other special information. Boaters and shippers use nautical maps that show waterways and bodies of water. Military maps are necessary for a nation's defense. This map of the United States shows the amount of rainfall different regions receive in a year.

Studying Maps

Regardless of the type of map, most maps will usually include a map title that tells you what the map is about. Maps also include other useful information to help you study and compare history and geography.

Map Symbols

Maps often have symbols on them. A **map key** tells you what the symbols on a map represent. On this map, the different colors represent the amount of rainfall.

Gus has found the **compass rose**. It is a small design that tells you the directions on a map. There are four main or **cardinal directions**: north, east, south, and west. Sometimes a compass rose will indicate the **intermediate directions**, which are halfway between the cardinal directions. The intermediate directions are northeast, southeast, southwest, and northwest.

Map Scales

A map cannot be as large as the earth, so it is drawn to scale. A **map scale** compares a distance on a map to a distance in the real world. Each map has its own scale. A map scale usually shows miles or kilometers on the earth as fractions of inches or centimeters. The scale is different depending on the area of the earth that is shown.

Rainfall in the U.S.A.

Inches
- Less than 10
- 10 to 20
- 20 to 40
- 40 to 60
- 60 to 80
- More than 80

Sometimes you need to see a small area of land and many details. Other times, you need to see a large area of land and not as many details.

Look at the trails on the *Western Trails* map. So that you can locate all the trails, the map shows a large area of the United States. Notice the map scale. One inch represents 800 miles. Find the Santa Fe Trail. Using the map scale, you can determine the distance from Independence, Missouri to Santa Fe, New Mexico. Are you able to locate the rivers you would cross traveling along the Sante Fe Trail from Independence to Santa Fe?

Now look at the map of the Santa Fe Trail. This large-scale map of the Santa Fe Trail gives you more detail about the cities and area along the trail. Can you now locate the rivers you would cross traveling along the

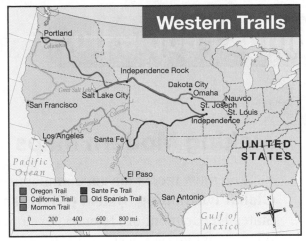

In the 1840s, people on horseback and in wagons traveled these trails.

trail from Independence to Santa Fe? Look at the map scale. One inch represents 120 miles. Which map has a larger map scale?

Different map scales give you different kinds of information. You need to decide which map scale would best give you the information you are looking for.

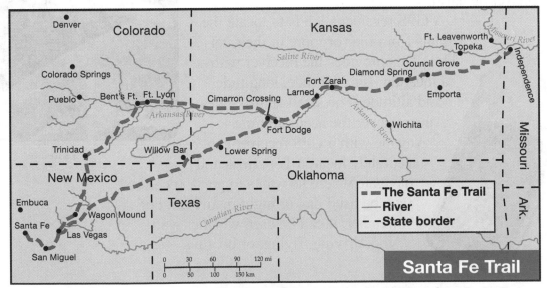

The Santa Fe Trail opened in 1821, the year Mexico gained independence from Spain. Ten years later the trail had two main routes: the Mountain Fork and Cimarron Fork.

17

Making Modern Maps

The most recent advance in mapmaking is the **Global Positioning System (GPS)**. The United States Department of Defense developed this satellite navigation system for military use. Today it can be used by civilians for navigation. It is a useful tool in mapmaking and land surveying. It also aids farmers, geologists, military personnel, and many others in their work.

Twenty-four GPS satellites circle the earth.

The GPS is made up of satellites orbiting the earth, control and monitoring stations on earth, and GPS receivers owned by users. There are twenty-four GPS satellites orbiting the earth. Each satellite weighs about 3,000 pounds and travels around the earth every twelve hours. Each satellite broadcasts signals from space that are picked up by a GPS receiver on earth.

A GPS receiver's job is to locate the signals from four or more of the satellites. This provides the receiver with a location using latitude, longitude, and altitude. The satellite also gives the receiver the accurate time.

GPS satellite

Anyone with a GPS receiver can accurately locate where he is and navigate where he wants to go. A receiver can be used day or night in any kind of weather. It can be used whether walking, driving, flying, or boating.

GPS receiver

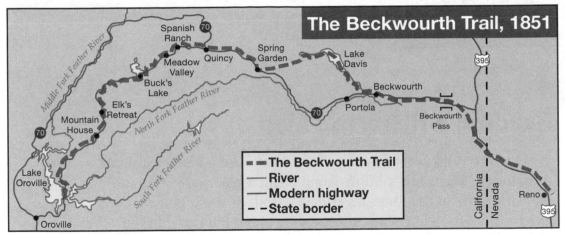

A trail map was the forerunner of a road map. This map shows the trail of James Beckwourth, a black pioneer who found a pass through the Sierra Nevada Mountains.

Reading a Road Map

A **road map** shows the cities and the roads that connect one place to another. Main roads are numbered, and the numbers are inside different shapes. These shapes are used to identify the kinds of highways. In the map key of the *Northern California* map, you find each shape and the kind of road it represents. Some road maps may also mark points of interest, natural features, and even rest stops.

A road curves and bends, making it difficult to measure the distance between cities. On some maps, small red numbers are used to show the mileage along sections of road. Find I-80 on the *Northern California* map. What is the mileage from Sacramento to Auburn?

States publish large flat road maps for tourists. These maps include smaller maps of the large cities in the state. A city map helps tourists navigate the main roads in that city.

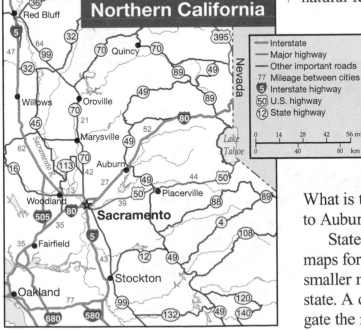

19

Reading a Historical Map

One way to study a historical event is to use a historical map. A *historical map* shows information about a place as it was in the past. Look at the maps on page 17. Both of these maps are historical maps. They show information about the trails in the United States as they were in the 1800s. Look at the maps on page 11. These maps show the United States and its borders in 1803, 1850, and 1861. Compare the maps to see how the borders have changed through history.

1. You will need your Activity Manual, a pencil, and the maps on Student Text pages 11 and 17.

2. Compare the modern map of the United States on the Activity Manual page to the historical maps on the text pages.

3. Complete the page.

Chapter 2

Getting There Faster

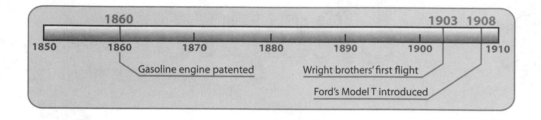

1850   1860   1870   1880   1890   1900   1910

1860

1903   1908

Gasoline engine patented   Wright brothers' first flight

Ford's Model T introduced

The Automobile

Try to imagine for a moment the streets and roads around your school without any cars or trucks on them—only wagons and horses and people walking. What would be different? Noise levels? Speed? The number of people going by in an hour? Indeed these would be significant differences. But other things would have to change as well. Think of the students who go to your school. Do they live close by or far away? If they live far away, how would they get to school without cars or buses?

Those who worked on inventing the automobile wanted to increase people's **mobility**, or ability to get from place to place. They did not imagine the many other changes the automobile would bring.

Henry Ford

Young Henry wanted to sleep late and tinker with watches and get out of all the farm work he could. His father got up early every day and let Henry sleep in. Mr. Ford generously gave Henry more tools

than most boys in those days could ever hope to have.

Henry was the oldest child. His parents worked hard and long. They made a good home for their children. Everything seemed rather slow and changeless to Henry. And then something happened that changed his life forever—and in turn changed America.

In May of 1876, Henry's mother died. Twelve-year-old Henry was stunned. His mother had been the light of the whole house, his own guiding star. Henry blamed the hard work of the farm for her death. And somehow the horses that pulled the plow represented in his mind all the work that he believed had killed his mother. He promised himself that he would build a machine that would replace horses.

Henry Ford at age seventeen

That boy was Henry Ford. When he grew up, he made an automobile that the average person could afford. Automobiles put the horse out of the carriage business almost entirely. Later, Ford's tractors put the plowhorses out to pasture as well. Eventually there were more cars and tractors in America than there had ever been horses. The little farm boy from Michigan became the man who revolutionized modern transportation.

Early Autos

As early as 1801, some Englishmen had put steam-powered carriages on the road.

Cugnot, a French engineer, designed this steam tractor to carry artillery in the 1770s. It was the first self-propelled vehicle.

In 1860, Thomas Rickett drove all around England in his steam carriage. He caused a stir with his "noisy" machine. Soon there was a big debate over such "horseless conveyances."

People who wanted to stop steam cars were happy when the **Red Flag Act** was passed in **1865**. This English law said that such vehicles could go only two miles an hour in town and four miles an hour on the open road. Furthermore, someone had to walk in front of each slow-moving car and carry a red flag. However, carriages pulled by horses could go ten miles an hour. This discouraged people from using steam carriages. Most people chose to continue using horses and railroads.

Besides such laws, the steam cars themselves had many drawbacks. For one thing, the cars were large and heavy. Steam engines needed water and fuel to make the steam. Each steam car had to be large enough to carry water and fuel for the trip. The body of the car had to be heavy enough to hold up all the machinery that made it run. Some early cars looked more like the train engines of that time period.

A steam carriage of the mid-1880s

A steam-powered tricycle

The bicycle was extremely popular in the 1880s and 1890s. A few people tried to make steam-powered bicycles. A Frenchman, Leon Serpollet, produced a much lighter steam engine for his tricycle than had ever been made before. In the 1860s, Jean Joseph Lenoir (luh NWAHR) patented the first gasoline engine. This kind of engine ran on gasoline rather than steam. Later, the German inventor Gottlieb **Daimler** (DYM lur) improved the gasoline engine. His engine provided the basis for most car engines that are used today.

The American Motor Car

Although some wealthy people in Europe had motor cars, the cars were not trustworthy. In fact, most drivers took a team of horses with them in case of breakdowns. But in America, **Henry Ford** was determined to make a reliable car that average people could own. In 1896, Ford built his first car and called it the *Quadricycle*. He continued working for several years. Finally in **1908**, Henry Ford introduced the *Model T*. At last he had made an affordable, sturdy car.

Henry Ford built this Quadricycle in his small workshop behind his home in Detroit, Michigan.
From the Collections of The Henry Ford.

25

The Model T became one of the most famous cars in history. It sold faster than any other car in the United States as well as in other countries. Also, it was easy to drive and easy to fix, even if it broke down on the road.

At first, a driver did not need a license to operate a car. He could pay for two hours of instruction from the Ford Motor Company and then drive off on his own. Or, if he preferred, he could simply drive off right after buying a car. This is very different from getting a car today.

Owning cars changed the lives of Americans. Driving gave people more freedom than they had before. People could now live in one town and work in another. And they could take trips according to their own schedules, not the railroad's schedules.

A flat tire on a Model T could often be easily pumped up again.

The Model T was large enough for a family to ride in comfortably.

Names from the Past

When you go past a car sales lot and see cars called Dodge or Chevrolet, you are seeing a little piece of the past. Early in the twentieth century, some people started car companies that are still around today.

A 1904 Buick

David Dunbar Buick, born in Scotland and reared in Detroit, opened the Buick Motor Company in 1903. His cars had better engines than earlier cars. Buick's cars could travel farther on one gallon of gasoline. One of Buick's workers, Walter Percy Chrysler, became president of the Buick company. Chrysler later founded the Chrysler Corporation that made Chrysler automobiles.

Louis Chevrolet came to the United States from Switzerland to sell an invention. Instead he became a driver in the newest sport in America—car racing. He had ideas of his own about how cars should be made. In 1911, he helped form the Chevrolet Motor Company. The company later became part of the General Motors Corporation. Louis and his brother Arthur tried to start an airplane company too.

Louis Chevrolet behind the wheel of an early racing Buick

27

John and Horace Dodge were a wild and brawling pair who owned a machine shop in Detroit, Michigan. They had invested in the Ford Motor Company. The brothers also sold car parts to Ford's factory. With the money they made, the Dodges started their own line of cars in 1914. Their cars had twenty-four **horsepower**. But Ford's Model T had only twenty. The Dodge Company became part of the Chrysler Corporation in 1928.

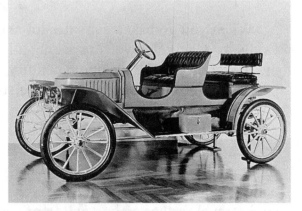

Stanley Steamers, powered by steam engines, continued in production until 1924.

Other brothers were also in the car business. Francis and Freelan Stanley made the respected "Stanley Steamers." Fred and August Duesenberg produced an automobile that many people think was the finest car of its time. And John and Warren Packard had been making luxury cars since 1900.

A Duesenberg from the late 1920s

The names of these early carmakers "echoed" in showrooms and car lots for decades. Some, like Ford, are still "echoing" today.

A 1940 Packard

Changes Ford Made

Henry Ford changed America by successfully making a car many people could afford. However, he also changed the way America manufactured goods. When Ford first started making cars, each one had to be put together in his shop. They were made at the rate of one car every fourteen hours. The Model T sold for $850. That rate and that price did not suit Ford. "We can do better," he said.

Why would he want to do better? He had sold six thousand Model T cars in one year. Ford was sure that a lower-priced car would benefit everyone. More people could have cars. He would also benefit by making more money.

Ford had heard of a meatpacking business in Ohio that used an **assembly line**. In an assembly line, each worker does one part of a total job instead of doing the total job alone. In the meatpacking company, each person did his task on a piece of meat and then moved to the next piece. Some companies making rifles and typewriters were also using assembly lines. Ford thought cars could be made the same way.

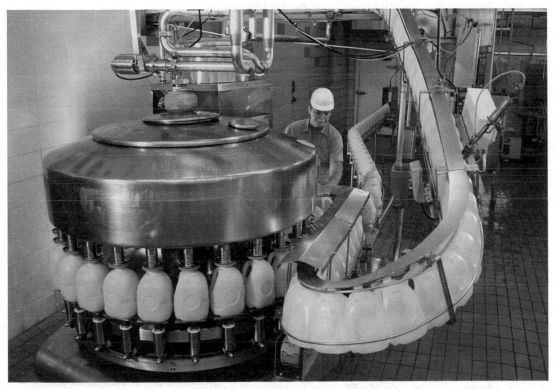

The assembly line is used in many factories today.
This assembly line is bottling orange juice.

Henry Ford's assembly line increased car production.

America's comfortable living is due to the assembly line.

Ford's company made more than fifteen million Model T cars. The last one was made in 1927. There was not another car as popular until the German Volkswagen was sold in America in the late 1940s.

Other carmakers had tried the assembly line and had given up. Ford used it but made a major change. Rather than having the workers move from car to car, the cars moved from worker to worker. Ford built a factory with conveyor belts and overhead cranes to move the cars. The new system was a success. Now a Model T rolled out of the factory in ninety minutes.

Ford's idea benefited business and American people as it spread to other companies. Before long, clothes and household goods were being made quickly on assembly lines. This caused prices to go down. More people could afford to buy more things. Today, much of

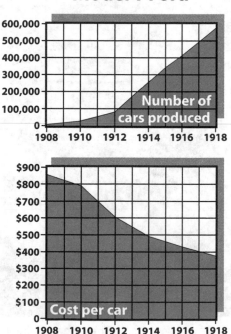

Model T Ford

Number of cars produced

Cost per car

Collecting Antique Automobiles

Some people collect and drive antique cars. **Antiques** are things that were made long ago. People have different reasons for owning antique cars. One reason may be that a car is a reminder of earlier good times. Another reason may be the pleasure of owning something unique. Collecting an antique car may be like buying a gem or a work of art. If the car is rare, it may be valuable.

Other people like to own vintage cars. Vintage cars are collectible autos known for their style. Collectors think these cars are beautiful, historical, or remarkable for some reason. They want to preserve and enjoy a part of the past.

Collecting antique and vintage cars can be a hobby or a business. The old cars may need to be restored to look and run like new. Restoring and maintaining the cars take skill and money. Collectors may take their cars to shows all over the world. At these shows, collectors can look at other automobiles and display their own.

A 1932 Pierce Arrow (above),
a 1928 Chrysler (upper right),
and a restored 1911 Model T (right)

Working on an Assembly Line

1. Get the materials your teacher assigns you.

2. Go to the "station" you have been assigned.

3. Read the instructions for your station.

4. Begin your work when the whistle blows. Continue doing your job until the whistle blows again.

5. Assess your production rate. How can it be improved? How can you do your part more efficiently?

The Airplane

A Greek myth tells of a boy named Icarus, who made a pair of feathered wings and learned to fly. His father warned him not to fly too high, but Icarus did anyway. He got too close to the sun, and the wax holding the feathers on his wings melted. The boy fell from the sky into the sea.

The First Flying Machines

In more modern times, there have been other people like Icarus. They dreamed of flying, but with much the same results. In England, about AD 1050, a man named Eilmer made some wings from linen stretched over wooden frames. He went to a high tower and pushed off into a fair wind. After flying almost an eighth of a mile, he crashed. He broke his legs and was lame for the rest of his life.

Later, people tried to glide on the air currents rather than fly like birds. Around 1890, a German man named Otto Lilienthal made **gliders**. Gliders are machines that fly without engine power. His gliders looked much like birds' wings and tails. In fact, he made sixteen kinds of gliders and tried over two thousand flights with them. He never could stay in the air for longer than fifteen seconds. But he helped prove that flying might not be an impossible dream after all.

Otto Lilienthal kept his gliders balanced by shifting his weight back and forth.

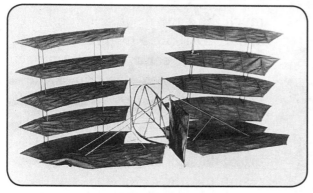

Chanute's glider

Other people were also trying to make flying machines. Octave **Chanute** (shuh NOOT), an American, had seen Lilienthal and his gliders. Chanute returned home full of ideas for a better glider. He made one with rubber joints so that the wings could move with the wind.

Samuel **Langley**, head of the Smithsonian Institution in Washington, D.C., was building a flying machine that he called an aerodrome. His aerodrome had a gasoline engine. Small models of the aerodrome had flown quite well. For one demonstration, Langley's *Great Aerodrome*, with Charles Manly as its pilot, was set to launch off the top of a houseboat on the Potomac River. But instead of flying, the *Great Aerodrome* lurched and slid right into the water. The newspapers jeered at Langley's soggy flying machine. The next day the *New York Times* claimed that man would not fly until scientists had worked for another ten million years.

Two months later, however, the newspaper would be proven wrong. On a windy beach in North Carolina, two brothers were about to change the world beyond anyone's wildest expectations.

Langley's aerodrome catapulting into the Potomac River

The Wright Idea

When **Orville** and **Wilbur Wright** were boys, their father bought them a toy helicopter made of paper, cork, and bamboo. They played with the "bat," as they called it, until it completely wore out. Then they used it as a model to make other toy helicopters that were bigger. Later Wilbur said it was the bat that caused him and Orville to become interested in flying.

When Orville was seventeen, he made his own printing press and set up a shop. Business was good and he had to hire a helper. Wilbur and Orville also had a bicycle repair shop. This business became so large that they had four shops running. The brothers put the hired helper in charge of the print shop and they began to design bicycles. Then, during the winter when the bicycle business was slow, Wilbur and Orville used their tools and knowledge in their lifelong hobby—making a flying machine.

The Wrights wanted to know all that they could about flying, so they wrote to the Smithsonian Institution. They received a list of books, some written by Langley and Chanute. The Wrights wrote to both men and received replies. Before long, the Wright brothers and Chanute were good friends.

This building in Dayton, Ohio, housed the Wright Cycle Company.

Wilbur and Orville read everything they could about new inventions and discoveries. When they read about gliders, they decided to build one for themselves. They took their glider by train from Dayton, Ohio, all the way to **Kitty Hawk, North Carolina**. Kitty Hawk was an ideal place to try out a glider. At Kitty Hawk, good winds always came in from the ocean. The hills were layered with soft sand for landing.

The glider flew, but only for a few seconds at a time. The brothers went home to experiment some more. They built a **wind tunnel**, a six-foot-long narrow box with a fan

A model of the Wright brother's wind tunnel

at one end and a glass top. When they flew a small model glider in the tunnel, they could watch what happened to it at different wind speeds. The wind tunnel helped the brothers accurately calculate the effects of air on different wing surfaces.

After they finished the tests in the wind tunnel, the brothers built a better glider. They went back to Kitty Hawk to try it. Then the next year, they took a third glider to the outer banks of North Carolina. The brothers were greatly pleased with how this one flew. Now they were ready to add an engine to their flying machine.

Wilbur flying a glider in 1902

The Wrights knew they needed a light, powerful engine. They asked several engine makers to design an engine for them. It needed to be an eight-horsepower engine that would not weigh more than two hundred pounds. Everyone the Wrights asked said that it could not be done. So the brothers set to work and built their own engine. It weighed just 179 pounds and had more than twelve horsepower. They had accomplished this job that "could not be done" in only six weeks.

But before the Wright brothers could complete their flying machine, they needed to make one more invention—a **propeller**. For several months, they tested many different shapes of propellers. They filled up five notebooks with formulas and sketches. Orville wrote in his diary that the problem took up so much of their time that they "could do little other work." Then they made a major discovery. They found that each end of the propeller should be shaped like a wing on the flying machine. This shape would allow the propeller to slice forward through the air.

The Wright brothers were now ready for their most important trip to Kitty Hawk.

The shape of the propeller was important for the machine to fly.

The First Flight

On December 17, 1903, the wind at Kitty Hawk was brisk and the air was cold—so cold that the Wrights had to keep going into the camp building to warm their hands. They put up the red flag to signal their helpers to come. The Wrights were going to test the **Flyer**, their newest machine.

Four men and a boy showed up. With their help, the Wrights laid out the track and set the *Flyer* on it. Orville and Wilbur shook hands. One helper said they shook hands for a long time, "like two folks parting who weren't sure they'd ever see one another again." Then Orville got onto the *Flyer*.

Orville let the engine run a little while. Then he slipped the wire that held the flying machine, and the machine started forward. It moved slowly against the wind for about forty feet. Then, on its own power, the *Flyer* lifted from the ground. It went up about ten feet and then dipped and rose again, swaying and lurching in the wind. Wilbur and the others cheered. One man operated the camera that Orville had set up, catching forever the first moment a man really flew.

Orville Wright aboard the *Flyer* as it lifted from the ground at Kitty Hawk

The *Flyer* stayed up for twelve seconds and traveled only 120 feet. But it had stayed up by its own power and had landed on high ground. The Wrights had truly done what many said was impossible. They flew the *Flyer* three more times.

The *Flyer III* stayed aloft for 39 minutes—a new record.

The *Flyer II* could fly for five minutes at a time.

That afternoon Orville and Wilbur walked four miles to send their father a telegram. In part it said, "Success four flights Thursday morning . . . inform Press home Christmas."

That winter, the brothers worked on improving their flying machine.

In the spring they went to a neighbor's field and began testing the *Flyer II*. In order for the airplane to be useful, it had to do more than fly in a short, straight line. So Wilbur began to experiment with turning in the air. Soon both brothers were flying in complete circles over the field.

The next winter, they built the *Flyer III*, a plane that gave the pilot more control over turns and landings. With this airplane, they could stay in the air for more than thirty minutes at a time. They could land many times without making repairs. Now they were ready to show the world. However, there were few people in the world ready to believe that man could fly.

Orville Wright demonstrated this airplane's capabilities for the army in 1908.

could fly a distance of 125 miles at forty miles per hour with two men aboard. So Orville and Wilbur began working to meet the army's requests. Charlie Furnas, a mechanic and friend, was the passenger during the practice flights. Orville demonstrated the plane for the army. And in **1909**, the army bought the first military plane.

There could be no more doubt. The age of air travel had arrived.

The Wrights offered their invention to the United States War Department. But they were turned down immediately. No one even came to see the airplane. The army had given much money to Langley, only to see his aerodrome fall into the river. The army leaders were not ready to spend more money on another flying machine. For two years, the brothers did not fly or show their invention to anyone. The Wrights were waiting for a **patent** so that no one could steal their idea. They still hoped the United States government would give them a contract to make airplanes for the army.

Finally in 1908, the army decided to give the Wright brothers a chance. But the army wanted proof that the Wrights' machine

The Wright brothers on the back steps of their home

Air Traffic Controller

Who in 1903 would have guessed that, only a few decades after the first plane flight, air traffic directors would be needed because of so many airplanes? Air traffic controllers talk to all pilots. They tell them when and where to take off and land. Without towers and the quick, sharp-eyed people in them, large airports would be in chaos. The air traffic controller's job is to get the most aircraft in and out of the airport in a safe and efficient way.

Although controllers have good eyesight, there are days when heavy fog or other weather conditions limit what they can see. At these times controllers must rely fully on their equipment. The Instrument Landing System uses radio signals to locate planes. Large airports also use the Microwave Landing System, which gives even more precise information to the controllers and pilots. Systems that use information from satellites also help keep the air traffic flowing smoothly.

The most important characteristic of an air traffic controller is an ability to remain calm. This is very important during hectic hours and emergencies. Some busy airports like Chicago O'Hare International and Dallas-Fort Worth International each have nearly one million takeoffs and landings in a year.

From Then Until Now

God made people to rule over His world. Throughout history, they have used parts of God's world to help them travel. In the last century, people have made amazing progress in how they travel.

Consider today how it would be to ride to church in a buggy or travel to another state in a wagon. It would certainly slow down life in this decade. Think how our sleek modern cars would look to Henry Ford.

Imagine what Wilbur and Orville Wright might think of space travel. In 1903, the Wright brothers made the first short flights in their simple flying machine. Little did they dream that only sixty-six years later, Neil Armstrong would step down from a far different craft onto the surface of the moon. Or that Armstrong would carry with him a small piece of cloth from the *Flyer*, which had skimmed the air at Kitty Hawk one cold December day.

> "Thou madest him to have dominion over the works of thy hands: thou hast put all things under his feet."
>
> **Psalm 8:6**

God has allowed man's progress to happen. Even though many people may not have believed this, God still used them to have control over what He made. Perhaps in the future, you will help make advances in transportation.

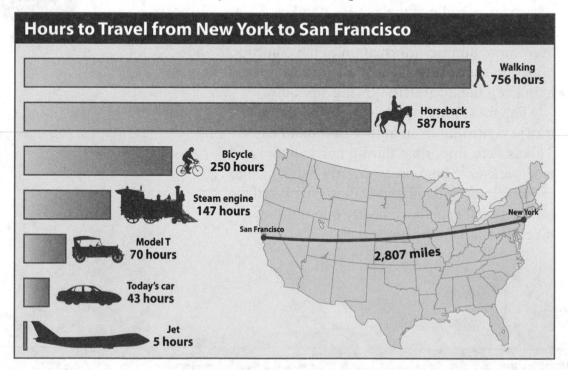

Hours to Travel from New York to San Francisco

- Walking — 756 hours
- Horseback — 587 hours
- Bicycle — 250 hours
- Steam engine — 147 hours
- Model T — 70 hours
- Today's car — 43 hours
- Jet — 5 hours

San Francisco — New York: 2,807 miles

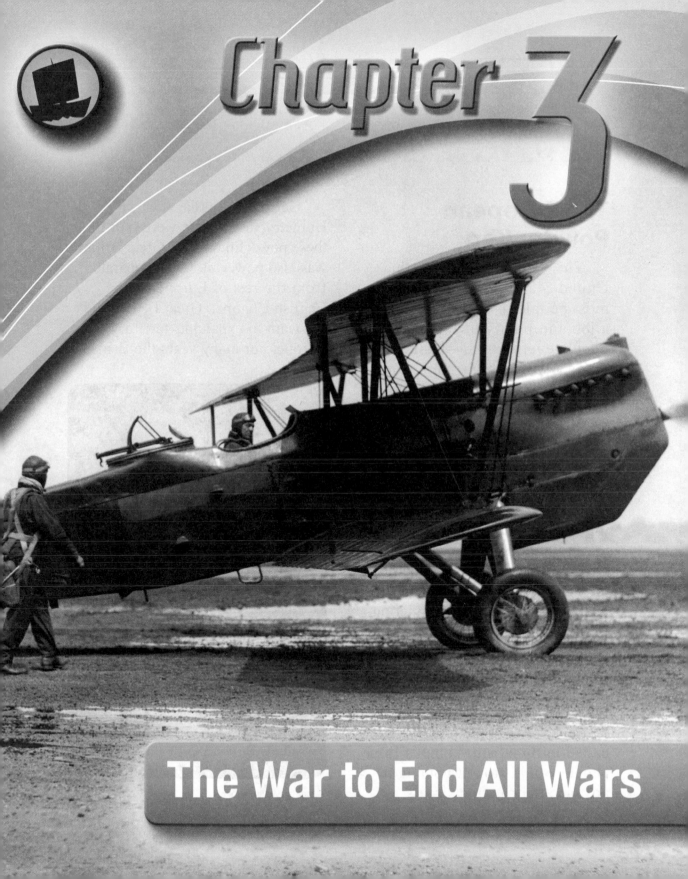

Chapter 3

The War to End All Wars

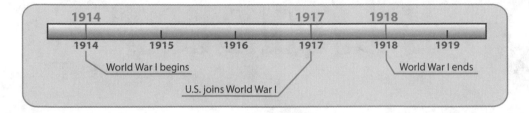

1914			1917	1918	
1914	1915	1916	1917	1918	1919

World War I begins

U.S. joins World War I

World War I ends

The European Powder Keg

The year was 1914. In the United States, life was good for most people. Nearly everyone had a job and plenty of food to eat. People everywhere—bankers, factory workers, farmers, and college students—talked about President Woodrow Wilson's recent election.

But across the ocean in Europe, life was not so peaceful. Several nations wanted to become more powerful. They wanted to enlarge their boundaries. Often this meant taking land that other countries already owned. They wanted to have the strongest armies and navies. They were all competing with each other to make the best and to sell the most products. The people of each nation thought that their nation was the best one in Europe. Their strong patriotic feelings for their own nation were called **nationalism**. Some of these people would stop at nothing to advance their nation's goals.

Germany, Russia, Austria-Hungary, and France were four of these powerful nations. Great Britain was also powerful. It was separated from the rest of Europe by the English Channel. Great Britain did not want to expand its territory in Europe. For many years the British

Woodrow Wilson

navy was the strongest navy on the seas. Great Britain wanted to stay out of the tension in Europe.

But Great Britain would not be able to avoid tension for long. Several years earlier, it had made an agreement with France and Russia. They would help each other if any one of them went to war. This kind of agreement between nations is called an **alliance**. France, Russia, and Great Britain named their alliance the Triple Entente (ah*n* TAH*N*T). Germany, Austria-Hungary, and Italy had also made an alliance. They called their group the Triple Alliance.

European Alliances		
Triple Entente France, Russia, Great Britain		
Triple Alliance Germany, Austria-Hungary, Italy		

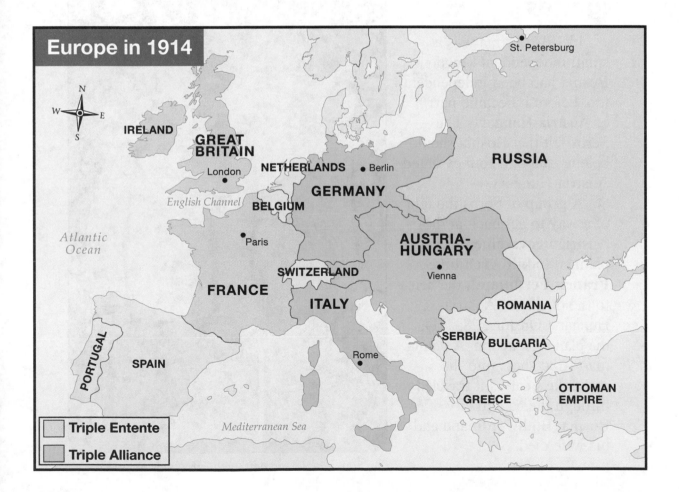

Europe in 1914

Triple Entente

Triple Alliance

Some people referred to Europe in 1914 as a powder keg. A powder keg is a small container that holds gunpowder. Gunpowder will explode the moment a spark touches it. In Europe, relations between the nations were so tense it would take only a "spark" of a problem for the nations to explode into war. The spark came on June 28, 1914.

The government of Austria-Hungary was outraged. Kaiser Wilhelm II, the ruler of Germany, urged Austria-Hungary to attack Serbia immediately. Instead, Count Leopold von Berchtold, Austria's foreign minister, sent Serbia a note. The note had some harsh demands. He wanted Serbia to give up most of the rights it had as an independent country.

The Powder Keg Ignites

In 1914, Serbia was a small independent kingdom. Bosnia had been independent too, before it became part of Austria-Hungary. The Serbs felt that Bosnia should belong to them, so they hated Austria-Hungary.

A group of Serbs thought of a way to get back at the Austrian government. They planned to kill **Archduke Francis Ferdinand**, the heir to the throne of Austria-Hungary. On June 28, 1914, the plan took action. A young man fired shots into the archduke's car as it traveled through the capital city of Bosnia. Both Ferdinand and his wife died.

Archduke Ferdinand (left) with Emperor Franz Josef

During the German invasion of Belgium, Belgian troops used straw for camouflage in the straw-covered field.

Nations Declare War

Serbia agreed to some, but not all, of Austria-Hungary's demands. That was not good enough for Austria-Hungary. It took the advice of Germany and declared war on Serbia on **July 28, 1914**.

Serbia could not fight Austria-Hungary alone. It had to have help. Russia prepared its army to help Serbia. When Russia's army began preparing for war, Germany declared war on Russia.

Do you remember the Triple Alliance and the Triple Entente? Italy had promised to side with Germany and Austria-Hungary in a war. But now Italy decided to withdraw from the Triple Alliance.

Great Britain had promised to help France and Russia. The British did not want a war. But they became angry when Belgium was invaded by the Germans. Belgium was a small neutral country under Great Britain's protection. A **neutral country** is one that does not take sides in a war between other countries. So the British declared war on Germany and Austria-Hungary. It seemed as though an entire continent had gone to war.

European Rulers (pre-WWI)	
Germany	kaiser
Austria-Hungary	emperor
Italy	king
France	president
Russia	czar
Great Britain	king

Early in the war, the German soldiers wore helmets like this one.

The German poster encourages German men to protect their country and enlist in the army.

The French poster declares, "One last effort and we will get them [the Germans]."

The Glory of War

It seemed like a holiday in each of the countries at war. Crowds of people swarmed the streets. Bands played and people sang. Long lines of volunteers waited to join the army. Posters went up in every city, urging men to join the armed forces. Newspapers and magazines published political cartoons that poked fun at the enemy.

"War is a glorious thing," most people thought. "How noble it would be to fight for one's country!" No one expected the war to last very long.

Sir Edward Grey, the British secretary for foreign affairs, was one of the few people with a solemn face. "The lights are going out all over Europe," he told a friend. "We shall not see them lit again in our lifetime."

French troops marching through a village on their way to the Battle of the Marne

The Fighting Begins

Germany and Austria-Hungary called themselves the **Central Powers**. The German army was much larger and better trained than that of Austria-Hungary. So the Germans did most of the actual fighting. Russia, Serbia, France, and Great Britain called themselves the **Allies**.

Alliances: Early War		
Allies		
Russia, Serbia, France, Great Britain		
Central Powers		
Germany, Austria-Hungary		

The Central Powers had a plan to conquer the Allies. They named it the **Schlieffen** (SHLEE fen) **Plan**, after the German official who had thought of it. The plan called for the Germans to attack France and quickly capture the capital, Paris. Then the Germans planned to march east and defeat Russia.

A German general sent home a telegram to Kaiser Wilhelm II of Germany. The telegram read, "In six weeks it will all be over."

But things did not happen that easily for the Germans. Before they got to Paris, they met French troops at the Marne River. The French soldiers fought so fiercely that the German troops had to retreat. After the **Battle of the Marne**, the Germans realized they would have to abandon their Schlieffen Plan. The French were not going to be defeated quickly.

Now Germany had to fight France and Russia at the same time.

War on the Western Front

The Germans and the Allies began what was called the "**Race to the Sea**." Both sides wanted to take control of the ports along the English Channel. If Germany could control the ports, it could prevent the British from sending help to France.

At the Belgian city of Ypres (EE pruh), the Allies finally stopped the German advance toward the English Channel. The battle lasted an entire month. Thousands of soldiers died. Today Flanders, Belgium, has fields dotted with white crosses where many of these men are buried.

By the end of November, both armies had dug **trenches**. Soldiers used these for protection and shelter. These trenches snaked for nearly six hundred miles from Belgium to Switzerland. This line of trenches between the two sides became known as the **western front**. The war along the western front had reached a **deadlock**, which means that neither side was gaining ground. Most people had thought the war would be over by Christmas. But now they began to doubt this.

Europe During WW I

Life in a Trench

Trenches were about six and a half feet deep and only wide enough for two men to stand side by side. Sometimes soldiers tried to cover the muddy ground with boards. But often mud was knee-deep on the floor of a trench. Lice and bad smells were problems as soldiers had to go without bathing for days at a time. Rats constantly ran around the soldiers' feet.

Some of the officers lived in underground rooms. The officers' rooms had furniture. But most soldiers slept in crude dugouts cut into the trench walls.

At the top of the trenches were **parapets**. Parapets are walls made of dirt, sandbags, and tangles of barbed wire. The parapets discouraged enemy attacks. Soldiers in the trenches fired their machine guns over the parapets.

Each army had a system of up to four trenches. There was a frontline trench with two support trenches behind it. A reserve trench was farther back. Soldiers could move between the trenches through tunnels.

The land between the front trenches of opposing armies was called "**no man's land**." Littered with dead bodies, barbed wire, and muddy shell holes, the area was hard for any soldiers to cross during an attack.

Western Front
Christmas of 1914

A dusting of snow covered the muddy battlefields of the western front. It was Christmas Eve, 1914. Soldiers had hung paper lanterns along the trench lines. Some even decorated Christmas trees.

A familiar sound rose from the lines in the hushed darkness. The men were singing. Germans and British alike blended their voices in Christmas carols.

The soldiers in their dugouts heard the music. They climbed over the parapets of their trenches to join the singing. Germans in pointed caps shook hands with British in khaki-colored berets. Christmas greetings were exchanged in German and English.

The guns were silent all Christmas day. Some soldiers exchanged gifts. A few held soccer matches. For just that one day, the men forgot about the war and celebrated a holiday.

Many officers on both sides were angry with their troops. They did not believe it was right to make friends with the enemy, even on a holiday. After 1914, a Christmas **truce**, or a temporary halt to fighting, was forbidden.

In 1915, it became clear that the war would last a long time. Soldiers were able to defend themselves easily from their trenches. Direct attacks were too risky to be tried often. So the fighting went on.

World War I was the first war that used airplanes.

Weapons of World War I

Machine guns had only been in use since the late 1800s. These new guns were the most important for airplanes. His invention allowed a machine gun to shoot between spinning propeller blades without hitting them.

Another new weapon was **gas**. This kind of chemical weapon was contained in canisters called shells. The gas spread through the air when the shell exploded. At first, only tear gas was used. Then the Germans introduced more deadly gases like chlorine gas and mustard gas. These gases were poisons that choked the victims and burned their skin. Mustard gas was especially hard to defend against because it was invisible and had no odor. To protect themselves, soldiers wore large, clumsy gas masks that covered their entire heads.

Machine gunners protect themselves with gas masks at the Battle of the Somme.

weapons of the war. In one minute a soldier's rifle could fire fifteen shots. His machine gun, however, could fire 450 shots a minute. Aircraft were also equipped with machine guns. A Dutchman named Anthony Fokker had invented a mechanism

Gas mask

During 1915, the Germans and the Allies tried several **offensives**, or attacks, against each other. None of these were successful. The western front remained deadlocked. So the war continued.

The western front was only one part of the war. In the east, France and England had wanted to open a supply route to Russia. The route would go through a peninsula in Turkey. The **peninsula**, or piece of land almost surrounded by water, was called Gallipoli. The Allies made an unsuccessful attempt to take control of Gallipoli. The Russian army had retreated from the smaller German army. Meanwhile, on the **eastern front**, the Germans were winning.

On the high seas, the British navy swept the sea clear of German surface ships. So the Germans used submarines, called **U-boats**. These boats traveled underwater to sink enemy ships.

A German U-boat

Writing Poems

A soldier huddled on the dirt floor of an Allied trench. He held his pen in his hand. Distant machine-gun fire rattled like popcorn. Somewhere, a shell exploded. A man's cry of pain echoed over the battlefield.

The soldier closed his eyes for a moment. He ran his hand over his damp brow and began to write:

> Our brains ache, in the merciless iced east winds that knive us. . .
> Wearied we keep awake because the night is silent…
> Low, drooping flares confuse our memory of the salient. . .
> Worried by silence, sentries whisper, curious, nervous,
>   But nothing happens.
>
> Watching, we hear the mad gusts tugging on the wire,
> Like twitching agonies of men among its brambles.
> Northward, incessantly, the flickering gunnery rumbles,
> Far off, like a dull rumour of some other war.
>   What are we doing here?

> —from "Exposure" by Wilfred Owen

People often write poems to express something in a new way. The poems written during World War I help us to understand how people felt about the war. Wilfred Owen wrote many of the best poems about World War I. He died shortly before the war ended.

In a famous poem called "In Flanders Fields," John McCrae expressed his feelings about the soldiers who died.

> In Flanders fields the poppies blow
> Between the crosses, row on row,
> That mark our place. . . .
> . . .Short days ago
> We lived, felt dawn, saw sunset glow,
> Loved and were loved, and now we lie
> In Flanders fields.

The *New York Times* reports the sinking of the *Lusitania*.

Alliances: Mid-War

Allies
France, Russia, Great Britain, Italy

Central Powers
Germany, Austria-Hungary, Turkey, Bulgaria

More Nations Join the Alliances

The *Lusitania* was a passenger ship traveling from New York to Liverpool, England. On May 7, 1915, a German U-boat torpedoed the ship. Over one thousand people died when the ship sank. One hundred twenty-eight of them were Americans.

Americans were shocked and angry. Some felt that the Germans had disobeyed important warfare laws. The ship had been unarmed and had carried defenseless passengers. Many Americans believed that the United States should become involved in the war.

Before the war, Italy had been part of the Triple Alliance with Germany and Austria-Hungary. After the *Lusitania* was sunk, Italy joined the war on the side of the Allies. The Allies promised Italy lands in Austria, Africa, and Turkey if they won the war. The offer was too good for the Italians to refuse.

Some nations joined the Central Powers. Turkey joined after defeating the British at Gallipoli. Bulgaria joined just in time to help the Central Powers defeat Serbia. In the east, the Central Powers were winning.

Battles and Bravery

Early in 1916, the Germans on the western front decided it was time to break the deadlock. They planned to capture Verdun (ver DUHN). Verdun was a French city surrounded by three rings of fortresses. Many of the French soldiers who normally protected the fortresses had left their posts to fight on the front. The Germans thought that Verdun would be defeated quickly.

For two days in February, the Germans bombarded Verdun's fortresses. They used shells, machine guns, and poison gas. Then German foot soldiers began marching forward. They expected to find all the French defenders dead. Instead, French soldiers rained gunfire on them when they tried to advance. The French were not defeated yet.

The Battle of Verdun

General Henri Pétain arrived two days later to take command of the French forces. Under his leadership, the French rallied. "*Ils ne passeront pas!*" they cried, meaning "They shall not pass!" The French were determined that the Germans should not have Verdun. For ten months the French fought bravely. Their determined efforts saved the city. But more than five hundred thousand French soldiers died in the **Battle of Verdun**. German losses were almost as great. Verdun was the longest and bloodiest battle of the war.

The city of Verdun was severely damaged.

Military cemetery at Verdun, France

The Battle of the Somme

In July of 1916, British commanders on the western front began a plan to help the French soldiers fighting at Verdun. The British attacked the Germans at a point along the Somme River. They hoped that this might lure some of the Germans away from Verdun and relieve the French.

The **Battle of the Somme** lasted four months. The Germans finally retreated. But over one million lives had been lost on both sides. A British soldier called this battle "the glory and the graveyard of our army."

During this battle, the Allies introduced a new weapon they called the **tank**. The Allies wanted the Germans to think that tanks were water carriers. But the tanks were equipped with huge guns. Soldiers driving tanks could crush anything in their paths. They could even drive tanks over the tops of trenches. When Germans first saw the tank, they called it a *Schutzengrabenvernichtungsautomobile*. This meant "an automobile built to destroy trenches dug in the ground."

Tanks advance through the Argonne Forest in France.

HMS *Warspite* participated in the Battle of Jutland.

The Battle of Jutland

During the Battle of Verdun, another important battle took place at sea. The **Battle of Jutland** was fought in the North Sea off the coast of Denmark. The British Grand Fleet was the finest navy in the world. It clashed with the German High Seas Fleet in May of 1916.

The battle was quick and bitter. It lasted less than thirty minutes. The British lost fourteen ships. Among them was the *Queen Mary*, with a crew of 1,266 men. The Germans lost eleven ships. Neither side could really claim victory, and neither wanted to admit defeat.

Sides Deadlocked

It was now 1917, the third year of the war. The battles had cost millions of sacrificed lives. But the Allies and the Central Powers were still deadlocked. Every country was tired of fighting. Woodrow Wilson, the president of the United States, encouraged the European leaders to consider settling for "peace without victory."

Both the Allies and the Central Powers believed that "peace without victory" would mean giving in to the enemy. Neither was willing to do that.

America Joins In

In November of 1916, **President Woodrow Wilson** was re-elected. His campaign slogan had been "He kept us out of war." But now people in the United States and President Wilson were leaning more and more toward joining the war in Europe.

Early in 1917, the Germans did two things that outraged the Americans. First, Kaiser Wilhelm II declared all ships to be fair game for German submarine attacks. There were to be no restrictions. Second, the Germans planned to convince Mexico to join the war on the side of Germany. If Mexico agreed, it would receive Texas and other land in the southwestern United States.

President Wilson spoke to Congress on April 2. He persuaded them of the need to make the world "safe for democracy." On **April 6, 1917**, the United States declared war on Germany and joined the Allies.

American soldiers marching onto French soil were a welcome sight for the Allies. These new soldiers in the war were nicknamed "doughboys."

President Wilson before Congress

On the Home Fronts

At home in each of the countries at war, life had changed. Most of the men had gone to the battlefronts. Women took over men's jobs in factories and on farms. Women were delivering the mail and working as chauffeurs or waiters. They were even making weapons for the soldiers.

Woman welding in an arsenal

Children helped the war effort too. Girls sewed clothing and rolled bandages to be sent to the battlefields. Boy Scouts ran errands and wrote letters for wounded soldiers in war hospitals. Some teenage boys trained to be army officers while still in school.

Food was in short supply. So most families planted gardens and grew their own vegetables. Products like meat, bread, butter, and sugar had to be carefully rationed or saved for special occasions. In the United States, Herbert Hoover created a system of "meatless days," "sweetless days," and "heatless days." This system was to help with the rationing.

People who lived in towns near the fronts in Europe had to take special precautions. The cities on the fronts were often bombed or

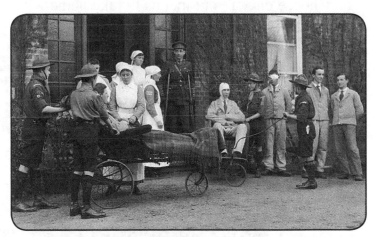

Boy Scouts help wounded soldiers in Great Britain.

raided during the war. Schoolchildren and mothers learned how to put on gas masks. They learned where the nearest bomb shelters were in case of an enemy attack.

Conserving Food

1. Label three separate sheets of paper with the headings "Day One," "Day Two," and "Day Three."

2. Under "Day One," plan a menu for a "meatless day" meal. No meat may be included.

3. Under "Day Two," plan a menu for a "sweetless day" meal. No dessert foods may be included.

4. Under "Day Three," plan a menu for a "heatless day" meal. None of the foods included may require cooking.

5. Choose one of your menus to take home with you. Prepare the foods listed for a meal one day this week.

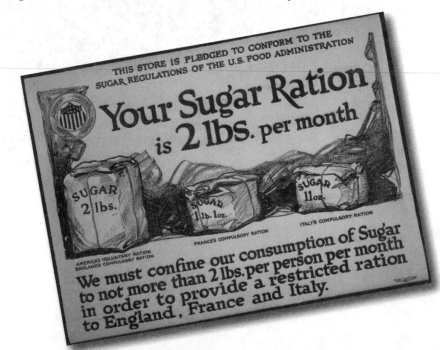

THIS STORE IS PLEDGED TO CONFORM TO THE SUGAR REGULATIONS OF THE U.S. FOOD ADMINISTRATION

Your Sugar Ration is 2 lbs. per month

SUGAR 2 lbs.
AMERICA'S VOLUNTARY RATION
ENGLAND'S COMPULSORY RATION

SUGAR 1 lb. 1oz.
FRANCE'S COMPULSORY RATION

SUGAR 11oz.
ITALY'S COMPULSORY RATION

We must confine our consumption of Sugar to not more than 2 lbs. per person per month in order to provide a restricted ration to England, France and Italy.

Trouble in Russia

While America was entering the war, Russia was changing politically. For several years there had been political unrest in Russia. In March of 1917, many Russians revolted in their own country. This and other events forced their czar, Nicholas II, to give up his throne.

A man named **Vladimir Lenin** came to Russia in April of 1917. Over the next several months, Lenin organized his own political party. His followers were called Bolsheviks. The Bolsheviks staged a second revolution in November. Lenin promised the Russian people bread, land, and peace.

With all the hardships of war, the Russians listened to Lenin. Many men left the war and went to St. Petersburg, Russia's capital. They helped set up Lenin's new government. In 1918, Lenin signed a peace treaty with Germany. Germany now had to fight on only the western front.

Alliances: 1917
Allies
France, Great Britain, Italy, United States
Central Powers
Germany, Austria-Hungary, Turkey, Bulgaria

Political conditions in Russia were so tense that, only a few months after being publicly welcomed by his party members, Lenin had to disguise himself as a Finnish railway worker to avoid arrest.

Can you name the Allied nations these flags represent?

Hassam, Childe (1859–1935). Avenue of the Allies, Great Britain, 1918. 1918. Oil on canvas. Bequest of Miss Adelaide Milton de Groot (1876–1967), 1967. The Metropolitan Museum of Art, New York, NY, USA.

By the spring of 1918, over six hundred thousand American troops had arrived at the fronts. This gave fresh help to the Allies. Eventually, over two million American soldiers came. By July, the Allies were under the command of the French General Ferdinand Foch. They were ready to move forward against the Germans once again.

The Allies Move Ahead

The war dragged on through 1917. Offensives from both sides ended in more casualties. After one battle, many French soldiers deserted the battlefield, or gave up, and went home. Nearly three hundred thousand British soldiers died after their attack against the Germans at Passchendaele in Belgium.

At the Second Battle of the Marne, the Allies drove the Germans behind the Marne River as before. Then they broke through the Germans' mighty Hindenburg Line in the forest.

The fighting became more fierce than ever before. It was becoming more and more apparent that the Germans were losing.

Sergeant Alvin York

Sergeant Alvin York grew up on a farm in the hills of Tennessee. As a boy he learned how to shoot a rifle and a pistol. He became a skilled marksman. He also learned that Jesus Christ had died for him, and he accepted Christ as his Savior.

York was a young man when World War I began. He believed that it was wrong for a Christian to kill people, even in war. When the United States entered World War I, he asked that his name be left out of the draft pool.

But the government would not listen to York's protests. He was drafted into the United States Army. After thinking and praying for a long time, York changed his mind. He decided that it would be wrong for him to refuse to serve his country. So York went off to Europe to fight in the war.

On October 8, 1918, York performed a deed that made him a hero. At the time, York was a corporal in a battalion of seventeen men. As they neared the goal of their mission, they met and fought a brief battle with Germans. Soon, only eight American soldiers were left. But York did not give up. He forced the remaining Germans to surrender. The other men from his battalion assisted as he took 132 German prisoners.

"For he hath said, I will never leave thee, nor forsake thee."
Hebrews 13:5

While still in the war, York was promoted to sergeant. Then on April 18, 1919, Sergeant York was awarded the Congressional Medal of Honor for his bravery. He had saved many American lives by his heroism. When congratulated, he gave the Lord the credit for his actions. "God will be with you if you will only trust Him," he said.

The End at Last

By early November, all of the Central Powers except Germany had surrendered. The people in Germany were starving. Nearly every German family had lost one of its members in the war. At last, weary German leaders met with General Foch in a railroad car in the Compiègne Forest of France. They signed the **armistice**, or agreement to stop fighting. On **November 11, 1918**, at 11:00 a.m., the war officially ended.

The Allied troops went wild with joy. Soldiers cried and laughed and slapped each other on the back. Four years of fighting were finally over.

But there was sadness, too, for many families. More than six million people received wounds in the war. They would have physical disabilities for the rest of their lives. And more than ten million people had lost their lives. Rows and rows of white crosses on battlefields were silent reminders of the high cost of peace.

After the War

Woodrow Wilson met with David Lloyd George, the British prime minister, and Georges Clemenceau, the French premier. Leaders of twenty-nine other Allied nations joined them. Their job was to write a peace treaty. Discussions were held in Paris to determine what they would put in the treaty.

Wilson wanted the treaty to include fourteen points that he considered important. But not all of the other leaders agreed with him. Many of the leaders wanted the treaty to punish Germany.

Delegates from various countries watch as the German leaders sign the Treaty of Versailles in the Hall of Mirrors.

In the end, the treaty placed all of the blame for the war on the Germans. The treaty required Germany to pay for the damages they had caused. It took away a great deal of territory from Germany, Austria-Hungary, and other nations who had fought on the side of the Central Powers. The treaty limited the number of men Germany could have in its army. It forced Germany to give up many of the ships in the German navy. The Allies wanted to weaken Germany so that it would be unable to cause more trouble in Europe.

On June 28, 1919, German leaders met with the Allies in the Hall of Mirrors at the Palace of Versailles. There, the leaders signed the Treaty of Versailles. The Germans were then obligated to meet the demands in the treaty.

The war had involved countries on two continents. It had cost many, many lives. People described World War I as "the Great War" or "**the war to end all wars**." However, people soon realized they had been too optimistic in assuming there would be no more war after this one.

Many problems had been left unsolved. Germany remained extremely bitter about its defeat. Europe was still divided into systems of alliances between nations. And several countries were developing dangerous new political ideas.

But for a while, the world enjoyed peace.

From left to right: Allied leaders David Lloyd George of Britain, Vittorio Orlando of Italy, Georges Clemenceau of France, and Woodrow Wilson of the United States

"Come, behold the works of the Lord, what desolations he hath made in the earth. He maketh wars to cease unto the end of the earth; he breaketh the bow, and cutteth the spear in sunder; he burneth the chariot in the fire."

Psalm 46:8–9

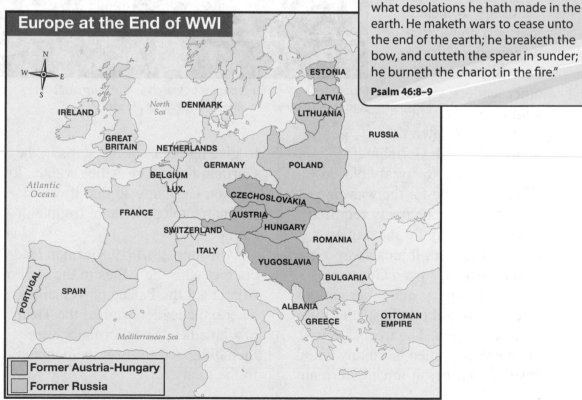

Europe at the End of WWI

N
W E
S

ESTONIA
LATVIA
LITHUANIA
RUSSIA
IRELAND
North Sea
DENMARK
GREAT BRITAIN
NETHERLANDS
GERMANY
POLAND
BELGIUM
LUX.
CZECHOSLOVAKIA
Atlantic Ocean
FRANCE
AUSTRIA
SWITZERLAND
HUNGARY
ROMANIA
ITALY
YUGOSLAVIA
BULGARIA
PORTUGAL
SPAIN
ALBANIA
GREECE
OTTOMAN EMPIRE
Mediterranean Sea

Former Austria-Hungary
Former Russia

Chapter 4

Nations of the Earth

The earth belongs to God. He governs each nation even though we cannot see Him. A **nation** is a large group of people that has a common culture, history, and land. These people mostly share the same beliefs, language, and race. When a nation has its own rights, land, and government, it is recognized as a country. Learning about the nations helps us begin to understand how God rules over them.

It is difficult to think of studying the whole world at once. There are so many people, so much land, and so many events through so long a time. Because of this, the study of places is organized by historians and geographers. They group the information by culture, history, and geography. These divisions make it easier to understand more about people and places.

Cultures

At seven o'clock in the morning in America, an alarm clock rings. A boy rolls over to turn it off and thinks of a race he will run at school that day. In Syria, a bell chimes, and a boy goes to prayers with his father. In China, a buzzer sounds, and a boy begins to study. All over the world, every day, people go about their routines with many different purposes.

All peoples of the world have **customs**, or practices, that make them different from all other people. These customs are part of a country's culture. **Culture** is a way of life. It is the combination of languages, religions, government, economy, customs, and arts of a group of people. Most people cherish their cultures and strive to preserve them. Your country or city has some things that make it different from other countries or cities. We live in an interesting world filled with variety.

This church is a group within a culture in Ghana, Africa.

Hudson Taylor was an English missionary to China. He believed in learning the culture of others. Taylor had his head shaved except for a section in the back. Into those remaining hairs, he had a braid woven until his own hair grew long enough to braid. He also wore Chinese clothing. This included a long silk outer gown with full sleeves that marked him as a teacher. Other English missionaries disapproved of Taylor's change in appearance. However, he was eventually received by the Chinese—and so was the gospel.

The culture to which you belong consists of many smaller groups. For example, your community is a small group within your state. And your church is a small group within your community.

You make many choices during the day. What you have been taught by parents, teachers, and friends affects what you believe and the choices you make. These people close to you form another group to which you belong. You are an important part of many groups within your culture. You make a difference in your family, church, community, state, and country. It is a Christian's responsibility to make the right choices so that he can have a godly influence on those around him.

A Christian also has a responsibility to learn about the cultures of other places. This knowledge will make him a better ambassador, or representative, for Christ.

Hudson Taylor

History

History is the record of activities and events in the lives of all the people who have ever lived. Every nation has a unique history that is a small part of the whole story of man on the earth. **Historians**, or people who study history, use many sources to put these stories together. Sources supply information about something and can be written or non-written.

Primary Sources

Some information used by historians comes from primary sources. A **primary source** is an original object or document from a particular time period.

Objects are non-written sources. They can be natural objects, such as fossils or bones. They can also be objects made by people, such as **artifacts**. Some examples of artifacts are pottery, clothing, or even buildings. Photographs and paintings done during the time period they represent are also non-written primary sources. Besides studying objects, historians may also learn

Decorative vase from China

The Parthenon in Greece

about a time or event by listening to people who experienced it.

Historians also read documents and other written sources. These are primary sources if they were written by people who lived in the times they wrote about. Some examples of written primary sources are old letters or journals. Such accounts are valuable to historians. The Gospels are primary sources. Because it is the Word of God, the Bible is a primary source.

This journal was written by a soldier during World War I.

Some primary sources are written during the same time as the events, but the writer may not have actually seen what he writes about. For example, a newspaper may print a story from another newspaper without sending out its own reporter. Such a story is a primary source but not a firsthand report.

Replica of the Wright brothers' 1909 military plane

Secondary Sources

Sometimes people create new sources based on their study of primary sources. These new sources are called **secondary sources**. Like primary sources, secondary sources may be written or non-written. They are made after the events of the original sources have passed.

In AD 79, Mt. Vesuvius, a volcano in Italy, erupted. Artifacts preserved

This secondary source tells us what it may have been like to travel in Old Testament times.

Preparing to Depart for Canaan. Leandro Bassano, called Leandro da Ponte. From the Bob Jones University Museum & Gallery Collection.

in the ash were a record of the event. These artifacts are primary sources. In 1785, the eruption was portrayed in a painting by a Swiss painter named Angelica Kauffman. She had studied primary sources. But she did not live during the time period the volcano erupted. Therefore, her painting is a secondary source.

Another secondary source can be found in the Lincoln Memorial in Washington, D.C. The statue of Abraham Lincoln was completed by sculptors who used primary sources. The statue was made about fifty years after Lincoln's death.

Many books with history topics are secondary sources. The writers may use written or non-written primary sources to gather information as they write.

Stories, legends, and folk songs may also contain historical information. These can serve as secondary sources and are often passed from generation to generation.

Digging Up the Past

Until the early 1900s, most people who dug into places of the past were in search of treasures to sell or hoard. An ancient site that yielded incredible wealth was the tomb of Tutankhamen, an Egyptian pharaoh. Solid gold artifacts were found there. One artifact was a gold mask, an art treasure itself. Some discoverers of the tomb were mainly interested in the money the artifacts would bring. They enjoyed the prestige of owning things that once belonged to a famous king.

Today, the goal of such searches is usually to learn about the people of long ago. Some great Viking ships, for example, have been carefully removed from where they were buried in the earth. These ships are preserved for what they can tell us about how the Vikings lived.

Archaeologists are people who excavate and study ancient sites. They work with soil specialists, chemists, and even botanists and zoologists. It is important for archaeologists to look at every part of a dig and search for clues that can help unravel the mystery of earlier days. Workers use small spades and soft brushes to carefully clean each item. Archaeologists and their helpers sort through everything, even ancient trash dumps. To archaeologists, even broken pottery is a treasure of information.

Geography

Geography is the study of a place on earth. This study includes a place's land, climate, natural resources, and influence on its people. Chapter 1 of this book discussed other characteristics of geography, such as the earth's latitude and longitude, and natural boundaries. Together, these are all parts of a good geography study.

Natural Resources

Psalm 33:5 tells us that the goodness of the Lord fills the earth. We can see and know God's goodness by noticing the many treasures in and on the earth. God placed these **natural resources** on earth for our use. The very soil we walk on, the plants that grow from it, and the minerals beneath it are all gifts from Him. God has also given us the sun, fresh water, wildlife, and the oceans. How we use these gifts shows our respect for the Giver, the Lord. Sadly, some people choose to worship the gifts instead of worshipping God.

Some regions of the world have more natural resources than others. People must use the resources that they have to meet their basic needs of food, shelter, and clothing.

> "The earth is full of the goodness of the Lord."
> **Psalm 33:5**

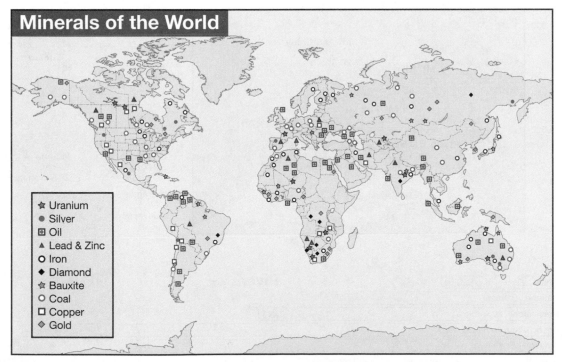

Minerals of the World

- ☆ Uranium
- ● Silver
- ⊡ Oil
- ▲ Lead & Zinc
- ○ Iron
- ◆ Diamond
- ✩ Bauxite
- ○ Coal
- □ Copper
- ◇ Gold

This map shows the major kinds of minerals found all over the world.

Land Features

The study of land features and their elevations is called **topography**. You already know many of the land features found around the world. Mountains, valleys, caves, and canyons are land features. But land features are not limited to the land. They also include rivers, lakes, swamps, and waterfalls.

An area may have one or more land features. The Great Plains in the central United States is such an area. It has mostly flat plains, but rivers, lakes, and even some hills are also found there.

No two land features are the same. God made each river, lake, and mountain unique.

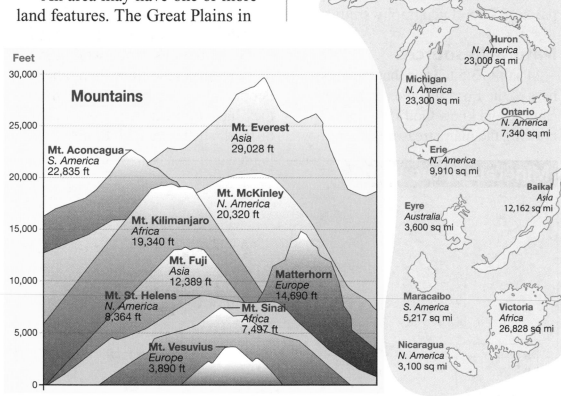

Mountains

Mt. Everest *Asia* 29,028 ft
Mt. Aconcagua *S. America* 22,835 ft
Mt. McKinley *N. America* 20,320 ft
Mt. Kilimanjaro *Africa* 19,340 ft
Mt. Fuji *Asia* 12,389 ft
Matterhorn *Europe* 14,690 ft
Mt. St. Helens *N. America* 8,364 ft
Mt. Sinai *Africa* 7,497 ft
Mt. Vesuvius *Europe* 3,890 ft

Feet: 30,000 / 25,000 / 20,000 / 15,000 / 10,000 / 5,000 / 0

Lakes

Superior *N. America* 31,700 sq mi
Huron *N. America* 23,000 sq mi
Michigan *N. America* 23,300 sq mi
Ontario *N. America* 7,340 sq mi
Erie *N. America* 9,910 sq mi
Baikal *Asia* 12,162 sq mi
Eyre *Australia* 3,600 sq mi
Maracaibo *S. America* 5,217 sq mi
Victoria *Africa* 26,828 sq mi
Nicaragua *N. America* 3,100 sq mi

Rivers

Rhine	*Europe*	820 mi
Danube	*Europe*	1,776 mi
Mississippi	*N. America*	2,315 mi
Chang Jiang (Yangtze)	*Asia*	3,964 mi
Amazon	*S. America*	4,000 mi
Nile	*Africa*	4,160 mi

People can see an overview of a land's features by using **physical maps**. These special maps show hills and mountains, rivers and valleys, plateaus and canyons, and other land features. There are many kinds of physical maps. A relief map uses shading to show the height of landforms. An elevation map uses colors to show how far above or below **sea level** the land is. Sea level is shown as 0 on an elevation key.

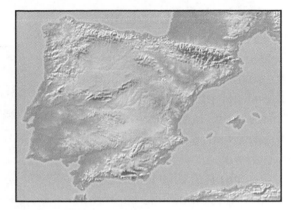

In this relief map of Spain, the shading helps you see where the mountains are.

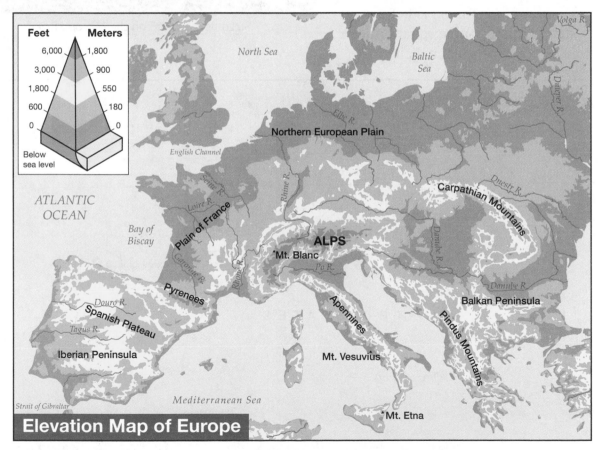

Elevation Map of Europe

Compare this map with the map on page 68 (*Europe at the End of WWI*). Notice the land features that form natural boundaries between some of the countries.

Nations and Capitals

Along with natural land features, man-made features are important. Cities are included in the study of geography. Many cities were built near useful land features such as rivers or other waterways.

A **capital** city is the chief city of a nation. The capital of the United States is **Washington, D.C.** This city makes up the entire District of Columbia. The District of Columbia is not a state, but sixty-nine square miles set aside for the capital city.

St. Louis is located on the Missouri River.

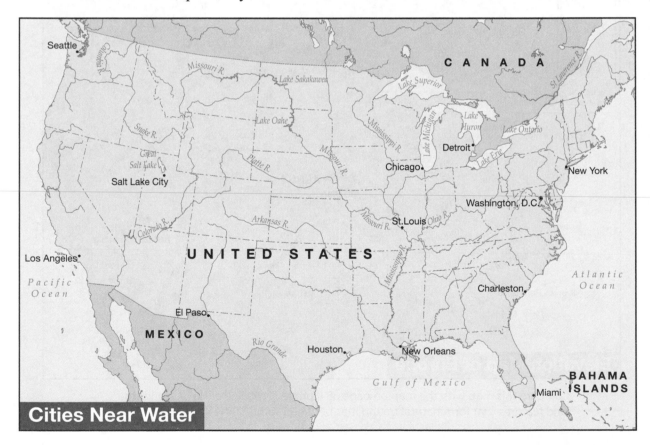

Cities Near Water

L'Enfant's plan for the city of Washington

The site for Washington, D.C., was chosen by President George Washington. Part of the land he chose belonged to Maryland and part to Virginia. Both states gave land to the United States government for the city. In 1791, President Washington hired the French engineer, Pierre Charles L'Enfant, to plan the city.

In 1800, the United States government moved from Philadelphia to Washington, D.C. The streets of the new city were made of dirt. L'Enfant designed a broad strip of land known as the "Grand Avenue." The Capitol building sat at one end of it. Today the Grand Avenue is known as **"the Mall."**

"The Mall," Washington, D.C.

During the War of 1812, British troops came in 1814 and burned many of Washington, D.C.'s, buildings. Among these buildings were the White House and the Capitol. But by 1819, the buildings were rebuilt. The Capitol was even bigger and grander than before.

Although many people had hoped that the city would grow quickly, it did not. Washington, D.C., remained much smaller and less influential than the older cities of New York, Boston, and Philadelphia. By looking at the graph on this page, you can see the rise and fall of the population of Washington, D.C.

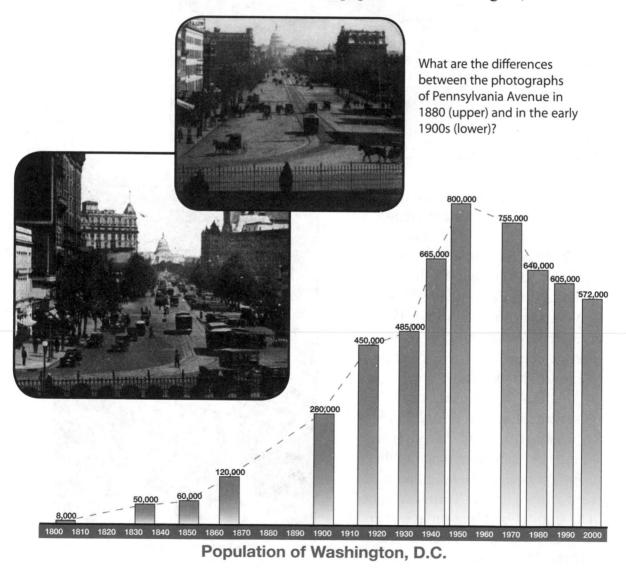

What are the differences between the photographs of Pennsylvania Avenue in 1880 (upper) and in the early 1900s (lower)?

Population of Washington, D.C.

Every country has a capital. In a capital city, the government meets to conduct much of its business. The country's laws are made there. Like Washington, D.C., capital cities contain the government buildings. These buildings include a residence for the country's ruler. Often many of the country's officials live in or near the capital city.

London

Berlin

Paris

Madrid

European Capitals After World War I

FINLAND
Helsinki

NORWAY
Oslo ⊛

SWEDEN
Stockholm ⊛

Tallinn ⊛
ESTONIA

Riga ⊛
LATVIA

Moscow ⊛

North Sea

DENMARK

LITHUANIA
Vilnius ⊛

RUSSIA

IRELAND
Dublin ⊛

Copenhagen ⊛

NETHERLANDS
Amsterdam ⊛

Berlin ⊛

Warsaw ⊛

GREAT BRITAIN
London ⊛

Brussels ⊛
GERMANY

POLAND

BELGIUM

LUX.
Luxembourg

Prague ⊛

Atlantic Ocean

Paris ⊛

CZECHOSLOVAKIA

FRANCE

Vienna ⊛

Budapest ⊛

Bern ⊛

AUSTRIA HUNGARY

ROMANIA

SWITZERLAND

Belgrade ⊛

Bucharest ⊛

YUGOSLAVIA

BULGARIA
Sofia ⊛

Lisbon ⊛
PORTUGAL

SPAIN
Madrid ⊛

ITALY
Rome ⊛

Tirane ⊛

ALBANIA

OTTOMAN EMPIRE

GREECE

Mediterranean Sea

Athens ⊛

Symbols

Every country is different. The differences include the kind of government and ruler the country has. The people of a country may speak different languages or work different kinds of jobs than those living in other countries. These differences help form a country's identity to the rest of the world. A country's identity is represented by national symbols. Two **national symbols** are flags and anthems.

National Flags

Perhaps you think that nations have always displayed flags to represent their countries. However, **national flags** have been around only since AD 16. Earlier flags, along with banners and streamers, were used to represent rulers, such as kings or lords, and ideas, such as a religion or courage. Some Chinese art from 3000 BC shows cloth attached to the tops of poles. These early flags were probably made of silk.

Early flags were used in battle. Sometimes they indicated the direction of the wind to help those who had to shoot arrows at the enemy. Flags also helped leaders locate their armies. Eventually, flags bore symbols that stood for the people they represented.

This banner was carried by the troops of Edward III of England in the 1300s.

Flags often stir patriotism in people. Every country has a national flag that represents that nation to the world. These flags are displayed at international events such as the Olympics. An **international** event is one where two or more nations are present.

A country may also have flags that represent a government leader, such as the president of the United States. Flags are also used to represent large international organizations, such as the United Nations.

Regions within a country may also have flags. Each state in the United States has its own flag.

National Anthems

Another national symbol of each country is its national anthem. A **national anthem** is the official song that represents a nation. It may be played before official government events.

This symbol appears on the flag of the president of the United States.

Some anthems are military marches. Others have a soft, calm tune. The national anthem of the United States is "**The Star Spangled Banner**."

Most anthems have words that can be sung. In some countries, the national anthem is played or sung before ball games, plays, or other special events. Whether played or sung, an anthem increases the citizens' feelings of patriotism.

Flags and anthems represent nations to the world. In much the same way, Christians are to represent Christ to the world. A Christian's actions are like a flag, and his words like an anthem. A good testimony shows and tells others of Christ's love for them.

At the Olympics, the national anthem of the gold medalist is played.

83

Researching a Country

1. Choose a country to research.

2. Find information about your country by looking in books and other resources.

3. Complete the information cards in your Activity Manual.

4. Prepare a map of your country on poster board or cardboard. Cut out your information cards and attach them to the map with string. Now you have a mobile displaying your information.

5. Present your mobile to the class.

Chapter 5

States in the Spotlight

Prologue

Imagine what it would be like to present the entire history of the United States as a play on a stage. The fifty states could be the characters.

Now think about what the costumes for this play would look like. Each costume would need to show characteristics of the people who live and work in the state it represents. The character of a farming state may wear denim overalls. A costume may also represent past or present events of a state. Some characters might wear the colored beads of the Comanche Indian warriors. We could even see one character wearing the dusty hat and boots of a cowboy. Think of the type of clothing your state's character would wear in our play.

Your character will need to have a specific role, or part. Some roles might be joyful, and others, sad. Some might be a little frightening. And some would even involve hardship and bloodshed. Yet each role would be an honor to portray. All the characters would have one important thing in common—freedom.

The background scenery for this play is a map of the United States. Each region of the map has a different color. Locate your state and its capital. Find the region your state is in.

Regions of the United States

NORTH DAKOTA
*Bismarck

SOUTH DAKOTA
*Pierre

MINNESOTA

WISCONSIN
*Saint Paul

IOWA
*Des Moines

NEBRASKA
*Lincoln

KANSAS
*Topeka

MISSOURI
*Jefferson City

OKLAHOMA
*Oklahoma City

TEXAS
*Austin

MICHIGAN
*Lansing
*Madison

ILLINOIS
*Springfield

INDIANA
*Indianapolis

OHIO
*Columbus

KENTUCKY
*Frankfort

W. VIRGINIA
*Charleston

VIRGINIA
*Richmond

ARKANSAS
*Little Rock

TENNESSEE
*Nashville

NORTH CAROLINA
*Raleigh

SOUTH CAROLINA
*Columbia

LOUISIANA
*Baton Rouge

MISSISSIPPI
*Jackson

ALABAMA
*Montgomery

GEORGIA
*Atlanta

FLORIDA
*Tallahassee

NEW HAMPSHIRE
VERMONT
*Montpelier

MAINE
*Augusta
*Concord

NEW YORK
*Albany
*Boston **MASSACHUSETTS**
*Providence **RHODE ISLAND**
*Hartford **CONNECTICUT**

PENNSYLVANIA
*Harrisburg
*Trenton **NEW JERSEY**
*Dover **DELAWARE**
*Annapolis **MARYLAND**

Pacific
Rocky Mountain
Southwest
Middle West
Southeast
Northeast

87

The Northeast

The **Northeast region** includes eleven states. Many of these states would have major parts in a play about America's history.

One of the leading roles would belong to *Pennsylvania*. In 1776, the Declaration of Independence was written. It was signed at the Second Continental Congress in Philadelphia. Another important date for Philadelphia was 1787. This was the year America's leaders wrote the United States Constitution. Philadelphia was also one of the early capitals of the United States.

Massachusetts would also have a leading part in our historical play. Boston, the state capital, was a center of activity before and during the American Revolution (War for Independence). In an event called the Boston Massacre, British soldiers killed five colonists. Several years later, American patriots dumped British tea into the harbor. They did this because they thought Britain's tax on tea was unfair. This event was called the Boston Tea Party.

Maryland would have a singing part in our play. During the War of 1812, America's national anthem, "The Star-Spangled Banner," was composed. Francis Scott Key wrote it as he watched a battle from the deck of a ship. He saw the flag flying over Fort McHenry at Baltimore's harbor.

The American flag still flies over Fort McHenry today.

Ethan Allen led the Green Mountain Boys.

What about costumes for the states of the Northeast? Perhaps *Vermont* would enter dressed as a Green Mountain Boy. The Green Mountain Boys were a group of Vermont settlers that formed a military force in 1770. They made history when they captured Fort Ticonderoga from the British.

New York might wear a crown and a long gown, and carry a raised torch to represent the Statue of Liberty. The statue was a gift to the United States from France. It stands in New York Harbor. Also known as "Lady Liberty," the statue has become famous as a symbol of America's freedom.

Rhode Island might choose the costume of the Narragansett (NAR uh GAN sit) people. These were one of Rhode Island's earliest Native Americans. A Narragansett wardrobe might include buckskin leggings and a necklace of bone, shells, and beads. Rhode Island's Narragansett Bay takes its name from this early people.

Narragansett woman

Statue of Liberty

Delaware would likely wear the colorful clothing of a Dutch or Swedish settler. A group of colonists from Hoorn in the Netherlands were the first European settlers in the Delaware region. Later, Swedish people also formed a settlement there.

Maine might come on stage dressed in work clothes and carrying the tools of a shipbuilder. People have been building ships in Maine for a long time. In 1607, English colonists built their first ship in North America. They called it the *Virginia*. The first sea battle fought during the American Revolution took place off the coast of Maine. Today, boats and ships built in Maine are often used for fishing, one of the state's largest industries.

For our remaining northeastern states, perhaps we could use costumes that represent famous people. In *New Jersey*, George Washington made his famous crossing over the Delaware River. Nathan Hale was a schoolteacher and a patriot from *Connecticut*. Before he was hanged by the British, he supposedly said, "I only regret that I have but one life to lose for my country." Alan Shepard Jr. was born and raised in *New Hampshire*. He was the first American astronaut to travel into space.

District of Columbia

The District of Columbia is not a state. It is located between two regions—the Northeast and the Southeast. Remember that the people of Maryland and Virginia each gave part of their land to America's government. The government wanted to use these lands to build the city of Washington, D.C. This city is now the capital of the United States. It is where the president lives and the government makes laws for the country.

The Capitol Building in Washington, D.C.

The Southeast

The **Southeast region** is made up of twelve states. The states of this region have had difficult roles to play in America's history. Many of them have battle scars from the Civil War.

In the early 1860s, the United States had thirty-four states. But eleven southeastern states decided to secede, or break away, from the United States. These eleven states formed a new country called the **Confederate States of America**. The eleven states were known as the Confederacy. The remaining twenty-three states were called the Union. Some of our play's most tragic scenes would show the Confederacy fighting against the Union. Often family members, even brothers, fought against each other in the Civil War.

The graves of many Confederate soldiers are in this Chattanooga cemetery.

91

The surrender ending the Civil War took place in the McLean House in 1865.

called Appomattox Court House. There General Robert E. Lee and Lieutenant General Ulysses S. Grant reached an agreement to end the war.

South Carolina would play a key part in scenes about the Civil War. It was the first state to secede from the United States. The Civil War started in the harbor of Charleston. The fighting began when Confederate troops fired upon the Union troops in Fort Sumter.

Virginia would have a major part in the play. Eight United States presidents were from Virginia. And many important events happened there. The first permanent English settlement was at Jamestown in 1607. Two major wars ended in Virginia—the American Revolution and the Civil War. The American Revolution ended at Yorktown, where Lord Cornwallis surrendered to George Washington. And the Civil War ended at a small town

Tennessee would have some tragic scenes in its role. During the Civil War, a major battle was fought at Shiloh. Although the Union eventually won the battle, each side lost over ten thousand men. Later, in 1878, an epidemic, or outbreak, of yellow fever swept through the city of Memphis. Out of 19,600 people in Memphis, over 5,000 died.

Fort Sumter in Charleston Harbor

Georgia's role in our play would require a special prop called the cotton gin. This machine was invented by Eli Whitney in 1793 near Savannah. The cotton gin could quickly separate cottonseeds from the fibers. This process used to be done by hand. But the cotton gin could do much more work in less time. This gave the United States a successful and leading cotton industry.

Mississippi would probably have a part right before a scene change in our play. A major turning point in the Civil War occurred in 1863. This was the year Union soldiers won a battle at Vicksburg, a busy port city on the Mississippi River.

Some of *Louisiana*'s lines in our play might be in French. Louisiana was part of the region that the French explorer La Salle (lah SAHL) claimed for France. The first European settlers in Louisiana were from France. Later, French-speaking people from Canada settled there as well. These immigrants were called "Cajuns." Today the city of New Orleans has a neighborhood known as the French Quarter. Some people who live there still speak a French dialect and enjoy French cooking.

Vicksburg National Military Park

The French Quarter in New Orleans is famous for the lacy ironwork that adorns its buildings.

93

Daniel Boone

Perhaps *Kentucky* would dress for our play in what Daniel Boone wore—a black felt hat and rugged clothing. Daniel Boone cut the first path for travelers through the Appalachian Mountains. He led a group of pioneers from Virginia to Kentucky through the Cumberland Gap. Boone called his trail the Wilderness Road.

West Virginia might wear the costume of a coal miner. In the early 1700s, a man named John Salling discovered coal in West Virginia. After further growth of the railroad in the mid-1800s, coal mining became one of the state's largest industries.

Florida might choose the plumed hat and full-sleeved coat of a Spanish explorer. Ponce de Leon (PONS duh LEE-uhn) discovered and named

Florida. He was searching for the "Fountain of Youth" that he had heard of in legends. Later, at St. Augustine, Spaniards formed the first permanent European settlement in 1565.

North Carolina might wear the costume of Sir Walter Raleigh. He sent a group of men to explore Roanoke Island. They mysteriously disappeared. The vanished people are often referred to as the Lost Colony.

Alabama might dress as George Washington Carver, who discovered over three hundred uses for the peanut. He was the agriculture director at Tuskegee Institute, a college for African Americans.

George Washington Carver

For *Arkansas* we might have a rocky formation on stage. The formation located on the banks of the Arkansas River is what gave the capital city of Little Rock its name.

Interpreting and Graphing Data

1. Get some colored pencils and your Activity Manual.

2. Look at the chart on the Activity Manual page. It is similar to one you can find in an almanac or other research sources. Choose a city from the chart. Write the name of the city in the title of the graph.

3. Study the almanac page to find information asked for on each graph.

4. Record the information on each graph.

5. Answer the questions to help you interpret the information.

The Middle West

The middle of our play would bring the states of the **Middle West region** to the stage. This region has twelve states. Many of these states were part of the territory the United States bought from France. This purchase of land was known as the Louisiana Purchase.

Iowa was one of the states carved out of the Louisiana Purchase territory. Its part in our play would have some battle scenes. Chief Black Hawk was the leader of the Sauk and the Fox people. His people wanted to stay on the land they lived on. They fought against United States troops for it. In the end, Black Hawk was forced to give up a section of Iowa's land to the white settlers. People called it the Black Hawk Purchase.

Chief Black Hawk

Lincoln's tomb in Oak Ridge Cemetery

Illinois would have a main part in our play. One of America's greatest leaders, Abraham Lincoln, lived and worked there. Today, he is buried in Springfield, the state capital. Chicago is another famous city. It was nearly destroyed by a great fire in 1871.

Michigan is made up of two separate land areas. The areas are called the Upper Peninsula and the Lower Peninsula. What part would Michigan have in our play? Perhaps

The Detroit River connects Lake St. Claire (upper lake) and Lake Erie (lower lake).

we would have an old-fashioned car on stage. Henry Ford's automobile factory was in Detroit. Detroit was first known as Fort Pontchartrain du Détroit, a French port built on the Detroit River. The city's name comes from the French word *détroit*, which means "strait."

Missouri's part in our play would involve some arguing. It became part of the United States as a result of the Missouri Compromise in 1820. Many people wanted Missouri to be a slave state, while others wanted it to be a free state. The Missouri Compromise was a legal agreement. It had two parts. One part admitted Missouri as a slave state. And the other admitted Maine as a free state.

Another event that caused people to argue was the Supreme Court's ruling about a slave from Missouri. The slave's name was Dred Scott. Scott had lived in a free state for a while and he sought his freedom through the court. But the Supreme Court decided that Scott could not have his freedom. The ruling also stated that slavery could not be against the law in United States territories.

Dred Scott

Kansas would be involved in some violent scenes in our play. Before Kansas became a state, people fought over whether it should be a slave state or a free state. John Brown was an abolitionist, or a person who was against slavery. He led a raid on a Kansas settlement at Pottawatomie Creek. He and his men killed five settlers. Other incidents like this gave this state the nickname "Bleeding Kansas."

John Brown

South Dakota's part in the play would stir up some excitement in the audience. General Custer's soldiers discovered gold in the Black

Sitting Bull

Hills. Gold hunters rushed to South Dakota, and many found what they came for. Gold is still the chief product of South Dakota's mines today. This state's history also had a tragic event. Tension had been building between white settlers and the Native Americans. As a result, in 1890, the United States Army arrested the Sioux (soo) leader, **Sitting Bull**.

Indian warriors tried to rescue their chief, but Sitting Bull was killed in the effort. Later, hundreds of Sioux were killed at Wounded Knee Creek in a battle with the United States Army.

The city of Deadwood served as the "capital" for Black Hills gold hunters.

The Cincinnati Red Stockings were undefeated in their first season of professional play.

The costumes of the Middle West would be colorful and varied. *Ohio* might come dressed in the uniform of a Cincinnati Red Stockings baseball player. The Red Stockings were the first professional baseball team. Today the Cincinnati team is called the Reds.

Wisconsin might wear the blue uniform of a man from the Iron Brigade. This group of men, mostly from the state of Wisconsin, fought for the Union during the Civil War. The troops were commanded by several different Wisconsin generals.

Perhaps *Minnesota* would wear

the white lab coat of a medical doctor. William Mayo and his two sons started St. Mary's

Mayo Clinic

Hospital in Rochester. Later, the name of the hospital was changed to Mayo Clinic. It is one of the world's foremost centers of medical research.

The *Nebraska* character might dress as a farmer. About 95 percent of the state is farmland. Wheat, corn, and cattle are its main products. It is called "The Cornhusker State," and cornhusking contests are held there.

A view of the badlands in Theodore Roosevelt National Park in North Dakota

North Dakota's character could be dressed as a rancher or a coal miner. Nearly all of the state is covered with ranches and farms. This state is also one of the country's top producers of coal. The badlands region of the state has beautiful rock formations. Many of the formations resulted from soft coal burning under the surface of the earth.

Indiana's character may play the part of a racecar driver. The state is famous for its Indianapolis 500 race. Also, the first professional baseball game was played in Fort Wayne.

The Southwest

Let's bring the **Southwest region** to center stage. This region has the fewest number of states—only four.

Oklahoma's part in our play would include the **Trail of Tears**. This was a journey made by people from five Native American groups. Oklahoma was set aside to be Indian Territory. Groups of Creek, Choctaw, Chickasaw, Seminole, and Cherokee had to leave their homes in the southeastern states and move to Oklahoma. Many grew sick and died on the journey. Later, even the land that was supposed to belong to them was opened for white settlers. More than fifty thousand people poured into Oklahoma to build homes on the first day that the land opened. These people were nicknamed "boomers." Some even entered the land before it was open for settlement.

Arizona was part of the land the United States gained from Mexico after the **Mexican War**. Its part in our play might include a treasure hunt. The first European to explore Arizona was a Spanish priest named Marcos de Niza (NEE sah) in 1539. He was looking for the legendary Seven Cities of Cíbola (SEE buh luh). They were thought to contain gold.

Cold weather was only one of the many hardships the Native Americans endured on the Trail of Tears.

Think of some costumes the Southwest states would wear. Perhaps *New Mexico* would come on stage in the fur robes and feathers of the **Anasazi** (AH nuh SAH zee) people. The Anasazi were farmers who grew corn, beans, gourds, and cotton. They made their homes in the walls of cliffs. The Spanish explorer Coronado found their villages. He, like Marcos de Niza, searched for gold.

Texas might choose to carry the Lone Star

In 1835, Texan men formed a group called the Rangers to defend settlers from bandits and outlaws.

Fragments of Anasazi pottery

flag and a rifle. These would be in memory of the state's struggle for freedom from Mexico. Another symbol for freedom would be the Alamo Mission, a military fort. There, a small group of Texans defended the fort from the Mexican army. But the Mexicans held the fort under siege, and most of the Texan defenders were killed. The struggle did not stop there. A month later, under the command of Sam Houston, Texans defeated the army of Mexico at the Battle of San Jacinto. For the next ten years, Texas was an independent republic. It flew a flag with a single, lone star. This is still the state flag today.

Anasazi homes in the cliffs

Designing Costumes

Have you ever seen a play that made you wish you could be in it? What did you like about that play? Maybe you liked the costumes of the characters. Costumes help audiences better understand a play. They tell about a play's place and time. Costumes also give clues about the personalities of the characters.

The first thing a costume designer must do is research. He reads the script of the play. Perhaps he even watches a rehearsal or two. He must be familiar with the play's setting, or the location and time period in which the action happens.

Historical plays require a designer's special attention. He needs to find out exact details about how people from that time period dressed. Even the kind of fabric and color of fabric are important. A designer would never use a yellow fabric for a Puritan costume. Puritans believed the color yellow was a symbol of pride. But yellow would work well for an early American colonist costume. Colonists considered the color yellow as a symbol of hopefulness and happiness.

Designer's board of fabrics

Costume designers use different sources to find out the details needed to design a costume. Library books are always a helpful source of information. The designer could also study letters or paintings from the era of the play. These might give him extra hints about fashions of the day. He might fold up one corner of an apron or give a plume a stylish tilt over the brim of a hat.

Next, the designer makes a sketch of his idea to show the director of the play. The stage crew might also need to give its approval of the sketches. Full hoop skirts for a play set in Civil War times might not be practical on stage. The actors may have only a small amount of room to move around.

The last step is actually making the costumes. Cast members must be measured first, and then the fabrics must be purchased, cut, and sewn. But the work is worthwhile when performance night arrives. The lights brighten the stage as the actors come out in their different costumes. The designer knows he has done his job well when he sees the satisfied smiles and admiring eyes of the audience.

Scene from *Hamlet*, Bob Jones University Classic Players

The Rocky Mountain Region

Our play's next act belongs to the **Rocky Mountain region**. Six north-western states make up this region. The Rocky Mountain Range runs through all but one of these states.

Montana would have some unruly scenes in the play. General George Custer and his men fought Sioux and Cheyenne (shahy AN) warriors near the Little Bighorn River. The two tribes defeated Custer and his men. The battle was called **"Custer's Last Stand."** A year later, Chief Joseph, the Nez Perce (NEZ PURS) leader, tried to move his people from Oregon to Canada. He wanted them to settle there. But the United States government wanted the Nez Perce to settle on a reservation in Idaho. After a one-thousand-mile trek, he and his people were captured at Big Hole in the Montana Territory.

Jim Bridger, fur trader

General George Custer

Utah's part in our play would begin with a fur trader named Jim Bridger. He explored the Utah region. When he tasted the water in the **Great Salt Lake**, he thought he had found the ocean. Why do you suppose he thought that? Later, members of the Mormon religious group came to live in Utah.

We would see some different costumes as the Rocky Mountain states enter our play. *Colorado* might wear boots and carry a backpack as mountain climbers do. Explorer **Zebulon** (ZEB yuh lon) **Pike** discovered one of the most famous peaks in the Rocky Mountain range. He named the steep mountain with its curved top Pikes Peak. The tallest mountaintops of the Rockies are in Colorado.

Nevada might carry mining tools as part of its costume. Henry Comstock found a rich **lode**, or a source of ore, that contained silver and gold. He discovered it near Virginia City and named it the

Buffalo Bill

Henry Comstock, miner

Comstock Lode. Miners poured into Nevada hoping to become rich, and many did.

Perhaps *Wyoming* would be dressed in a fringed jacket and a cowboy hat like "Buffalo Bill" Cody might have worn. He was one of Wyoming's famous people. Before retiring to his Wyoming ranch, Buffalo Bill acted in a traveling show. The show gave people his view of the Wild West.

Idaho might come dressed as missionary Eliza Spalding. She and her husband established the Lapwai (LAP wy) Mission Station in the Idaho Territory. Eliza was one of the first white women to settle in the Northwest.

The Pacific

The final act brings the **Pacific region** to the stage. This western region contains five states.

Alaska and Hawaii would be the two youngest characters in our play. *Alaska* joined the United States in January of 1959. Secretary of State William Seward (SOO urd) had purchased the territory from Russia in 1867. At first, people called the large barren land of Alaska "Seward's Folly" or "Icebergia." But Americans soon learned that Alaska was rich in resources. One of these resources was oil. In 1977, workers completed the **trans-Alaska pipeline**. This pipeline can carry two million barrels of oil a day. Today, the oil still flows from Alaska's north coast to its south coast.

When the oil reaches the south coast, it is carried by ship and sold.

Hawaii became the fiftieth state in August of 1959.

Trans-Alaska pipeline

Liliuokalani was the last queen of Hawaii.

The first people to live on the islands were Polynesians. Presently, people from many different countries live there. Hawaii has over a hundred islands. Eight of the largest islands are known as the main islands and are where most of the people live. At first, kings and queens ruled the islands. Then the islands formed a republic. On December 7, 1941, the naval base at **Pearl Harbor** on the island of Oahu (oh AH hoo) was bombed by Japan. This caused the United States to join World War II.

This memorial at Pearl Harbor honors those who died aboard the USS *Arizona*.

Let's look at some of the costumes the Pacific states might wear. The state of *Washington* might wear a warm coat and carry a bundle of furs. Traders sailed to this territory to trade for furs. One trader was Robert Gray, a merchant sea captain. Captain Gray made several trips to trade for furs with the Chinook people. On one trip, he named the **Columbia River**. The Columbia River is part of the boundary between Washington and Oregon.

Oregon might dress as explorers Meriwether Lewis or William Clark. Their expedition traveled from St. Louis, Missouri, to the mouth of the Columbia River in Oregon, then back again. The route of their expedition became the **Oregon Trail**. Between the 1840s and 1870s, the rugged Oregon Trail was traveled by hundreds of thousands of settlers.

Perhaps *California* would dress as one of the Hupa or Yurok people. These people lived in the northwestern part of California before any white settlers came. They were skilled woodworkers and even made their own tools. They fashioned canoes for traveling on rivers and on the sea. They were also expert fishermen.

Lewis and Clark recorded their findings in a journal. The men gave peace medals to the Native American chiefs they met.

Epilogue

How do you think the audience will react to our play? Certain scenes might make them laugh, and other scenes might bring tears to their eyes. A lot of scenes might make people think about the future.

But this play is not over yet. It will keep going on as long as there is a United States of America. What parts do you think your state will play in future scenes? Christians must do their part to keep their country looking toward God. One way to do this is for Christians to fear the Lord and to serve and praise Him as they perform public responsibilities.

"Only fear the Lord, and serve him in truth with all your heart: for consider how great things he hath done for you."

1 Samuel 12:24

Chapter 6

The Roaring Twenties

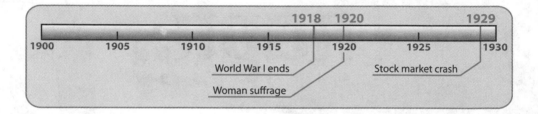

| 1900 | 1905 | 1910 | 1915 | 1918 | 1920 | 1920 | 1925 | 1929 | 1930 |

World War I ends

Woman suffrage

Stock market crash

Changes in Life

The doughboys had come home. Ticker tape parades and waving flags greeted the soldiers as they marched through American streets again. Brass bands played and crowds cheered. Americans were glad that the Allies had won the war. And they were even gladder that the war was finally over.

But when the cheers died away, many people felt let down. It was time to turn from patriotism to the practical business of daily living. Many people realized that life in America would be different. Life would never be the same as it had been before World War I.

After World War I

President Harding promised a "return to normalcy" for the United States after World War I. Most Americans wanted nothing more than for life to return to normal. The soldiers wanted to forget the horrible sights they had seen on the battlefields. People were ready to stop rationing their food and reading

A ticker tape parade in Minneapolis welcoming returning WWI soldiers

the lists of names of dead soldiers. Everyone wanted to relax. They wanted a chance to become rich. They wanted to enjoy life again.

As time went by, life picked up speed. Business was booming. More people were driving cars. And clothing styles were changing. Many women were wearing silk stockings and skirts above the ankles. Even the music was faster.

The decade of the 1920s has been given several names. A few of those names are the Jazz Age, the Dazzling Decade, and the Roaring Twenties. The 1920s had different names because many events happened during those years. It was indeed a decade of change.

New York City During Prohibition

Izzy Einstein and Moe Smith in disguise

The Eighteenth Amendment made it illegal for anyone to make or sell alcohol. This ban on alcohol became known as **Prohibition**. Many people disobeyed the law. Some people made their own alcoholic drinks. Some restaurants, soda shops, and even candy shops had back rooms or basements where alcohol was illegally sold in secret. Such places were called **speakeasies**.

Sometimes policemen accepted money to keep quiet about these illegal businesses. But two New York police agents, Izzy Einstein and Moe Smith, stood up for the law. They often wore creative disguises to get into the secret speakeasies. One time, Izzy pretended to be a musician carrying a violin. Another time, he wore a football uniform. Once inside a speakeasy, Izzy and Moe would pour some alcohol into the flasks they carried in their pockets. The liquor was the evidence that allowed them to make arrests.

The two agents worked only in New York City at first. But soon, other cities wanted to hire them for difficult jobs. Over a five-year period, Izzy and Moe made 4,392 arrests.

Despite the ban on alcohol, police often discovered underground breweries like this one in Detroit.

1830s, Susan B. Anthony, Elizabeth Cady Stanton, and other leaders fought for this cause. They were known as *suffragettes.* Suffragettes collected women's signatures on petitions that asked the government to let them vote. A **petition** is a written request for a right or a benefit from someone in authority.

By 1920, the efforts of the suffragettes caused a big change. A new amendment was ratified. The Nineteenth Amendment allowed women to vote for the first time. That same year, women voted in the election that made Warren G. Harding president.

Amendments

Shortly after World War I, two important *amendments*, or changes, were made to the United States Constitution. These changes were the Eighteenth and Nineteenth Amendments.

In 1919, the Eighteenth Amendment was **ratified,** or approved. This amendment made it illegal to manufacture, transport, or sell alcoholic beverages in the United States.

Women had been working for many years to have another amendment approved. These women wanted **suffrage,** or the right to vote. Since the

Sometimes suffragettes held parades in city streets.

Making a Petition

The suffragettes used petitions to change the Constitution. Petitions can be used to cause other changes as well. Even you can write a petition that may cause a change. What kinds of things might you change? Perhaps you can suggest a change to the order of classes taught each day. Or you could ask for additional playground equipment.

1. Think of an idea for a change in your classroom or school. Make sure your idea is a positive one and something that would be helpful for many people. It may be something that would make the school run more smoothly.

2. Write your idea for a change on the Activity Manual page. Explain your idea and why it is needed.

3. Present your idea to other students, teachers, and parents. Collect signatures from at least six people who have heard your idea and agree with the change you are suggesting.

4. Present your petition and its signatures to your class.

Changes in Attitudes and Behavior

In the 1920s, there were many temptations facing a young person just as there are today. Partying and movie-going were favorite pastimes. A new style of music called **jazz** was popular. And many people were learning a fast new dance called the Charleston.

Standards of dress and behavior that families had upheld for years were changing. Until the decade of the twenties, women were expected to wear ankle-length skirts. Makeup was considered immodest. And young ladies wore their hair long.

Now women's skirts fell just to their knees. Rouge and lipstick grew fashionable. Women all over America sat in barbers' chairs and had their hair cut short around their faces in the new "bobbed" style. Women who dressed in this nontraditional way were called **flappers**.

Your parents have probably taught you certain ways in which you should or should not act. These guidelines of behavior are called **manners**. During the 1920s, many people began ignoring some of their manners. It became acceptable for boys and girls to ride alone together in cars. People "crashed" parties that they hadn't been invited to. Some girls smoked cigarettes and drank alcohol along with boys. Many thought the idea of manners was old-fashioned.

But there were some who refused to go along with the new ideas. Those who did not accept the new ideas often found it hard to be different from their friends.

The Lost Generation

The young people of the 1920s often referred to themselves as "the lost generation." At first, this name had referred to those who lost their lives during the war. But the young people were "lost" in other ways. Many were not trusting in Christ as their Savior from sin. Many had lost their moral values. They were headed in the wrong direction spiritually and morally.

In spite of efforts by policemen like Izzy and Moe, the drinking went on. People crowded into speakeasies all over America. They wanted to drink alcohol, dance, and "have a

A speakeasy

good time." But they did not find lasting happiness in these activities.

One young man often seen at the tables of such places was F. Scott Fitzgerald. He was a writer, and his novels were very popular. He wrote about the younger generation of his day. His stories were based on things he had actually experienced and observed. But despite his fame, Fitzgerald felt empty inside. He went restlessly from one party to the next. He even went to Paris for a time with his wife and young daughter but returned penniless. He never quit drinking and spending money carelessly. Fitzgerald died of a heart attack at the age of forty-four.

F. Scott Fitzgerald's writings are still read and studied today. They reflect the attitudes and values of a whole generation. He once wrote, "In the real dark night of the soul, it is always three o'clock in the morning."

F. Scott Fitzgerald

Francis Scott Key Fitzgerald (1896-1940). American Author. 1935. Oil on canvas, 24 x 20 in. National Portrait Gallery, Smithsonian Institution, Washington, DC, U.S.A.

Spiritual Revival

Some people during the 1920s were concerned about souls. They saw people around them searching for joy in places where they would never find it. And those who cared wanted to help.

One man with such a concern for souls was Billy Sunday. Before he became a Christian, Sunday was a baseball player for the Chicago White Stockings. He heard the gospel in a service at the Pacific Garden Mission in Chicago. He trusted Christ to save him from his sin and give him a new life. A few years later, Sunday gave up generous contracts from two different baseball teams. He believed the Lord wanted him in full-time evangelistic work. So he quit baseball and became a preacher.

During the 1920s, Billy Sunday preached to thousands of people in cities and towns all over the United States. He told them that Christ had died to pay for their sins. He encouraged them to put their trust in the Lord

Billy Sunday

Bellows, George (1882-1925); William Ashley Sunday "Billy" (1862-1935), Evangelist. 1923. Lithograph. Location: National Portrait Gallery, Smithsonian Institution, Washington, DC, U.S.A.

Billy Sunday played for the Chicago White Stockings.

and not to look to alcohol and a sinful lifestyle for happiness.

Bob Jones was another evangelist who ministered during the 1920s. He held most of his meetings in the southern part of the United States. Meetings like his and Billy Sunday's were called **revivals**. At revivals, many people repented of their sin and trusted Christ as their Savior. Often they changed their lifestyles too. But not everyone trusted Christ.

"For whosoever shall call upon the name of the Lord shall be saved."
Romans 10:13

Bob Jones Sr.

116

Admiring Celebrities

Some people in the 1920s were more interested in famous people than in God. Many spent time watching or thinking about their favorite celebrities. For many, celebrities were more important than thinking about God, going to church, or reading the Bible. Anyone or anything that becomes more important to someone than God can become an idol. Worshiping celebrities was very common. It is also common today. Deuteronomy 6:5 tells us that we are to love the Lord with all our hearts and might.

Babe Ruth

Some celebrities in the 1920s were sports figures. Fans flocked to baseball games, hoping to see Babe Ruth hit a home run. People listened to Jack Dempsey's boxing matches on their radios. They cheered Gertrude Ederle with a ticker tape parade after she swam across the English Channel.

Some celebrities were famous actors and actresses. In the early 1920s, films had no sound. People had to read words that appeared on the screen to know what the actors were saying. One of the most popular actors of silent films was Rudolph Valentino. After his death, mourners lined the street for nine blocks outside the funeral parlor.

Some celebrities were not always of noble character or action. One man did not lead an honest life, but he was still held in awe by the public because of his wealth and power. His name was Al Capone. Capone was the leader of a gang of men in Chicago. This group earned millions of dollars through illegal activities in what was known as the underworld. Al Capone and other criminals like him were known as **gangsters**, or mobsters. On February 14, 1929, Al Capone and his gangsters were blamed for the murders of seven of their enemy gangsters. This event was known as the St. Valentine's Day Massacre.

Al Capone

Charles Lindbergh
(1902–1974)

The 1920s was an age when people admired famous people. Some famous people were heroes. One man stood out above the others as the greatest hero of the decade.

Dawn had just broken over Roosevelt Field, Long Island, on May 20, 1927. A crowd of five hundred people had gathered. They watched as a twenty-five-year-old pilot from Minnesota stepped up into his gray-and-white monoplane, the *Spirit of St. Louis*. Charles Lindbergh was about to attempt to fly solo from New York to Paris, France. This was a feat that had never been done before.

Lindbergh started his engines. Armed with sandwiches, a bottle of water, and four hundred fifty gallons of fuel, he felt he was prepared. The *Spirit of St. Louis* sped down the runway and lifted into the air.

The long flight was a fairly smooth one. Toward morning of the second day, Lindbergh became worried when sleet began to cling to his plane. For a moment, he wondered whether he should go back. Later he said, "I decided I must not think any more about going back."

Charles Lindbergh

In the early afternoon of May 21, 1927, Lindbergh flew over Ireland. He knew he was on the right track to France. Once over France, he followed the Seine (SAYN) River into Paris. He landed at the city's airport, Le Bourget (luh boor-ZHEY).

French people swarmed up to the plane, surrounding it almost before Lindbergh brought it to a stop. His first words to the crowd were, "Well, here we are. I am very happy."

Lindbergh's flight of over 3,600 miles had taken a little over thirty-three hours. He was hailed as a hero, not just in the United States and France, but all over the world. In the next few days, he was showered with praise, fan letters, job offers, and even some proposals of marriage. People nicknamed him the "Lone Eagle" and wrote songs about "Lucky Lindy." But through it all, Charles Lindbergh kept his modest smile. "My flight has not done anything to advance the cause of civilization," he said. "Yet I am not unaware that it marks a date."

On leaving Paris, Lindbergh circled the Eiffel (AHY fuhl) Tower twice in his gray-and-white plane. Just before flying away, he dipped the plane low over the Arc de Triomphe (ARK duh tree-OHMF). A message fluttered down onto the Place de la Concorde. "Good-bye, dear Paris," it read. "Ten thousand thanks for your kindness to me."

The Harlem Renaissance

Some famous people of the 1920s were African Americans. Many African Americans lived in Harlem, a neighborhood in New York City, New York. It was during this time that African Americans began to research and preserve their culture. They used forms of literature and art. They wanted to tell others about their culture and heritage. This artistic movement among the black people of Harlem was called the *Harlem Renaissance*.

A man from Harlem named Arthur Schomburg (SHAHM burg) had an idea. He decided to start a collection. He collected books, pamphlets, poems, and pictures. All of the works in his collection were either by or about African Americans. Schomburg's collection grew larger and larger. African American poets and writers began coming to look at it. They wanted to find out about their history and to get ideas for writing.

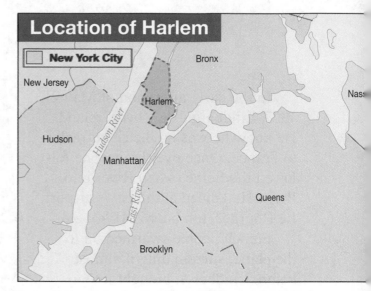

Location of Harlem

New York City

New Jersey

Bronx

Nass

Hudson

Harlem

Hudson River

Manhattan

East River

Queens

Brooklyn

Harlem is in the New York City borough of Manhattan.

Arthur Schomburg kept collecting during his travels to other parts of the world. By 1926, he had collected over five thousand books, three thousand manuscripts, and two thousand pictures.

The Carnegie Foundation bought the collection from Schomburg. The foundation donated the collection to the New York Public Library. Today this collection is located in Harlem at the Schomburg Center for Research in Black Culture.

Arthur Schomburg

Langston Hughes contributed to the Harlem Renaissance. He is best known for his poetry as well as writings about a black man named Simple.

Changes in Interests

Laws, attitudes, and behaviors were not the only things that were changing. Businesses and the ways people made and spent money were also changing.

Model Ts at a Ford factory in 1925

Products and Pastimes

The presidency experienced a sudden change. President Harding died in 1923 after an illness. Calvin Coolidge became the next president. He was elected to the presidency for a full term in 1924. President Coolidge commented on how important business had become. He said, "The chief business of the American people is business."

Business was successful in the 1920s. Factories found ways to **mass produce**, or make large quantities of their products. Often, a product had interchangeable parts. These are parts that can easily be replaced with other parts identical to them. In the 1700s, Eli Whitney promoted the idea of interchangeable parts. Interchangeable parts and the assembly line made products cheaper to make and repair.

For example, Henry Ford's automobile corporation produced interchangeable car parts. Parts like steering wheels and switches were made exactly the same so that they would fit in any car. Ford's company was able to make more than one thousand cars per day because of interchangeable parts and the assembly line.

Henry Ford gradually reduced the price of his automobiles. In 1908, the Model T sold for $850. Woodrow Wilson had called the automobile a "picture of the arrogance of wealth." But in the 1920s, many more people than just wealthy people were driving cars. By 1925, the price of a Model T was down to $260. Between 1920 and 1929, the number of cars driven in America skyrocketed.

The Model A was developed because people became discontented with the Model T.

121

As more and more people bought cars, they traveled more often. They also traveled farther away. The more they traveled, the more money they spent. Businesses such as gas stations, hotels, and restaurants profited from the increase in travel.

People in the 1920s were finding other things to spend their money on as well. More and more people were putting electricity into their homes. Now these people could use appliances like washing machines and refrigerators for the first time.

Radios were becoming more common. Families who had radios would often spend entire evenings listening to them. With radios, people could hear the news and other information. There were also sports and comedy programs that listeners enjoyed. And though people might live miles apart, they could hear the same information. This helped Americans feel closer to each other.

Family listening to a radio

About fourteen thousand homes were damaged or destroyed in the 1926 Miami hurricane.

Florida Boom

Buying land was another one of the many interests Americans spent time and money on. In 1924 and 1925, the most popular way to invest money was to buy real estate, or property, in Florida. Advertisements declared Florida "an emerald kingdom by the southern seas." The value of land in this warm state was high because so many people wanted to live there. Some land that was worth about one hundred dollars in 1910 was selling for over a hundred thousand dollars in 1925.

Not everyone who bought property in Florida moved there. Some people resold their land to someone else for a higher price and made large profits.

But the "Florida boom," as it was called, did not last forever. Soon sales and land values started to go down. Then, in 1926, a hurricane hit the Florida coast, killing over one hundred people in Miami. Over a hundred million dollars of property was lost. Hundreds of people in other parts of Florida lost their lives in flooding. The popularity of owning land and living in Florida decreased after the hurricane.

Other people earned extra money by investing in **stock**. At the stock exchange, people purchased parts of companies. These parts were known as shares. If you owned shares, you were said to own stock in a company. When the company made money, part of that money would go to you, the shareholder.

Before this time, very few people could afford to buy stock. Stock trading had been done mostly by wealthy businessmen. But in the 1920s, businesses were doing well and more people were prospering. These people now had extra money to buy shares in companies.

Credit and Stocks

Americans were enjoying the new conveniences that came with new technology. But electricity and other new products cost money. As a result, many people chose to buy items on **credit**. This process meant that a bank loaned a person the money to buy an item. The person would gradually pay the bank back in small payments called **installments**.

Big Bull Market

In the 1920s, people called times of economic growth *bull markets*. Times of economic loss were called *bear markets*. Today, these terms are still used in the business world.

Back in 1928, the prices of stock were higher than they had ever been before. Prices continued to rise.

More than one and a half million people were involved in buying and selling stock. This time period was so prosperous that experts called it "the Big Bull Market."

In 1929, *Herbert Hoover* became president of the United States. The nation seemed to be prospering. It looked as if America's economy was getting better and better.

The number of stocks purchased continued to rise until 1929.

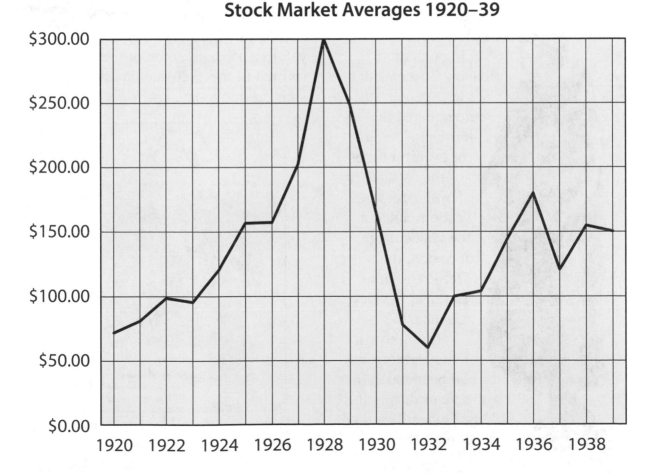

Stock Market Averages 1920–39

The End of the Roaring Twenties

The wealth and economic growth could not last forever. In October of 1929, America's prosperity came to a sudden end. The stock market "crashed." The prices of stock fell before people could sell what they owned. Most stocks were worth almost nothing. Thousands of people became poor overnight.

For many, the fast-paced life of the Roaring Twenties slowed down. Travel and parties became less common. Laughing faces became much more solemn in the decade to follow.

Although the Roaring Twenties did not last, people still remembered the more prosperous or eventful times of the decade. For this reason, people called it the Golden Age of Sports, the Get-Rich-Quick Era, and the Dry Decade.

Even though fame and fortune had been much of the focus during the 1920s, God still worked in people's lives. In the revival meetings of the 1920s, God saved many people from the "lost generation." These people could trust that God was in control of their lives. They could understand what Jesus meant when He said in Matthew 6:20 to "lay up for yourselves treasures in heaven, where neither moth nor rust doth corrupt, and where thieves do not break through and steal."

Think about the decade in which you live. Perhaps some of the lessons learned in the 1920s could apply to your decade today.

Many people listened to Billy Sunday preach on the radio.

126

Chapter 7

Why Prices Go Up

The way a country handles its money and products is called its **economy**. Each country has a slightly different economy. However, each economy includes the same basic parts—the production of goods, the selling of goods, and the buying of goods.

Supply and Demand

You can probably name different brands of shoes or soft drinks. Not all people like the same brands of products. Companies and businesses offer a variety to choose from.

When you buy any product, you are a **consumer**. Consumers have much influence over the kinds of things that are produced by the **manufacturers**, or those who make the products.

What and how much the consumer wants to buy is called the **demand**. In a sense, he "demands" that the manufacturers make certain things. One way that a consumer tells companies what he wants is by what he actually buys.

The items that businesses or companies produce are called the **supply**. Supply can come from sources such as farms, ranches, factories, or stores. The supply depends on the demand. Companies try to produce only what will sell the most. They want to make a good profit.

Profit is the money a company earns when the amount the company makes from selling its products is more than the amount it spends to make its products.

Imagine that you live on a busy street. You decide to make lemonade and sell it at a lemonade stand. The first day, you sell all your lemonade by lunchtime. When more people come to buy in the afternoon, you have no more lemonade. There are more consumers than there is lemonade. This situation is an example of *demand exceeding supply.*

The next day, you make more lemonade. The people yesterday seemed to like the drink and wanted more even after you ran out. You think they will pay more for it, so you raise the price. By the end of the second day, you sell all of your lemonade. And this time, there was enough for everyone. This situation is an example of *demand equaling supply*.

Notice how the prices affected supply and demand. Prices help consumers decide how much they want to buy. Prices also help a manufacturer decide how much product to make.

Now imagine that your friend Lori sets up her own lemonade stand down the street from yours. She has seen how much money you are making. Now there is more lemonade being sold in the neighborhood. But the number of customers stays the same. This situation is an example of *supply exceeding demand*.

Lori makes the same lemonade that you make but sells it cheaper. Because people are also buying lemonade from Lori's stand, you do not sell all of yours that day. You have to decide whether to lower your price or make different or better lemonade to try to increase the demand for your product. This whole situation is what economists

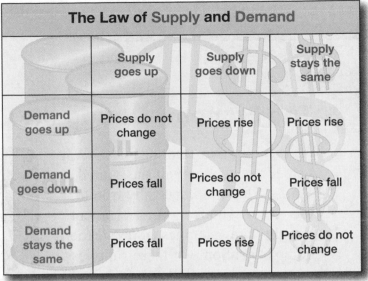

The Law of Supply and Demand			
	Supply goes up	Supply goes down	Supply stays the same
Demand goes up	Prices do not change	Prices rise	Prices rise
Demand goes down	Prices fall	Prices do not change	Prices fall
Demand stays the same	Prices fall	Prices rise	Prices do not change

call the **law of supply and demand**. If either the supply or the demand changes, the prices may change. Sometimes the changes are small, but sometimes they are big.

When Lori opened her lemonade stand and offered lemonade at a lower price, she sold more lemonade than you sold. To compete with Lori, your lemonade must be a product that the consumer wants to buy at a price he wants to pay. The lemonade is an example of a consumer-driven product. Demand for such a product depends on the consumer's preference. Based on taste and price, the consumer decides which lemonade he wants to buy. You, as the supplier, must decide to lower your price or make your lemonade better or different so the consumer wants to buy it.

The Economy During the Civil War

At first, the American Civil War helped the economy of the United States. This was especially true in the North. The federal government bought many supplies from Northern companies. Some of these supplies were steel, iron, clothing, and food. The money the government gave for the supplies helped businesses in the North to expand and make more products.

As the war continued, however, money grew scarce. To pay for more products, the government printed more money. But more money did not help. The more money that was printed, the less the money was worth. Because the money had less value, it cost more to buy products.

Most of the artillery used during the Civil War was manufactured in the North.

In 1861, the first money printed by the United States Treasury was to help fund the Civil War.

The money printed by the Southern states had no value after the war ended.

People in the South had a harder time because they lacked many of the supplies that the North had. This lack of supplies caused the prices to soar for the products that the South did have. Prices became so high that a pair of regular shoes cost about two hundred dollars!

The effects of the war were not changed overnight. Rebuilding an economy is a long process. Balancing the supply and demand of the many products takes time too. After the war, the government could not even help by printing more money or by taxing the people.

Today the government continues to handle the amount of money in the economy. The law of supply and demand still exists. This practice "echoes" economics from the Civil War.

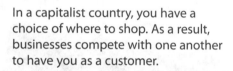

In a capitalist country, you have a choice of where to shop. As a result, businesses compete with one another to have you as a customer.

Capitalist, Communist, and Socialist Economies

In the United States, the government has little regulation, or control, of the supply of goods and services. Individual people and corporations own businesses. The consumers influence what and how much is produced. Companies make their decisions based on the demands of consumers. The kind of economy that uses supply and demand in this way is a **capitalist economy**. The economy in the United States is capitalist.

Not every country has a capitalist economy. In some countries, the government controls the supply. The government decides what items to produce. Then it decides the prices for those items. The kind of economy that handles supply in this way is a **communist economy**. In a communist country, the government owns all of the businesses.

There are many problems with this type of economy. Sometimes a government will not allow the production of what the people need. When not enough of an item, such as bread, is produced, there may not be enough for everyone. As a result, some people may go without.

132

When there is not enough of a certain item that people need, such as food, gasoline, or water, there is a shortage. Shortages are hard on the people. Often the shoppers must stand in long lines, sometimes not even getting what they waited for. Then they must pay high prices for the products they do get to buy.

These people are standing in line to buy meat in Russia when it was a communist country. By 1990, Russia began moving toward capitalism.

You may have stood in a long line at a store. Usually it was because people ahead of you were still paying for the items they bought. In a communist country, a shopper may be waiting for a long time in line, but may walk away without the items he needed to buy.

Some countries have a **socialist economy**. In these countries, some businesses are owned by the government and some by the people. Often the socialist government owns and controls one or more of the major resources and businesses, such as oil, transportation, or health care. Consumers pay high taxes for the government management of these businesses.

In Canada, the oil company Petro-Canada is owned by the government.

Colonial Economics

In colonial America, most of the land was managed by English companies or people in the courts of England. The American settlers were allowed to work on this land. Most of the crops they produced were used by everyone, whether the people worked or not. But neither the land nor the crops harvested belonged to the individuals who worked them.

"This we commanded you, that if any would not work, neither should he eat."

2 Thessalonians 3:10

In 1623, William Bradford put an end to the shared ownership of land and supplies in Plymouth Colony. He divided the land among the settlers, allowing each family to work its own land and to keep its own crops. The settlers could decide for themselves what they wanted to do with their property.

Captain John Smith noticed a good change in the people of Virginia after they were given individual plots of land. In his diary, John Smith wrote that when the people were fed from the common store, some were glad to slip away from their work. But after they each had their own land, they would do in a day the work that they used to do in a week. Why do you think the settlers worked harder on their own land? What "echoes" of this philosophy do you see in America today?

Have you ever seen several businesses of the same type on one street? How is this arrangement good for the economy?

Monopolies

In a capitalist system, both the manufacturer and the consumer have advantages. They can make their own choices about the ways they earn and spend money.

Competition is a benefit of a consumer-driven economy. Manufacturers of the same items compete for the consumers' business. Manufacturers try to please the buyers with quality products and lower prices.

When there is no competition between companies, a monopoly can occur. A **monopoly** is the control of the making and selling of a product by one company. That company can charge as much as it wants since it is the only company selling the product. With no competition, that company may choose to keep prices high. As a result, the consumer is affected.

The consumer does not have a choice when he selects a product with a monopoly. To understand how a monopoly works, go back to the lemonade stand example. At the beginning, you were the only stand

or "company" that made lemonade. A customer had no choice but to buy his lemonade from you. You had a monopoly on the lemonade market.

The consumer affects a monopoly differently than it affects consumer-driven supply and demand. Because your lemonade stand or company was a monopoly, you could charge as much as you wanted. The decisions of the company did not really depend on the tastes of the consumer. Why? The company got all the profit from any lemonade sold. A monopoly can become unfair to the consumer.

Resources

Monopolies affect consumers even more when they control items that people need, such as gasoline, food, or electricity. These types of products are called **resources**. Resources are valuable products like land, water, and sunlight that people must have in order to live. Some resources, such as coal, oil, and natural gas, give us power, light, and heat.

A monopoly of any resource can hurt the consumer. Because a consumer needs these things to live, he must buy them regardless of the cost. Everyone needs resources. The government makes laws to prevent companies from having monopolies of certain resources.

Many resources are found naturally in the earth. These resources are an important part of a nation's economy. Countries such as the United States have many natural resources. Developing these resources so that they may be used is important.

The supply of resources affects the way people live. Some countries are rich in resources and develop them well. These countries tend to have a higher **standard of living,** or the amount of goods and services that an average person views as necessary. In countries with a higher standard of living, the people have easy access to the resources. A more abundant supply allows the resources to be sold at lower prices.

The Lord provided the United States with many forests, a natural resource. These forests provide wood for fuel, paper, lumber, and other products.

The Economic Pattern in the United States

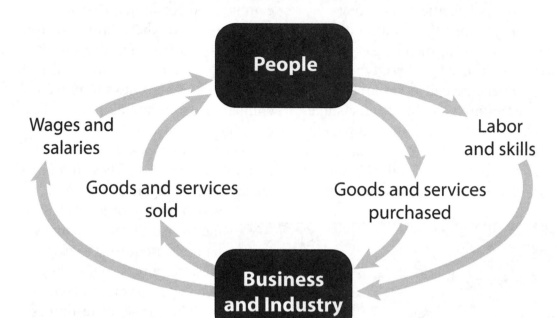

People

Wages and salaries

Labor and skills

Goods and services sold

Goods and services purchased

Business and Industry

Economics

Businesses and consumers depend on one another. Without businesses, consumers would have to supply their needs themselves. This process would take a lot of time. In some situations it would even be impossible. On the other hand, without the consumers the businesses would go **bankrupt**, or run out of money.

History of Money Use

There was a time when the consumer had to make a lot of the products he needed for himself. In the colonial days of America, people usually mastered one skill. Then they used that skill to produce goods that they could trade. Trading goods for other goods is called **bartering**.

As the nation grew, there was more money available. People could then pay for products with money instead of with goods or skills. Yet skills were still used to earn money. Production continued to be slow. Sometimes demand was not met by supply. By the time of the Civil War in the 1800s, the Industrial Revolution had begun. The assembly line allowed large quantities of goods to be produced. This mass production enabled businesses to meet the supply needed.

When you buy a book, you pay for it with money. Where did that money come from? Maybe your parents gave it to you as a present or as a payment for jobs you did. But where did they get the money?

People must work for the money they use to buy things they need and want. When people work, their employers, or bosses, pay them. Where do employers get money? Their money comes from the products they make and sell.

Working is important because it supplies money to buy the things that are needed and wanted. It is also important because God expects Christians to be dependable and busy. God honors those who work hard.

> "But rather let him labour, working with his hands the thing which is good, that he may have to give to him that needeth."
>
> **Ephesians 4:28**

Minting Money

Have you ever examined a quarter and wondered how it was made? **Minting** is the process of making coins. In the United States, coins are minted only at the United States Mint in Philadelphia, Pennsylvania, or in Denver, Colorado.

The minting of coins involves many steps. First, the government chooses a design for its coins. What design is on this quarter? An artist will then make the design out of a special type of clay. Some artists' designs are almost twelve times larger than a real coin. The artist can carve details more easily on the larger piece. Then a series of models of the design are made from plaster and other substances. Each model is carefully inspected for accuracy.

The coin-sized image is cut into a steel device called a hub.

These quarter dies were made from the hub at the top of the photo.

A special machine carefully traces and reduces the design of the final model. The machine then etches the design onto the steel *hub* that is the size of the final coin. This hub is used to make the many *dies* that will be used to stamp the design on coins.

Round *blanks* are cut from a huge sheet of metal the same thickness as the coins. Both sides of each coin design are stamped onto the blank at the same time. The finished coins are carefully inspected before they are ready for circulation.

Minting coins requires careful work. The design must be the same on each coin. The letters must be even. The United States Mint makes sure that America's national coins are of the highest quality.

Circulation of Money

The United States has a central banking system called the **Federal Reserve System**. This system controls the amount of bills and coins in **circulation**. Circulation is the movement of money from person to person or from place to place.

If there is not enough money in circulation, consumers will buy fewer things in order to save their money. When consumers buy fewer items, businesses slow down. Then manufacturers and businesses are left with too many products. Businesses would need to lower their prices in order to sell these products.

When prices are low for too long, businesses cannot make enough profit to stay in business. This makes it difficult for them to pay their employees. As a result, the businesses will reduce their number of workers. Being laid off or losing a job hurts the employees. They are not able to pay their bills or buy necessities.

When there is more money in circulation several results may occur. One result is that people are paid more. This causes consumers to demand more products. Manufacturers then hire more workers to meet this demand. This condition helps the economy by causing it to grow.

However, too much money may also hurt the economy. If the manufacturers cannot meet the consumer demand, prices go up. This increase in prices is called **inflation**. When this condition occurs in an economy, more money is needed to buy products.

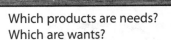

Which products are needs?
Which are wants?

Needs and Wants

When prices are high because of inflation, people must try to save money. One way they can save money is by buying only those things that are **needs**. Needs are those things that a person must have to live, such as food, clothing, and shelter. How are needs different from **wants**? Wants are things a person would like to own but could do without.

Another way to save money is by planning a **budget**. A budget is a plan that determines how money will be spent. With a budget, a person decides ahead of time how he will spend his money. A budget can help a person make wise decisions about spending and saving his money.

The way people spend or save money affects the law of supply and demand. When people do not spend as much, there is plenty of supply and prices are lower. When people spend more, the supply diminishes, and prices go up.

In the United States, when people earn their own money, they are free to spend it as they choose. A person may make wise choices or foolish choices. God gives us exactly the amount of money and things He wants us to have. We need to be good stewards of what God has given us. We need to use God's blessings in ways that are glorifying to Him.

143

Planning a Budget

1. Get your Activity Manual page and a pencil.
2. Pretend that you earn ten dollars each week. Decide how much money you will spend in each category on the page.
3. Fill in the amounts of money you will spend for each category. Remember that you have only ten dollars to spend.
4. Compare your amounts by answering the questions.

The Economy and You

Consider supply and demand, money, capitalism, and budgets. Someday you will have a job and will earn money to provide for your needs. In the future, and even now, when you buy things in the store, you are affecting the law of supply and demand.

You, as a consumer, are very important to the economy. You can affect not only your own community but also the nation, which in turn affects other countries.

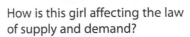
How is this girl affecting the law of supply and demand?

The economy is always changing. Some years are more stable than others. There are many factors that affect supply and demand. These factors include resources, jobs, trade with other countries, war, and the money supply. While you may not have control over these things, Christians are expected to be responsible for the money God gives them. You can be careful about how you spend your money and which products you choose to buy. God will reward Christians who are faithful even with the smallest amount of money.

"He that is faithful in that which is least is faithful also in much."
Luke 16:10

Learning How

Using the Market System

1. Get the Activity Manual page, a pencil, and the materials from your teacher.
2. Listen as your teacher tells you the rules of The Economy Game.
3. Play the game according to your teacher's directions.
4. The object of the game is to make the highest profit.

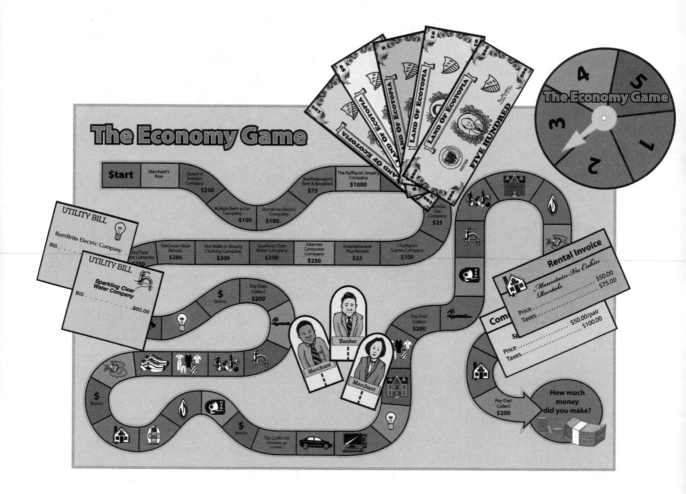

Chapter 8

Hard Times

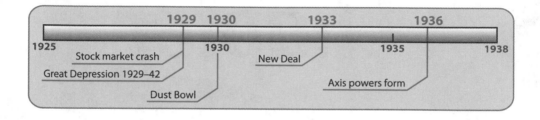

| 1925 | | 1929 | 1930 | | 1933 | | 1936 | | 1938 |

1929 1930 1933 1936

1925 1930 1935 1938

Stock market crash

Great Depression 1929–42

Dust Bowl

New Deal

Axis powers form

False Promises

Have you ever wanted something that cost a great amount of money? Perhaps you did not have enough money to buy it. But maybe you chose to save for it even though saving took a long time. Was it hard to wait and save your money? In the 1920s, many Americans decided not to wait and save money. They bought what they wanted whether they had enough money or not.

During this time money seemed plentiful. Wages were high and borrowing from banks was easy. People did not stop to think about the future and how much they were spending. But they were not as prosperous as they thought.

Many people spent more money than they earned. They bought new things such as cars, stoves, and washing machines on *credit*. Buying on credit means buying items using an amount borrowed from a bank or business. Then that amount is paid back in small payments called *installments*. If buyers can pay all of their installments, they and the businesses and banks are happy.

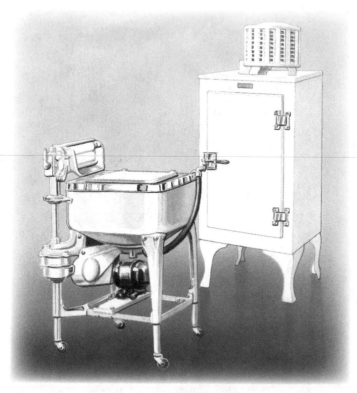

A 1920s washing machine (left) and refrigerator (right)

148

were needed, many workers lost their jobs.

Some people who lost their jobs had already purchased items on credit. Now these people did not have the money to make their payments. Businessmen who had sold the items on credit were not paid on time. As businesses began to lose money, they could not afford to continue paying all of their workers. They had to lay off some of their workers. More people were out of work and needed money. Those who had saved money in banks went to get it out.

Sometimes people bought more items on credit than they could pay for. When people could not make their installment payments, businesses and banks received less money.

Factory owners continued producing goods. But there were more goods than the American people could buy. As a result, the factory owners were not able to sell all of the goods they had made. These owners decided to produce fewer goods. Since fewer factory workers

Bankers had not been wise in their practices. By the late 1920s, banks had lent money to people who were not able to pay it back. Sometimes banks lent so much money that they had little left. Many people had already **deposited**, or put money, in the banks. These people now hurried to **withdraw**, or remove, their money. But the banks did not have enough money in the vaults to give to everyone who wanted it.

The Stock Market Crash

Investments

In the 1920s, buying and selling stocks was a popular way to make money. The business of buying and selling stocks is called the **stock market**. The New York Stock Exchange was one of the main stock businesses in the 1920s. It is still a leading business today.

People **invest**, or use money to make a profit, in the stock market. A portion of the profits earned by a company is divided among the people who invested in that company. These people are the shareholders. The profits they receive are called the **dividends**.

The stock market attracted many people. One reason was that

New York Stock Exchange in the 1920s

it seemed like an easy way to make extra money. A person did not have to work long hours to get the extra money. He only needed to have a little extra money to invest. Another reason was that investing in America's companies was considered patriotic. That is, it meant the investor supported America's future.

For many years, stocks brought in good dividends for shareholders. But toward the end of the 1920s, things changed.

A day at the stock exchange in 1920

The Stock Market

1. Get one hundred dollars in play money from your teacher.

2. Go to the "trading floor" and see the "stocks" your teacher has there. Check what the prices of the stocks are today.

3. Purchase some stocks.

4. Listen to the stock report from your teacher each day. Track what happens to your stocks in the "market." Record your losses or earnings in your Activity Manual.

Shaky Market

The stock market changes every day. It is not always financially stable. Sometimes stocks sell successfully. At other times, they do not.

When the economy is "on the rise" and stock prices are going up, the stock market is called a **bull market**.

At the stock exchange, people want to buy stocks at low prices. Then they hope to sell the stocks at high prices and make a profit.

Sometimes people are called "bullish on the market." This means they buy more shares, or stocks, than usual. These people hope the prices of their shares will go up. But at other times, many shareholders begin to sell their shares because they think the market prices will go down. When stock prices fall, the stock market is called a **bear market**.

In the late 1920s, there was a bull market. Many people put their money into stocks. But the prices went up too quickly, and the stocks were not earning the expected dividends. Shareholders were concerned that they would not earn a profit from the shares they had. They decided not to buy more stock.

Outside the New York Stock Exchange building, an anxious crowd waits for news about the market.

Black Thursday

As the prices of stocks rose and their values went down, shareholders tried to sell their stocks. But few people wanted to buy stocks. Shareholders saw that their stocks were losing value. So they lowered their prices and sold their stocks even faster, trying to gain some money before the stocks became worthless. This selling sped up the rate at which stocks lost their value. Prices began to go down. A bear market resulted.

The shareholders should have waited. They should have kept their stocks and waited for prices to level out. But they did not. The shareholders caused a financial panic, or alarm. This type of panic often results in a rush to sell. A rush to sell stocks happened on **October 24, 1929**, now known as **Black Thursday**.

Some large banks tried to help keep prices up. They bought a lot of stocks. This helped, but not for long. When the prices dropped again, the banks could not help. They had already put too much of their money into the market. The stock market was on the brink of disaster.

Black Tuesday

The **stock market crash** in America happened on Tuesday, **October 29, 1929**. That day, stock prices fell very low. The "crash" meant that the stocks quickly lost more than half their value. Not many people wanted to buy stocks, not even for a dollar a share.

Part of this financial crisis came from the way people had been buying stocks. Many had borrowed money to buy stocks, hoping to sell them at a profit. That way, people could pay off their loans and still make money. But things did not turn out the way people had planned. Prices at the time dropped very low, and it was difficult to sell stock. It was even more difficult to earn a profit from it. As a result, many shareholders who had borrowed money fell into serious debt.

The stock market crash was a lesson to the people. They learned that they could not keep borrowing and spending money the way they had been doing. It also meant that, for many people, life would change drastically—and suddenly.

In the late 1920s, operators at the stock exchange took many calls from people wanting to sell their stock.

New York City
A Morning in the 1930s

Imagine you were a child living in the 1930s, right after the stock market crash. What kind of day might you have?

Harold was a boy who lived in the 1930s. He got up very early every morning. He pulled on the same clothes that he wore the day before. And every day, he went to buy a loaf of bread for his family.

Harold would run all the way to the store with a nickel. He ran because he feared someone would take his money. Harold knew if someone offered to sell him a toy, he must not give that person his nickel. His family was counting on the bread for their meals. Many days the bread was the only food they would have. If the nickel was stolen, no one in Harold's family would eat that day.

When Harold went home carrying the bread, he ran even faster because someone always tried to grab the loaf from him. How is the beginning of your day different from Harold's day in the 1930s?

The Great Depression

The time period following the stock market crash was called the **Great Depression** (1929–1942). Most people, even people who had been rich before the crash, became very poor. Millions of people lost their jobs or had their pay cut drastically. A great number of people had very little to eat.

Run on Banks

Some of a bank's profits come from the bank's investment of customers' money in the stock market. Before the 1929 crash, many banks had bought stock to try to keep the prices up. Because the money was invested, the banks did not have enough cash on hand to pay out to those who wanted to withdraw their money. This caused a "run" on the banks. Customers hurried to withdraw their money. The first people in line got most of their money. Others got nothing at all.

The leaders of the Treasury Department predicted there might be trouble. So they closed the banks for a **bank holiday**. Customers knew that it was not an actual holiday. But most people quietly accepted the closings. They thought that surely things were already as bad as they could get and that these problems would be solved soon. The people did not anticipate what the next few years would bring.

> "He that trusteth in his riches shall fall; but the righteous shall flourish as a branch."
> **Proverbs 11:28**

People run to withdraw their money from a bank.

Loss of Jobs

Wealthy and poor alike lost their money and possessions. Nearly everyone became poor. One out of every four people who wanted to work could not find a job. Families lived on small amounts of food and could not buy new clothes. Try to imagine what it would be like to have only one or two shirts or dresses to wear.

In the cities, people worked for only pennies a week. Men who had once been successful businessmen sold apples on street corners. Others who had no work stood in long lines at **soup kitchens** to get a small portion of soup or bread. Many times people got what food they could from garbage dumps.

Soup kitchens were places that offered free food to the poor and homeless.

By the spring of 1930, more than four million people had no jobs. The next year there were eight million people without work. And ten months after that, thirteen and a half million workers were looking for jobs. Almost one-fourth of all the people in the United States who were able to work could not find work.

157

Farmers' Trials

Many farmers had borrowed money to purchase more land and improve their farms. But after the stock market crashed, these farmers could not pay their loans. Some of them had to give up their land and their homes. Others tried to make the best of the situation. They produced grain and raised animals to sell wherever they could.

The trouble was that farmers could no longer get the same prices for their goods. After the stock market crash, prices dropped. In 1929, wheat used to sell for $1.05 a bushel. But in 1932, wheat sold for only $0.39 a bushel. Cotton used to be $0.17 a pound. Then the price dropped to $0.06 a pound. At such low prices farmers were not able to make enough money to live on and to pay their debts.

Look at the *Fifty Years of Prices* chart. Notice that the prices of products increased from 1903 to 1913, then again in 1923. Now compare the prices in 1923 to the ones in 1933. Even though prices were low, people could not afford to buy items because of the drastic drop in their incomes.

Fifty Years of Prices

	1903	1913	1923	1933	1943	1953
Eggs 1 doz.	$0.26	$0.34	$0.50	$0.29	$0.57	$0.70
Milk ½ gal.	$0.14	$0.18	$0.28	$0.21	$0.31	$0.47
Potatoes 10 lb.	$0.17	$0.17	$0.30	$0.23	$0.46	$0.54
Sugar 5 lb.	$0.28	$0.27	$0.50	$0.26	$0.34	$0.53
Butter 1 lb.	$0.28	$0.38	$0.55	$0.28	$0.53	$0.80

Dust storms brought devastation to many farms. Families like this one took refuge in California.

Just when farmers thought the worst had passed, terrible droughts hit. A drought is a long period with little or no rainfall. The few farmers who had held onto their land could not produce anything to sell. When massive windstorms whipped through the dry land of the central United States, great clouds of dust covered the land. The farmers could not grow and harvest good crops. With no crops to sell, the farmers were unable to repay their loans.

Some farmers had plowed the prairie's natural grass to make fields for planting wheat. But the wheat did not hold down topsoil the way the prairie grass did. When the droughts came in the 1930s, winds swept up the dry topsoil. The loose soil became enormous clouds of dust. At times the blowing dirt was so thick that it blotted out the sun. In some areas, the loose soil was deposited in high piles that covered fences and tractors, and blocked barn doors. During this time the central United States was known as the **Dust Bowl**. This devastation was mainly in parts of Colorado, New Mexico, Texas, Oklahoma, and Kansas.

Presidents of the Great Depression

President Calvin Coolidge was in office from 1923 to 1929. He had said, "The chief business of the American people is business." He meant that as long as businesses were doing well, America would do well. Many businesses seemed to have money. And many people thought America was doing well. But many businesses were actually running on credit.

The man who took most of the blame, or at least the criticism, for the Great Depression was **President Herbert Hoover.** He was president from 1929 to 1933. Places where poor people lived in boxes or roughly made shanties were called "Hoovervilles." Old newspapers were called Hoover blankets. Cartoonists drew unkind pictures of the president. And many people said all the trouble was his fault. But the seeds of trouble had been growing years earlier.

Herbert Hoover

The spending habits and the use of the stock market had caught up with America. By this time, President Coolidge was out and President Hoover was in. Hoover signed into law a very high tax on imported goods. This tax further hurt businesses. He also used tax money to get the government involved in running farms. He had the government lend money to businesses that would never succeed. The government was getting involved in all areas of the economy. All of these actions only made the bad situation worse. They started America down a dangerous road.

A "Hooverville" in Seattle, Washington

Starting Over

In America, fear and unhappiness lasted for the next two and one-half years. People were looking for relief from their problems.

During Roosevelt's campaign in Indianapolis, he was welcomed by a two-mile-long parade.

New President

In 1933, **Franklin Delano Roosevelt** (often known as **FDR**) became the president. Roosevelt believed his inauguration speech would give everyone hope. This new president said, "The only thing we have to fear is fear itself—nameless, unreasoning, unjustified terror which paralyzes needed efforts to convert retreat into advance."

One of Roosevelt's campaign promises was to put an end to Prohibition (Eighteenth Amendment). In February of 1933, Congress proposed the Twenty-first Amendment to repeal, or cancel, the Prohibition law. The states quickly ratified the amendment. A few states kept the ban on alcohol until the 1950s or 1960s.

Roosevelt speaks at his first inauguration in 1933.

Franklin Delano Roosevelt
(1882–1945)

Franklin Roosevelt was a strong man and was used to outdoor activities. However, when he was thirty-nine years old, he became ill while on vacation. The next day he was so tired he could not get dressed, and one leg dragged. Soon he could not stand at all or hold a pen. He was diagnosed with polio.

Polio is a disease that attacks the nervous system. It can cause people to become weak and paralyzed. In the early years of the twentieth cenury, it was one of the most feared illnesses. Mostly children got it, but sometimes an adult came down with it. This was the case for FDR. People with polio rarely recovered fully. Roosevelt, however, refused to give up trying to walk again.

Before he got polio, Roosevelt had been running for vice president on the Democratic ticket. His running mate was presidential nominee James Cox. The Cox-Roosevelt team lost to the Harding-Coolidge team. But Roosevelt was making a name for himself in the Democratic Party. He had high hopes of winning another election. After his illness left him unable to stand alone or without leg braces, many told him to give up trying for public office.

Roosevelt with his family in 1919

163

Franklin Roosevelt was not about to give up. While he recuperated, he wrote letters to important Democratic leaders all over the country. In 1928, some of those leaders asked him to run for governor of New York. He did, and he won. Rather than allowing his struggle with polio to ruin his career, FDR overcame it in order to serve his country.

Franklin Roosevelt became president in 1933. The banks were failing and the country was sliding into the worst of the Depression. The new president gave many radio talks, which were known as the **Fireside Chats**. In them he explained what he was doing and what he hoped would happen with his plans. Some people liked him. Others thought he was taking too much power.

However, FDR pleased enough people to get re-elected in 1936 and again in 1940. After serving a third term, he was elected to a fourth. He was the first American president elected to more than two terms.

Roosevelt was re-elected as governor in 1930.

In his fireside chats, FDR explained his ideas for the nation's future.

He died just eighty-three days after his fourth inauguration. In a speech he had prepared for the next day, he had written, "The only limits to . . . tomorrow will be our doubts of today."

The New Deal

President Roosevelt promised everyone relief from the Depression. He had a plan called the **New Deal**. His idea was for the government to plan projects. Then the government would pay Americans to do the work.

Under the New Deal, millions of Americans went back to work. They built roads, bridges, and dams throughout the country. Besides giving people jobs, these projects improved transportation and helped prevent floods. One program was the Civilian Conservation Corps, also known as the CCC. This

Men clearing trees for a road

program planned and built many of America's national parks.

FDR had many new programs and organizations in action. Each one was called by its initials. There were so many initialed names that they were known as the "**alphabet agencies**."

This political cartoon presented FDR as a doctor trying to treat Uncle Sam's ailments. The cartoon is an example of a primary source from the 1930s.

Help for Businesses

Another New Deal program was the National Recovery Administration (NRA). The NRA allowed businesses to work together. Each business was assigned an amount of product to make, the maximum hours to be worked, and minimum wages. Big businesses seemed to be favored over smaller ones. By controlling how much of a product was made, a big business also controlled the price. The scarcer the product, usually the higher the price. This plan did not match the American ideal of fair competition in buying and selling.

When a business met the terms of the NRA, it was allowed to display the NRA's Blue Eagle seal.

The National Labor Relations Board (NLRB) opened the way for another change in business. It allowed workers to form groups within companies called **labor unions**. The unions could bargain with the owners. Before that, workers mostly had to either take the wages and the treatment of the employers without question, or quit. Now workers could unite and try to force the employers to pay them more or give them safer and cleaner places to work.

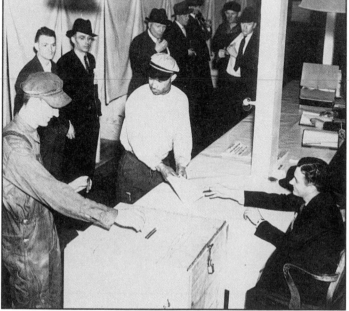

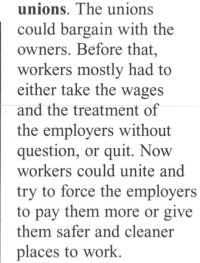

Many unions voiced their opinions through orderly methods like voting.

Help for Farmers

Special efforts were made to help farmers. The Farm Credit Administration (FCA) lent money to farmers at lower **interest** rates than banks could. Interest is a fee charged by the lender. The loans helped farmers who would have lost their land. To help raise prices, the Agricultural Adjustment Administration (AAA) was created. Through this agency, the government paid farmers not to produce as much. If there was not as much to sell, the prices would go up. The act also gave the government the right to buy surplus crops and the president the right to sell extra American products to other countries.

Many needy people used food stamps to purchase food the government designated as surplus.

Farmers began to learn about and practice **conservation**. This is the protection and wise use of natural resources. Never again did the farmers want to experience a dust bowl. With new ways of farming and with help from the government, farmers began to recover slowly from the worst of the Depression.

These farmers are learning to use their land more efficiently.

Legacies of the New Deal

The New Deal helped America in some ways. It also caused some problems. The government became more involved in the people's private lives and businesses. People did not like being told where and how to work. They were being told what fields to use and what crops to plant. Some people were sure the government programs were not right. These people took the government to court. In the end, some of the programs started by the New Deal were declared unconstitutional.

Another problem with the New Deal was that the government could not pay for all the programs. The government had to borrow money. The **national debt** kept growing. Today the national debt "echoes" as one of America's biggest problems.

Playing Miniature Golf

Golf had long been a highly revered game. Some people called it "the Royal and Ancient Game." But in 1916, James Barber brought golf down to size—or rather, made it undersized. He had a small version of a large golf course built on his estate, the first miniature golf course.

In ten years, little golf greens were showing up atop New York office buildings. Businessmen relaxed at lunch by playing a round of golf. Other cities offered luxurious indoor miniature golf courses. The courses had refreshments and lawn chairs to rest in.

Even during the hard times after the stock market crash, the game was popular. Perhaps it was the low admission prices. Perhaps it was the illusion of being master of the once elite game. Perhaps it was the momentary escape into a world where there still were country clubs and exotic places. Whatever the reasons, miniature golf became the "Madness of 1930." Later, the game gradually lost its appeal. But it returned in the 1950s. It is one of America's original pastimes and is still popular today.

Problems in Europe

America was not the only country to suffer from the Great Depression. European countries struggled with high unemployment and low production levels. The people in these countries thought their governments should do more to help them. Some men had ideas about how to help the people. They also wanted power, so they became rulers in countries like Germany and Italy. Once they were in office, these men changed the governments and took total control.

Adolf Hitler became the leader of Germany. He promised a cure to his country's economic problems.

During the Depression, poor people in Vienna, Austria, searched for food in garbage piles.

Benito Mussolini became dictator of Italy. In 1936, Hitler and Mussolini agreed to support each other in case of war. Together their countries were called the Axis powers. This agreement began the assembling of the countries that would fight against the Allies in the Second World War.

Adolf Hitler seemed eager to go to war. He wanted to prove to the world that the Germans were better than any other people. He used the German army to take land from smaller, weaker nations around Germany. The people of Britain and France did not like Hitler's actions. However, they did not try hard to stop him. They remembered the horrors of World War I. They wanted to avoid another war. They thought that if Hitler took a little territory, perhaps he would be satisfied and they would not have to go to war again. But great challenges still lay ahead that would change the world.

Adolf Hitler at a 1935 rally in Munich, Germany

Chapter 9

Rulers with Iron Fists

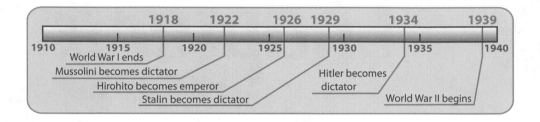

Have you ever tried to play with a bully? A bully is usually someone bigger or stronger than you are. He uses threats to frighten you and forces you to do things his way. You might obey a bully, not because you like him or agree with him, but because you are afraid he will hurt you if you do not do what he wants.

Imagine that you live in a country that is governed by a bully who has absolute power. Whatever he wants becomes law. All the people in the country must do what this bully wants. They must do it whether they agree with his ideas for the country or not. People are not allowed to talk about their own ideas or opinions. If anyone dares to disobey the man in power, that person may be taken away from his own family, put in prison, or even executed.

That is what life would be like in a country with a dictatorship. A **dictatorship** is a form of government in which the government has total control over the people's lives. Governments like these are led by one person, called a **dictator**.

Under a dictatorship, people have very little freedom. The people must agree with the government about everything. They may only go to the churches that the government says they can go to. They must live where the government places them. They must do whatever work the government wants them to do. Children must study the government's teachings in school. And if anyone has free time, he is often required to spend it in community service or a government-sponsored activity. Some countries with dictators have secret police who spy on the people to see that they are following orders.

Dictatorships Between WW I & WW II

Russia, Italy, Germany, and Japan were ruled by dictators.

America's government is a form of **democracy**. A democracy is a government in which the people work together to make all the important decisions for their country. Americans have freedoms that people in many other countries do not have. Americans can vote for their leaders and express their opinions freely. They can make decisions about where they live and work. They can also worship God in freedom.

After World War I, several European countries were left with weak, indecisive governments. Discouraged people were willing to follow anyone who might make a difference—anyone who might get their country back on its feet again. These countries were easy prey for dictators who made grand promises to help the people.

However, these dictators and their governments became too strong and controlling. They were harsh leaders. The lives of people were not valuable to them. Even some of their own citizens suffered. In the years leading to World War II, as well as during the war, many people lost their lives due to the actions of these men.

Joseph Stalin
(1879–1953)

Russia: The Man of Steel

Young Stalin

Joseph Stalin was born Joseph Vissarionovich Dzhugashvili in 1879. He was born in a Russian province called Georgia. The name Stalin, which he later adopted, meant "man of steel."

Stalin's childhood was not a happy one. His family was poor, and his father was often drunk. Smallpox left Stalin's face badly scarred. At age ten, his left arm was permanently disabled in an accident.

Despite these setbacks, and with his mother's encouragement, Stalin did well in school. He went on to attend a religious seminary where he had earned a scholarship.

About the time Stalin was finishing school, changes were taking place in Russia. The czar (ZAHR) had just died. He was succeeded by his son, Nicholas II. Nicholas II was a weaker ruler than his father and less interested in politics.

All over the Russian empire, people were unhappy with rule by

Stalin after an arrest

a czar. The Russian people wanted to have more say in how they were governed. Groups of men began to hold secret meetings. They talked of **revolution**, or rebellion against the government. Sometimes Stalin would attend these meetings.

Stalin read books by some of these men with revolutionary ideas. These kinds of books were forbidden by the seminary he went to. Stalin even adopted a name for himself from a political novel. He insisted that his classmates call him "Koba."

Some students liked Stalin. He had strong opinions and daring ideas that fascinated them. Others did not like him. When in a group, Stalin never wanted anyone else to take leadership. Sometimes he was defeated in debates or group discussions. He would become angry with the winner. Then he would withdraw from his friends to pout and plan revenge.

Stalin continued to read books that were forbidden by the school. He grew rebellious toward school authorities. In 1899, he did not attend his exams. He was expelled from the seminary.

Now Stalin was free to do as he pleased. He wanted to become part of the revolutionary movement. He became a devoted follower of Lenin. Lenin was the strongest leader of this movement. He wrote some of the articles that Stalin had read.

Soon Stalin was involved in political demonstrations and secret meetings. By 1901, he was writing for a political newspaper. He wrote about revolution. He tried to imitate Lenin's style of writing.

In 1902, Stalin was arrested for the first time. He was sent to prison in Siberia, a very cold and isolated northern region. Over the next fifteen years, Stalin was arrested many times.

Stalin's Rise to Power

During World War I, Russia fought against Germany and Austria-Hungary. In 1917, Nicholas II was forced to resign. This left the Russian government weak. Later that year, Lenin and his followers saw their chance to take over. These men were called Bolsheviks. The Bolshevik Revolution brought Lenin into power. He made Stalin one of the leaders in the new Russian government.

In 1922, Russia joined with other territories to become the Union of Soviet Socialist Republics (USSR). It was also called the **Soviet Union**. Soon the Bolsheviks renamed themselves Communists.

The kind of government they formed was called communism. **Communism** is a system in which the government owns all the businesses

Stalin and Lenin in 1919

and property. The government makes almost all the decisions for the people. A Communist country is run by a dictator. Usually the only political party allowed under communism is the Communist Party.

Lenin died in 1924. Stalin wanted to become the next leader of the Communist Party. He was determined to beat his rivals. One of them was Leon Trotsky. Trotsky had been second only to Lenin in authority. Stalin turned the people against Trotsky. Trotsky was forced to step down from his position.

Leon Trotsky

Stalin then removed the men who had helped him beat Trotsky. One by one, Stalin found ways to get rid of any man who stood in his way. On his fiftieth birthday in 1929, Stalin became the dictator.

Some people did not like the methods Stalin had used to gain his power. But no one dared to criticize the **"man of steel."**

In 1917, the Bolshevik Party seized control of the government.

The Soviet Union Under Stalin's Rule

The Soviet Union relied mostly on farming for its income. But Stalin wanted the Soviet Union to be more industrial like the more advanced countries. One of his goals was to increase Soviet industry by a series of Five-Year Plans. He sped up production by forcing people to work harder than ever before.

Stalin combined individual farms into large **collective farms** owned by the government. Some people were angry about Stalin's plans. These people did not want to give up their rights to farm independently. Some people opposed Stalin by burning their livestock, grain, and farm equipment. If they could not own their farms, they did not want the government to own them either.

But Stalin paid no attention to what the people wanted. He sent soldiers to the farms and forced the people to surrender at gunpoint. He sent about a million peasant families into **exile**. These people were forced to move far away from their homes. Most were sent to Siberia. Some people went to work on Siberian farms. Others were sent to prison work camps. Across the Soviet Union, as many as ten million people died of starvation as a result of Stalin's war on the farmers.

In one sense, Stalin's plans worked. By 1932, over half of all Soviet farms were collective farms. Industry was increasing each year. But in another sense, his system was failing. The morale of the people was low. Many had suffered or even died under Stalin's harsh working conditions. The people had no freedom to question anything Stalin ordered.

Another group of people in the Soviet Union suffered a different kind of oppression under Stalin. Writers, artists, and music composers were not allowed to create what they wanted. Their work had to be **censored**, or made to match what the government wanted. Stalin wanted to make sure their work supported his ideas before it was published.

Under Stalin's rule, religion was also restricted. Stalin was an **atheist**. He did not believe in God. He wanted everyone else to believe as he did. Stalin closed churches of all religions. Some people were arrested or killed.

Stalin trusted no one. He could not tolerate having anyone disagree with him. In the next several years, Stalin had nearly all the former Bolsheviks in the Communist Party killed. He went on to dispose of thousands of other Communists. Anyone who seemed a threat to his authority was imprisoned. Usually they were executed on some false charge. About one and a half million people were killed in four years. Those who were not killed were questioned, tortured, and starved in labor camps. People referred to these years as "the Terror."

Stalin expected every person to be a spy. He urged neighbors and family members to tell on each other. Stalin also had his own secret police force. People lived in constant fear of saying or doing the wrong thing—even in their own homes.

Winston Churchill of Great Britain, Franklin D. Roosevelt of the United States, and Joseph Stalin of the Soviet Union were the three major Allied leaders at the end of World War II.

farther across Europe after the war. He set up Communist governments in many Eastern European countries. Stalin cut off these countries from contact with the Western European countries. The country of Germany was even divided into two parts. This created an imaginary dividing line called the **Iron Curtain**. Stalin did not want the people under his control to know about the freedoms enjoyed by the Western countries.

After the war, Stalin's health gradually worsened. In 1953, he had a stroke. Soon afterward he died. After thirty years of oppression, the Russian people were relieved and hopeful for a better future.

By the time World War II began, Stalin had eliminated everyone he thought was a threat to his power. At the start of World War II, Stalin fought on the same side as Hitler. But by the middle of the war, Stalin was fighting against Hitler. The Soviet Union became one of the three major Allied powers.

Stalin used his position to spread his influence

Part of the Iron Curtain was the Berlin Wall which divided Communist East Germany from free West Germany for nearly thirty years.

Benito Mussolini
(1883–1945)

Italy: *Il Duce!*

Young Mussolini

Benito Mussolini was born in 1883 in the Romagna region of Italy. His father was a tough, strong blacksmith. He taught young Benito to stand up against anyone who bullied him. Benito's father was a socialist. As he worked, he often talked to Benito about politics.

Benito's mother was a schoolteacher. She was gentle and compassionate. She often worried about Benito's violent temper. Her desire was for Benito to become a teacher like herself. She persuaded his father to send him to the finest schools. Later, Benito graduated and earned a certificate to teach. He went on to teach at a school for a brief time.

Then Benito Mussolini left Italy and went to Switzerland. For months he went from job to job. He once worked in a chocolate factory. But no job satisfied him. Mussolini wanted to do something great. He wanted other people to respect him and follow him.

From his boyhood, Mussolini had been interested in politics. In Switzerland this interest continued.

Young Mussolini

Mussolini speaking at the Colosseum in Rome

Mussolini became a leader in the Socialist Party.

After World War I began in 1914, the Socialists did not believe Italy should join the war. But Mussolini saw advantages for the nation if they joined the Allies. He lost favor with the Socialists for taking this position. But he stood firm in his views. When Italy finally joined the war with the Allies, Mussolini fought on the frontlines.

He spent most of his evenings in cozy little restaurants called cafés. In these places he discussed political ideas with other Europeans. Mussolini listened excitedly to their ideas about government. One idea was to have a government run by ordinary, working-class people. These were the same ideas that Mussolini's father believed.

Mussolini returned to Italy and became involved in the Socialist Party. He wrote and edited articles for a Socialist newspaper. He stirred up workers in revolts and strikes. Once he led a violent mob in a riot through the city streets. He was even put in jail several times. Eventually,

Mussolini (foreground) stands with Fascist Party members and his friend Adolf Hitler (holding hat).

The Rise of Fascism

After the war, Mussolini met privately with a small group of men. His eyes scanned the group seated around him. They were daring men who wanted to change Italy's government. Many of them had been convicted of crimes. Several of them were former soldiers. They were tough men who sometimes used violence to reach their goals. These men would be the first **Fascists** (FASH ists) in Italy.

Mussolini was the leader of this new political party. He chose the title of **Il Duce** (eel DOO chay) for himself. *Il Duce* meant "the leader." Each man in the party wore a black shirt and a black, flat-topped hat, called a fez. These men, known as Black Shirts, fought any people or groups who opposed them.

The Fascists were a terror to Italy. They attacked those who were associated with socialism. Mussolini's Black Shirts could harm or kill anyone who did not agree with Il Duce.

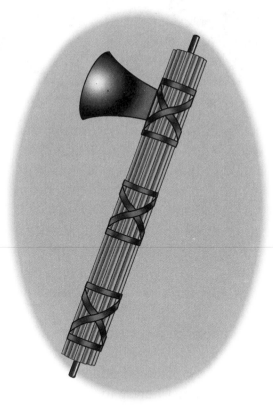

Mussolini named his political party after an ancient Roman symbol called a *fasces*. This symbol represents power and unity.

In spite of all its violence, Fascism was gaining more support. Many Italians were dissatisfied with their present king. They wanted a stronger leader. Others supported the Fascist Party because they wanted to own land or keep the land they already owned. Some supported Mussolini out of fear.

In 1922, Mussolini and fifty-two thousand Black Shirts marched into Rome. The king was forced to make Mussolini the prime minister of Italy. *"Duce! Duce!"* shouted Mussolini's followers.

Mussolini did some helpful things for Italy after he came to power. He built roads, schools, factories, and hospitals. He provided land for farmers. He introduced new welfare benefits and sanitation programs. He even improved Italy's railroad system so that the trains ran on time.

Mussolini charmed many Italians with his smile and his confident speeches.

But it did not take long for the Italian people to see what kind of ruler Mussolini was. He wanted total control over industry, education, and the media. "Obey because you must obey," the school children were taught. Il Duce carefully controlled the newspapers so that only good things were printed about him.

Mussolini also organized his own secret police force. His desire was to get rid of his enemies. The police force publicly humiliated or killed anyone who criticized Mussolini. All over Italy, people were afraid or angry. Some of them tried to fight against the government. But Mussolini's Black Shirts and secret police quickly squelched any uprising. Il Duce's reign of terror continued.

Ancient Roman Empire

Dictatorships existed long before World War I. Many dictators lived during Bible times. One dictator was Julius Caesar. Under his command, soldiers invaded much of Europe. In 46 BC, Caesar became dictator of Rome. The next dictator was Octavian. During Octavian's rule, all the lands under Roman control became known as the Roman Empire. An **empire** is a group of lands and countries under one government.

Jesus lived during the time of the Roman Empire. The rulers controlled most areas of the people's lives. Taxes were collected to support the cost of government. Luke 2:1–5 tells us that Caesar Augustus ordered that everyone return to his home city to be taxed. That is why Mary and Joseph had to make the long and difficult journey to Bethlehem. Jesus was born while they were there. Then, after the wise men spoke to Herod, soldiers were ordered to kill all the male babies in Bethlehem. God led Mary and Joseph to take young Jesus into Egypt during that time.

Jesus had several court trials and was severely beaten before He was crucified.

The people lived in fear of disobeying the laws. Soldiers enforced the laws and punished any lawbreakers. The treatment of Christ during His trial and death is an example of the cruelty of a dictatorship. After Christ's death, Christians were hated and persecuted throughout the Roman Empire for more than two hundred years.

Adolf Hitler
(1889–1945)

Germany: *Heil, Hitler!*

When Mussolini was at the height of his power, he received a fan letter. It was from a young Austrian man who asked for his photograph. Mussolini brushed off the request. He had more important things to do.

The young Austrian's name was **Adolf Hitler**. He had admired Mussolini's aggressive takeover of Italy and longed to imitate him.

Young Hitler

Adolf Hitler was born in 1889 in a town on the border between Austria and Bavaria. As a boy, he was a poor student. He was lazy and undisciplined. He did not fit in well with other children. He was often called a dreamer because he enjoyed passing the time by reading, listening to music, and drawing. He preferred these above other activities.

Hitler went to Vienna at the age of eighteen. There he hoped to be accepted at the Academy of Fine Arts. But he failed the entrance examinations twice. For several years he stayed in Vienna, trying to sell his paintings on the streets.

During his years in Vienna, Hitler began to hate the Jews. Perhaps he disliked them because many of them were accepted in the social circles of Vienna, while he was not. But his hatred for them kept growing. He read books by other men who hated them. Hitler developed a belief that there was a superior race of people in the world. These people were of Germanic heritage, like himself.

Adolf Hitler painted this scene while living in Vienna.

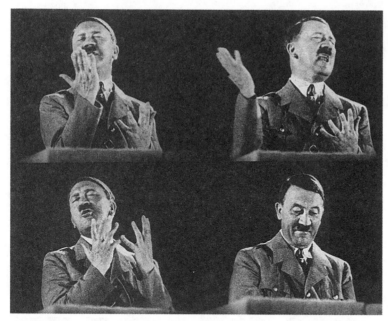

Hitler was known for his expressive gestures when speaking.

name to the National Socialist German Workers' Party. The German word for National Socialist was shortened to **Nazi** (NAHT see). Hitler took complete control of the Nazi Party in 1920. He designed the party's flag. It was red with a white circle and a black hooked cross called a **swastika**. The swastika became the Nazi emblem.

Hitler Becomes Dictator

Adolf Hitler became interested in politics while he lived in Vienna. He moved to Germany in 1913 and then fought in World War I. While in the army, Hitler was sent to spy on a small political party known as the German Workers' Party. Hitler agreed with the beliefs of this party and soon joined it. The party admired Hitler's speaking skills. He had a dynamic intensity in his voice that fascinated them. By 1920, Hitler became one of the party's leaders.

In only a few months, the number of members in the German Workers' Party increased from one hundred to one thousand. Now Hitler wanted to make some changes in the party. He changed the party's

Hitler borrowed several ideas from Mussolini. Just as Mussolini had his Black Shirts, Hitler had his own private army. They were called the storm troopers or Brownshirts. Hitler chose the title of **der Führer** (der FYOOR er) for himself. *Der Führer* meant "the leader" in German.

A brown-shirted Nazi soldier with a swastika on his armband

In 1923, Hitler and his Nazis tried to take over the government of Germany. But they were arrested, and Hitler was sent to prison. While in prison, he spent most of his time writing a book called *Mein Kampf* (mine KAHMPF), which means "My Struggle." The book told about his hatred for the Jews and his desire to rid Germany of all of them. It described his belief in a superior German race. Hitler also wrote about his policy on foreign affairs.

Another group Hitler hated was the Communists. He did not want the Communist Party to take control of Germany. When Hitler was released from prison, he pulled the weakened Nazi Party back together. The effects of the Great Depression led struggling workers to more easily accept Hitler's ideas.

In 1932, Hitler ran for president of Germany. He lost the election, but over two hundred other Nazis won offices in the government. Despite Hitler's loss, he still gained some power. In January of 1933, President Hindenburg appointed Hitler to be the chancellor. This position made Hitler the second in authority over all of Germany.

Just four weeks later, on a cold snowy night in February, a mysterious thing happened. A fire started in the building where the German government held its meetings. Soon the flames were leaping from the windows. Before the fire was put out, the building was badly damaged. Hitler's message spread through Germany almost as quickly as the fire had spread. "The Communists are responsible for setting the fire," he said.

After the fire, more than four thousand Communists were arrested. Hitler sent out his secret state police force, the **Gestapo**, to find enemies of the government. Anyone arrested was jailed or killed without a trial. Many went to **concentration camps**, places where people were kept as prisoners and forced to do heavy labor. Many people died at these camps. The government seemed to distrust everyone.

Hitler ordered many of his own storm troopers to be put to death. All the men he could think of who had ever made him angry were killed. Even so, many of these men shouted *"Heil, Hitler!"* as they died. They did not know why they were being killed.

Less than a year after the fire, President Hindenburg died. After this, Hitler achieved his goal. He became dictator of Germany in the summer of 1934.

Hitler wanted all German-speaking countries to be part of Germany. On March 14, 1938, Austria was the first country to be annexed, or added. Hitler and thousands of soldiers peacefully entered Vienna, the capital city.

Youth in Hitler's Germany

Hitler Youth rally in Nuremberg

Hitler wanted to establish a **Reich** (RIKE), or empire, that would last for a thousand years. The German people were expected to do everything possible to help him reach this goal. Even the young people were expected to help him.

If you had lived in Germany during Hitler's Reich, you would have no soccer teams or Bible clubs to be part of. You would join either the Hitler Youth or the Society of German Maidens. Your activities in these groups would take up most of your spare time.

You would wear a uniform and be given strict physical training to make you strong and healthy. If you were a girl, you would be given lessons in childcare and home economics. You would be told your duty as a woman was to bear as many healthy children as possible for Germany. If you were a boy, you would learn how to march and shoot guns. Your club leader would be a government official. He would keep military-style discipline at all times.

Every day you would have to recite this oath along with your friends: "I promise in the Hitler Youth, to do my duty at all times, in love and faithfulness to the Führer, so help me God."

A meeting of the Society of German Maidens

ARBEIT MA

The sign on this Jewish shop warned non-Jewish Germans not to buy anything there.

The Nuremberg Laws

Adolf Hitler hated the Jewish people. He felt that he belonged to a race that was superior to them. His beliefs disagreed with what the Bible teaches. Deuteronomy 14:2 says that the Jews are God's chosen people. Hitler disregarded God's love for His chosen people.

Hitler believed that a duty of all Germans was to hate the Jewish people as much as he did. The Jews were constantly ridiculed and shunned. Sometimes they were physically harmed by German soldiers. They lost their positions in the civil service. Jewish students could no longer attend the universities. The Nazi Party boycotted Jewish shops and other businesses. Many Jews left the country to find safer places to live.

In 1935, Hitler passed the **Nuremberg Laws**. These laws took away the Jews' freedoms as citizens of Germany. Jews could no longer vote or hold public offices. Jews could not marry Germans. Jewish children could no longer attend German schools. Jews were forbidden to ride public trains or own

"And I will make of thee a great nation, and I will bless thee, and make thy name great; and thou shalt be a blessing: And I will bless them that bless thee, and curse them that curseth thee: and in thee shall all families of the earth be blessed."
Genesis 12:2–3

Many concentration camps had this slogan, meaning, "Work makes free," on their front gates.

telephones. Many Jews were told they could no longer work. Every Jew had to wear a yellow Star of David on his clothing so that everyone would know he was Jewish.

The End of Hitler's Reich

Hitler's Reich did not last for a thousand years as he had hoped. World War II began in 1939. The following year, Mussolini of Italy joined forces with Hitler. The Axis powers, as they were called, won many early victories.

During the war, Hitler sent Jews from many different European countries to concentration camps. Most of the Jews died from mistreatment or were killed in the camps. This one man was responsible for the deaths of about two-thirds of the Jews in the lands he controlled. This time of persecution became known as the Holocaust.

By spring of 1945, the leaders knew the end of the war was near. Mussolini was captured by Communists and shot to death. His body was hung in a public square in Milan. The people did not mourn Mussolini's death. Hitler realized defeat for Germany was coming. He committed suicide in a bomb shelter in Berlin.

The crowds no longer shouted, "*Duce!*" and "*Heil, Hitler!*" Instead, they cheered because the men who had stolen their freedoms were dead.

Joseph McCarthy

After World War II, the fear of communism "echoed" in the United States. Some people thought Communists might be in the United States government. Senators were assigned to committees to investigate this. Joseph McCarthy, a Wisconsin senator, began to investigate people of whom he was suspicious. He made lists of the names of his suspects. He boldly accused people in the government of disloyalty to the United States.

People listened to McCarthy. When he accused someone, others also became suspicious of that person. Some people whom McCarthy had accused lost their jobs. Then they would not be hired by other companies.

Joseph McCarthy reveals his suspicions of alleged Communists in the U. S. Army.

Many Americans felt threatened. They were afraid of saying anything that might sound like criticism of the government. Someone might think they were disloyal and report their names to McCarthy.

McCarthy lost favor with the American public a few years later. The Senate did not believe he had enough proof to make his accusations. However, many years later, McCarthy was found to be right about some of his accusations.

Hirohito
(1901–1989)

Japan: The Showa Emperor

Before World War II, the leaders of Japan were called **emperors**. For many centuries the people of Japan thought of their emperors as gods. When **Hirohito** (HEER oh HEE toh) became emperor of Japan in 1926, he was no exception. The people carried their reverence for their emperor to extremes. No one could touch him and they were not even allowed to look at Hirohito in public. He was given the name **Showa** (SHOW ah) to represent his divinity or godlikeness. The title means "enlightened peace."

Hirohito was a thoughtful and reserved man. He enjoyed studying science. This helped Hirohito realize that he was not a descendant of the sun goddess as the people believed. He often expressed a wish to live closer to his people and to see how they lived.

Hirohito wears ceremonial attire at his formal enthronement in 1928.

Hirohito had a group of strong advisors. These men made most of the decisions for the country. They would ask Hirohito for his opinion. But he rarely objected to anything they recommended. The advisors decided that Japan should go to war against the United States during World War II. Hirohito went along with this decision. He signed all the necessary documents.

Hirohito and his family in 1934

Japan was proud of its military tradition. The nation had never been defeated in a war. The soldiers were fearless and not afraid of death. But World War II would be a different war for them.

The Japanese had high hopes when they first entered World War II. In 1941, their attack on American ships in Pearl Harbor was a great victory for them. But defeating the Americans would not be as easy as the Japanese thought.

Japan soon suffered serious defeats. Hirohito knew his people were in danger, but he did not take any action to end the war. He left the military decisions up to his advisors. The advisors refused to surrender and bring disgrace on Japan. If the United States did not act, the war would drag on and many more lives would be lost.

August 6, 1945, is a date Japanese people will never forget. The Americans dropped the world's first atomic bomb on the city of Hiroshima. Three days later, they dropped another atomic bomb on the city of Nagasaki. As a result, hundreds of thousands of Japanese people were killed.

On August 14, Hirohito met with his war council. In a broken voice, he asked them to surrender. He did not want his people to suffer any longer.

Hirohito had been set so far above his people that he had not understood their needs. He did not see the wounded soldiers lying on the battlefields or the mothers grieving over dead sons. He had remained silent when an order from him could have ended the war that took so many Japanese lives.

Hirohito in dress uniform

The Americans were generous to Hirohito after the war. They allowed him to keep his royal position as emperor of Japan. But he had to announce that he was not a god. He also had to announce that the Japanese were not better than other races, as his people had been taught to believe.

Under the leadership of General Douglas MacArthur of the United States, Japan's government changed to a democracy. In the new democratic Japan, the people elected representatives to govern them.

Hirohito lived the rest of his life peacefully. He toured places around

Hirohito and his wife enjoyed a leisurely life in their later years.

the world, spent time with his family, and studied science. The Showa Emperor died in January of 1989 from an illness.

As emperor, Hirohito was like a dictator. He was the ruler of the country. However, Hirohito was different from Stalin, Mussolini, and Hitler. He was not a heavy-handed tyrant as they were. But he made the same mistake that they did. None of these rulers used his power for the good of his people.

General Douglas MacArthur and Emperor Hirohito

"Lift not up your horn on high: speak not with a stiff neck. For promotion cometh neither from the east, nor from the west, nor from the south. But God is the judge: he putteth down one, and setteth up another."

Psalm 75: 5–7

Designing and Using a Map Key

1. Get your Activity Manual page and some colored pencils or crayons.

2. Study the maps.

3. Look at the rulers listed in the key. Choose a color to represent the country of the first leader. Color the box next to that ruler. Repeat by choosing different colors for the remaining countries.

4. Design a symbol to use on the map to indicate the national capital cities. Draw your symbol in the box in the key.

5. Complete your map according to your key.

Dictatorships Before WW II

Never Such a War

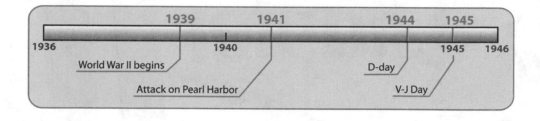

1936   1939   1941   1944   1945
1940   1945   1946

World War II begins
Attack on Pearl Harbor
D-day
V-J Day

The Gathering Storm

World War I, "the war to end all wars," was over. The victorious were wild to celebrate. And that carefree spirit spilled over into the 1920s. America grew richer. Europe began to rebuild its cities and heal from years of war.

Most people thought there could be no greater time of trouble than the world had just survived. But just over twenty years later, it was clear that the Great War had not ended all wars. An even bigger war was coming. The leaders who would cause this war were already working together.

Adolf Hitler of Germany and Benito Mussolini of Italy were dictators. Each of these men sought to re-create the greatness of the Roman Empire. They wanted to build their own empires. In 1936, Italy and Germany made an alliance called the *Rome-Berlin Axis*. The following year, Italy and Japan signed a similar agreement. This brought together the three major powers as the *Rome-Berlin-Tokyo Axis*. These three nations formed an alliance that would be known as the **Axis powers** during World War II. The leaders of all three nations believed that the good of the government was more important than the good of the people.

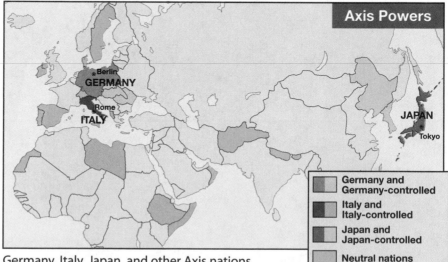

Germany, Italy, Japan, and other Axis nations fought Great Britain, the Soviet Union, the United States, and other Allied nations in World War II.

198

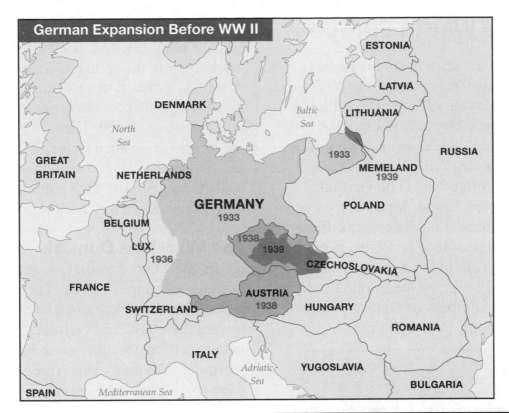

German Expansion Before WW II

Germany wanted control of Austria and also demanded part of Czechoslovakia (CHEK uh slo VAH kee uh). Great Britain and France agreed. The leaders thought it best to give in to Hitler's demands. They did not want to start another war. Hitler promised that he would be satisfied with the land in Czechoslovakia.

But Hitler did not keep his promise. Once he had Austria and part of Czechoslovakia, he also wanted Poland. This time, letting Hitler have what he wanted was out of the question. When Hitler was told he could not have Poland, he ordered his army to take it.

In this cartoon, Hitler has asked the driver to take him to Czechoslovakia. The driver thought it best to agree. The cartoon is an example of a primary source.

The War in Europe

The German forces moved quickly. In September of 1939, Germany took over Poland in eighteen days. This kind of fast-moving attack was known as a **blitzkrieg** (BLITS kreeg), or "lightning war." The German air force first dropped bombs on Poland's larger cities, killing many people. The Polish people were filled with terror. Then tanks rolled in. They were followed by huge numbers of German troops marching rank upon rank.

Successes of the Axis Nations

The blitzkrieg continued throughout Europe in the spring. Germany defeated Denmark in only one day. Norway lasted about three weeks before it was defeated. Then, in May, the Germans invaded Belgium and the Netherlands. Great Britain sent soldiers to help. But the German army could not be held back.

The Miracle at Dunkirk

In late May of 1940, German armies moved into France. They pushed English and French soldiers toward the coast. The Germans were so strong that they soon had surrounded thousands of Allied soldiers in northwestern France. The English and French were trapped on the beaches at the city of Dunkirk. It looked like certain defeat.

German soldiers advance into Poland.

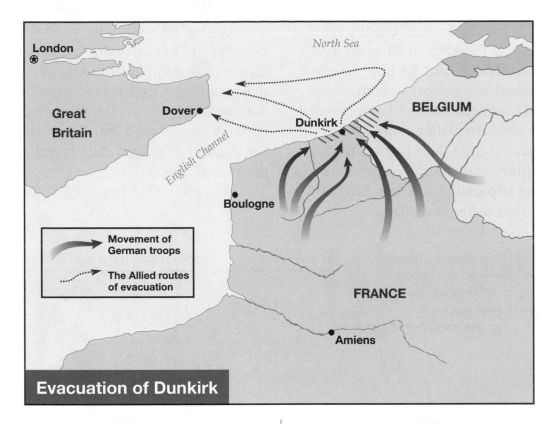

North Sea

London

Great
Britain

Dover

Dunkirk

BELGIUM

English Channel

Boulogne

Movement of
German troops

The Allied routes
of evacuation

FRANCE

Amiens

Evacuation of Dunkirk

Hitler thought the Allies had little hope of escaping. He ordered the German soldiers to halt. The soldiers stopped twelve miles short of Dunkirk. The Allies were surprised but quickly seized this opportunity to send for help.

The British leaders at Dunkirk asked the citizens of their country for help. King George VI called for a day of prayer for his nation. People throughout the British Empire began praying for God to deliver the Allied soldiers.

The British people responded with courage and determination. Soon thousands of boats, barges, yachts, and even fishing boats started across the English Channel.

Allied troops wait to cross the English Channel.

Winds and waves usually make crossing the English Channel by boat difficult. But for nine days the channel was almost smooth. Clouds and mists covered the harbor so that the German planes could not see where to drop their bombs. British military and civilian boats made trip after trip until more than 330,000 soldiers were rescued.

Winston Churchill, the prime minister of Great Britain, called the rescue at Dunkirk a **"miracle of deliverance."** Christians recognized it as an answer to prayer. God used both the people with their boats and the weather to answer the prayers of the British people.

"And call upon me in the day of trouble: I will deliver thee, and thou shalt glorify me."
Psalm 50:15

Troops shipping out from Dunkirk

The British used existing structures such as the underground railway stations, tunnels, and basements as shelters against air raids or attacks by airplanes.

SHELTER FULL except to reserved ticket holders

NEAREST PUBLIC SHELTER

Germans also wanted to prevent goods from entering Great Britain. So the Germans set up a **blockade**. German ships blocked or sank other ships trying to enter or leave British ports. But despite all of the danger and death, the British refused to surrender.

Many British people in the cities sent their children to live with families in the countryside. That way the children would be safer. In the cities and countryside alike, the British built shelters underground. When sirens sounded, the people fled into the shelters for safety.

The Fall of France

In June of 1940, France surrendered to Germany. France had fallen in just forty-two days. Now Hitler and the other nations in his alliance controlled most of Europe.

The Battle of Britain

Great Britain stood alone against the German forces. German planes roared across the English Channel to bomb cities in Great Britain. The

After the bombing of London, smoke swirled around St. Paul's Cathedral.

Winston Churchill
(1874–1965)

Winston Churchill was the son of a British lord and a beautiful American heiress. As a child, he showed little promise of becoming one of the greatest statesmen in history. He did poorly in school and was often in trouble.

However, in military school Churchill excelled in the study of tactics. He graduated near the top of his 150-member class. He then became a soldier and a war reporter. He was captured during the Boer War in Africa and made a daring escape. He returned to England as a national hero.

At the age of twenty-six Churchill was elected to Parliament. Shortly before World War I, he saw that war was coming. As First Lord of the Admiralty, Churchill prepared the British navy. For many years, he was in and out of popularity. Sometimes he was cheered, many times jeered. At one point he told a friend, "I'm finished." But Churchill was far from finished. His most important work was still ahead. He would

After his escape from the Boer War in 1900, Churchill became a lieutenant in the South African Light Horse Regiment.

become prime minister of Great Britain during World War II. After Dunkirk, Churchill realized that when France fell, England would be Hitler's next target. He stood before the British government and made one of the most famous speeches in history:

> The Battle of Britain is about to begin. . . . The whole fury and might of the enemy must very soon be turned on us. . . . Let us therefore brace ourselves to our duties, and so bear ourselves, that, if the British Empire and its Commonwealth last for a thousand years, men will say, "This was their finest hour."

The British proved they were able to fight this vicious enemy. Although the Royal Air Force was outnumbered and outgunned, it managed to protect its country and hold off Hitler's forces. The British people, as Churchill had declared in another famous speech, did not "flag nor fail." They never surrendered.

Much of the credit for the courage that the British showed in the worst of times goes to Churchill's amazing speeches. Late in his life, this great man of war said that it was many others who had "the lion's heart." It was his privilege, he said, "to give the roar."

Legend:
- Allies and Allied-controlled
- Axis and Axis-controlled
- Neutral nations

Europe in June 1941

weather. They could fight back. Hitler's lightning attack failed. The Germans, hindered by snow and cold, lost many soldiers.

The United States Stays Neutral

After World War I, Americans wanted to stay out of the problems of other nations. Some Americans thought that there was no reason for their men to die in another war. Others feared that America was not prepared and would be easily defeated. During the early years of World War II, Americans sent food, weapons, and other goods to the Allied nations. A law required American men to register for the draft. The **draft** was the system that chose men to go to war. After men signed up, the military could then select men as needed to train for war.

Late in 1941, something happened that changed the Americans' ideas drastically. It stunned the whole nation—and roused it to rage.

Invasion of the Soviet Union

In June of 1941, Germany and the other Axis nations surprised almost everyone. They attacked the Soviet Union, heading for the capital city of Moscow. But winter came earlier than usual to the Soviet Union. It was the coldest winter of the century. The German armies were trapped in that vast land. The Soviets were prepared for the

Unlike the Germans, these Soviet soldiers were well prepared for winter fighting.

The USS *Arizona* before the Pearl Harbor attack

The wreck of the battleship after the attack

Attack on Pearl Harbor

On the island of Oahu (oh AH hoo), Hawaii, there is a large **harbor** called Pearl Harbor. The Pearl Harbor Naval Base is located there. This base holds many American ships and aircraft. These are known as the U.S. Pacific Fleet.

Just before eight in the morning on **December 7, 1941**, nearly four hundred Japanese planes descended on Pearl Harbor. They bombed American airfields and seriously crippled the U.S. Pacific Fleet.

The Japanese attack destroyed two-thirds of the American aircraft. Eight battleships and three cruisers were sunk or seriously damaged in the attack. Over one thousand lives were lost on the USS *Arizona* alone. In the end,

over two thousand Americans were killed at Pearl Harbor.

The next day President Roosevelt said that December 7, 1941, was "a date which will live in infamy." He asked Congress to declare war on Japan. Congress voted to go to war. When America entered the war, its rallying cry was "Remember Pearl Harbor!"

A rescue boat helps seamen on the sinking USS *West Virginia*.

207

Propaganda

Using words and pictures to portray news or people in a certain way is called **propaganda**. Propaganda was widely used by both the Allies and the Axis nations during World War II. It was used in radio broadcasts, motion pictures, posters, and cartoons.

Germany is the topic of both posters shown. However, each promotes a different attitude toward Germany and its army.

Adolf Hitler had been impressed by the use of propaganda by the Allies during World War I. He felt it was a very important tool in war. Hitler established a government agency to handle all propaganda. He met each day with the agency chief to discuss world events. He censored the works of all artists, broadcasters, and journalists.

The British aired nightly radio programs about the war. They were heard on the European mainland. Hitler made it a crime for German people to listen to these programs.

This poster was to make the German army look good to the countries they were invading.

The United States used propaganda to support the war effort. President Roosevelt created the Office of War Information. One purpose of this agency was to make propaganda films to encourage the American people to support the war.

America also used posters to attract volunteers to join the military. These were very successful. Similar posters can be seen "echoing" today to bring in volunteers for military service.

This poster was designed by the Allies to show Germany as an evil force.

Allied tanks in North Africa

A Global War

The war that so many countries were now involved in was called **World War II**. The Americans fought in the Pacific and in North Africa. America also sent soldiers and a great leader to France.

Allied Preparation

Against the Axis leaders, the Allies had the "**Big Three**"—Winston Churchill of England, Joseph Stalin of the Soviet Union, and Franklin Roosevelt of the United States. In late 1943, these three men met at Tehran, Iran. They discussed military strategy. The decision was made to invade France. The Allies would sail across the English Channel and take France back from Germany. The Allies would push the Germans back to Germany.

The invasion of France was planned under the code name **Operation Overlord**. The code name for the day of the invasion was called **D-day**. The Allies worked for months in careful secrecy. They created an imaginary military force with its own commander. The Allies sent false messages and allowed the Germans to intercept them. The Germans were made to believe that an attack was coming near the French-Belgian border.

General Dwight D. Eisenhower encourages troops about to parachute out of airplanes to begin the invasion of France.

209

Great numbers of Allied troops gathered in England. They had thousands of trucks and tons of ammunition, food, and medical supplies. **Dwight Eisenhower**, the supreme Allied commander, decided to plan D-day for June. Everything had to be just right for the attack, including the weather. Finally, on **June 6, 1944**, in spite of threatening weather, Eisenhower ordered the attack.

Invasion of Normandy

The attack took place on five beaches along the coast of Normandy, France. Minesweepers went first to clear the water. About 2,700 ships sailed from England during the night. The ships carried over 150,000 troops and their supplies.

Shortly after midnight, thousands of Allied planes flew over the French coast. They bombed the beaches and German supply factories. Many Allied soldiers dropped by parachute behind the Germans. They captured bridges and railroad tracks.

At dawn, the Allied ships opened fire on the beaches of France and the troops stormed ashore. It was the biggest air and naval invasion in history. The Germans were taken by surprise. For both sides, the fighting was very hard. But in the end, D-day was a success for the Allies. The Allies won those beaches and began their march across France. Their final goal was to reach Germany.

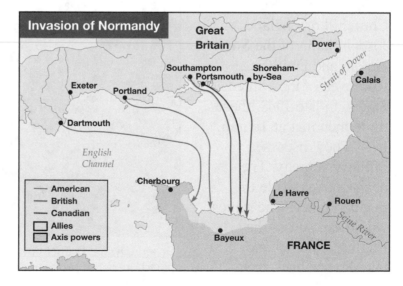

Dwight David Eisenhower
(1890–1969)

"Opportunity is all about you. Reach out and take it," said **Dwight D. Eisenhower**. He was describing some of the values his parents had taught him. Dwight, or "Ike" as he was called, was born in 1890 into a poor family in Texas. About a year later, the Eisenhower family moved to Abilene, Kansas. Dwight did well in school. His parents taught him to read the Bible and to live honorably.

Eisenhower did not have enough money to pay for his college tuition. He worked seven days a week, twelve hours a day, to save money for an education. He was accepted at West Point, the United States Military Academy. After he graduated, Eisenhower joined the army and worked at different posts. When World War I broke out, he trained soldiers for battle.

The Eisenhowers on their wedding day

During World War II, Eisenhower was selected to lead the Allied forces. His success as a five-star general made him very popular with the American people. When he returned home to the United States, he received a hero's welcome for his leadership in the D-day invasion.

After the war, Eisenhower became the president of Columbia University. Then President Harry Truman wanted Eisenhower to be the leader of a group of nations. This group was called the North Atlantic Treaty Organization, or NATO. Its purpose was to fight communism.

Because of his leadership abilities and popularity, Eisenhower was encouraged to run for the presidency. People carried signs and wore buttons that read, "I Like Ike." He swept the elections. In 1953, Eisenhower became the thirty-fourth president of the United States.

In a speech, Eisenhower said, "What counts is not necessarily the size of the dog in the fight—it's the size of the fight in the dog." He proved to be a good fighter and a hard worker throughout his life. He faced many difficult decisions and problems during his two terms as president. But Eisenhower seized every opportunity to serve his country. He worked to preserve freedom and peace, not only in America, but around the world.

Dwight Eisenhower spent his retirement years near Gettysburg, Pennsylvania. He died on March 28, 1969. In the hours before his death, he quietly stated his unwavering allegiance to America with the simple words, "I've always loved my country." His last words were, "I want to go; God take me."

The French people celebrate.

The Beginning of the End

The Allies now moved across France, pushing the German forces back. French people cheered the Allies. They wept for joy as the German soldiers withdrew from French villages and cities. As the Allies marched and fought, they freed any Axis prisoners.

The Allies fought from the east and from the west. They forced the German army into a smaller and smaller area. By March of 1945, American troops reached the Rhine River. One month later the soldiers reached the Elbe River farther east. There the troops waited for the arrival of their Soviet allies. The Soviets had been marching and fighting their way across Germany from the east.

On April 30, 1945, Hitler shot himself in his underground bunker in Berlin. A few days later, on May 7, the Germans surrendered. The Allies declared **May 8, 1945**, as "Victory in Europe Day," or **V-E Day**. On V-E Day, the Allies rejoiced. The war in Europe was over. But the Allies still had to defeat Japan in the Pacific.

Celebrating V-E Day

> "I have seen the wicked in great power, and spreading himself like a green bay tree."
> **Psalm 37:35**

The Holocaust

Early in the war, Hitler had ordered that all the Jews be rounded up. Hitler especially hated the Jews, God's chosen people. The Jews were forced to live in restricted areas. These areas were sealed off from the rest of the city. The Jews were forced to live and work in unbearable conditions. Their food was rationed.

Hungarian Jews stumble out of a freight c... upon their arrival at a concentration cam...

Many Jews were horribly mistreated and placed in concentration camps. The German leaders had built these camps for anyone who disagreed with their ideas. The largest group of camps was in the Polish village of Oswiecim (in German, *Auschwitz*). Three camps were built there to receive thousands of Jews from all over Eastern Europe. The Jews were brought to the prison camps in closed railroad cars. The cars were made to hold forty people, but as many as one hundred fifty people were crammed into each. They traveled for days before reaching a camp. Scores of people died during the trip.

Concentration camps had gas chambers. They also had furnaces where many of the bodies of men, women, and children were burned. Millions of Europeans, such as gypsies, mentally or physically disabled, and Jehovah's Witnesses were killed in these camps. But the Jewish race remained Hitler's primary target. An estimated six million Jews were murdered. This slaughtering of Jews became known as the **Holocaust**.

Even though Hitler tried to wipe out the Jews, the Bible says that God protects His chosen people. In the 1940s, the Jews were brought together again as an official nation of the world.

Prisoners in their bunks at the Buchenwald camp.

The War in the Pacific

After the Japanese attack on Pearl Harbor, many Americans feared anyone they met who was of Japanese heritage. They thought the Japanese Americans could be spies for Japan.

Because of this fear, President Roosevelt authorized the military to move the Japanese Americans. In February of 1942, about 120,000 Japanese Americans were forced from their homes in California, Oregon, and Washington. They were sent to relocation camps further inland. They lost their homes and their jobs. In 1988, the American government apologized for not trusting loyal Americans just because of their Japanese heritage.

Early Japanese Victories

For months after Pearl Harbor, the Japanese troops seemed to win everywhere they fought. Many islands and countries fell to the Japanese. The Japanese took thousands of prisoners and forced them into large concentration camps. They lived in terrible conditions with very little food or water. Many were tortured and killed.

China was also in the war against Japan. The Chinese army needed supplies, but the Japanese had control of China's coast. So the United States transported war supplies on the Burma Road. It ran through rough mountain country. The road linked Burma to China.

A relocation camp at Manzanar, California

Japanese Americans travel to relocation camps.

The Burma Road was about 700 miles long with many hairpin curves.

In April of 1942, the Japanese conquered Burma. They closed the Burma Road. Brave Allied pilots flew supplies over the Himalaya Mountains instead. The Himalayas, referred to as "the Hump" by Allied pilots, are the world's highest mountains.

The Fall of the Philippines

In the Philippine Islands, the Americans fought hard against the Japanese. Since early January of 1942, the food rations for the American troops had been cut in half. The troops gnawed on roots. They sometimes ate mules, monkeys, or dogs.

In spite of a lack of supplies, the Americans held the Japanese back for five months. But in May of 1942, the American and Filipino forces had no choice but to surrender. The American commander, **General Douglas MacArthur**, escaped. He promised, "I shall return." While the Americans were gone, the Japanese tortured and killed many Filipino soldiers and Christian missionaries.

Island-Hopping Campaign

In June of 1942, the Japanese attacked the United States air base on the Midway Islands northwest of Hawaii. Although the Americans were outnumbered, they turned back the Japanese attack. After the defeat, Japan was on the defensive for the rest of the war.

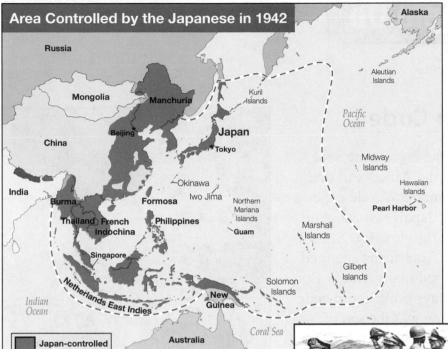

Area Controlled by the Japanese in 1942

Russia

Alaska

Mongolia

Manchuria

China

Beijing

Japan

Tokyo

Kuril Islands

Aleutian Islands

Pacific Ocean

Midway Islands

India

Burma

Okinawa

Iwo Jima

Formosa

Thailand French Indochina

Philippines

Northern Mariana Islands

Guam

Hawaiian Islands

Pearl Harbor

Marshall Islands

Singapore

Netherlands East Indies

New Guinea

Solomon Islands

Gilbert Islands

Indian Ocean

Australia

Coral Sea

■ Japan-controlled

The return of General MacArthur

Look at the map to find the islands that the Japanese controlled. The Americans knew that it would be hard to capture all the islands. So they followed an **island-hopping campaign**. This meant the military seized only the islands that offered good sites for air bases. Fighting was often difficult. Few Japanese troops surrendered. Most chose to die in battle or commit suicide rather than face the dishonor of surrender.

By October of 1944, the Americans' island hopping landed them in the Philippines. General MacArthur returned, just as he had promised. After wading ashore, he said, "People of the Philippines, I have returned. By the grace of Almighty God, our forces stand again on Philippine soil."

MacArthur came with a large American force. American ships attacked the Japanese off the coast. On the ground American soldiers had some success. But not until the end of the war did all the Japanese resistance in the Philippines cease.

Talking in Code

Radio war messages were sent in code by both the Americans and the Japanese. American code experts worked to break Japan's codes. And the Japanese tried to break U.S. military codes. The Americans changed the codes they used many times. But the Japanese always broke those codes.

Philip Johnston was the son of missionaries to the Navajo Indians in the American Southwest. He suggested letting Navajos be the radiomen. They could talk in their own language.

Navajo cousins Preston Toledo and Frank Toledo relay a coded message.

The U.S. Marine Corps trained more than 375 Navajos as "code talkers." The Navajos memorized everything. No code books were needed. These **Navajo code talkers** could decode a three-line message in only twenty seconds. It would take a decoding machine thirty minutes to decode the same message.

There are no words in the Navajo language for such things as airplanes and bombs. So they substituted other words for the military words. Bombers became *jaysho*, or "buzzards." And bombs were *ayeshi*, or "eggs." The radiomen made up colorful names for countries as well. They called Australia "rolled hat."

The Japanese tried but never could break this new secret code. Without the Navajo code talkers, the American marines could not have taken Iwo Jima in Japan. In 1982, President Ronald Reagan declared August 14 as National Code Talkers Day.

Communicating in Code

The Navajo language was used as a code to keep the Japanese from understanding American messages. You can write in code too. First, design your own code. Then write a secret message using your code. Imagine that a friend is an enemy spy. Will the enemy be able to decode your message correctly?

1. Find an existing code or invent one. Write it in the boxes above the letters on the Activity Manual page.

2. Make up a message. Write it in your code.

3. Let your message fall into "enemy" hands.

4. Intercept a message from an "enemy." Try to decode it.

Marines raise the flag on Iwo Jima.

Two Strategic Islands

The Americans fought their way toward Japan. As the troops got closer to Japan, the fighting became more fierce. The American troops needed good air bases from which they could launch bombing raids on the main islands of Japan.

Iwo Jima (EE-wuh JEE-muh) was less than 700 miles from Japan. Iwo Jima was a volcanic island with many underground tunnels. American planes bombed the island for seventy-two days. Then the American ground troops landed on the beaches. American casualties were high. But by mid-March, Iwo Jima was in American hands.

Kamikazes, or Japanese suicide pilots, attacked many American ships at Okinawa.

There was only one more island to take before reaching the Japanese mainland. Both the Japanese and the Americans knew the importance of the island of **Okinawa** (OH kuh NOW wuh). On April 1, 1945, the Americans invaded Okinawa. They fought the Japanese military for two and one-half months. The Japanese finally gave up Okinawa.

American fighters could now bomb the factories and cities on Japan's mainland. In a one-night raid on Tokyo, fire destroyed nearly sixteen square miles of the city. More than 80,000 people died. Japanese people wanted to see the war end. But Japan's military leaders refused to give up.

Douglas MacArthur
(1880–1964)

Douglas MacArthur was born in 1880 in Arkansas. His mother's ancestors had lived at the early Jamestown settlement in Virginia. His father was a hero in the Civil War and a United States military governor of the Philippines.

MacArthur's parents were his first teachers. They taught him about duty. They told him to do right, no matter what it might cost. "Our country was always to come first," he wrote of those days. There were "two things we must never do: never lie and never tattle."

MacArthur was an average student in elementary school. Later he did extremely well at West Texas Military Academy. He wanted to go to the United States Military Academy at West Point, New York. He studied hard for the entrance tests. He received high marks. "It was a lesson I never forgot. Preparedness is the key to success and victory."

MacArthur finished at West Point in 1903. He graduated first in his class. His first military assignment was in the Philippines. He then served his country in several foreign countries as well as in the United States. During World War I, MacArthur won numerous honors for his bravery.

MacArthur being decorated for bravery in World War I

General MacArthur in Korea

In 1919, he became the youngest superintendent of West Point. Then, in 1930, he became chief of staff for the whole army. He was also the youngest man ever to have that job. MacArthur retired from the army in 1937. He became the military advisor to the Philippine government.

During World War II, he was called to return to active duty. He commanded the American troops in the Pacific. At the end of the war, he became commander of the Allied troops sent to occupy Japan. He helped Japan write a new constitution. MacArthur made the royalty in Japan less influential. He led the government to give Japanese women the right to vote. And he invited Christian missionaries to bring the gospel to Japan.

In his retirement years, MacArthur went to West Point to receive an award. There he gave one of the most famous speeches in American military history. In it he declared "Duty, honor, country; those three hallowed words reverently dictate what you ought to be, what you can be, what you will be."

MacArthur greeting cadets at West Point after giving his famous speech.

Cloud from the atomic bomb at Nagasaki

Victory in Japan

The war was coming to an end. In April of 1945, President Roosevelt died. Vice President Harry Truman became president. The new president had a big decision to make. Should he use the atomic bomb, the new weapon invented by American scientists? The events in Okinawa had shown him that the Japanese would not easily surrender. The war would continue much longer if American forces invaded Japan. President Truman knew that hundreds of thousands of soldiers would be killed. He also knew that the **atomic bomb** would be more destructive than any weapon in history. It would change forever the way wars would be fought.

The United States tried to get the Japanese to surrender. American planes dropped leaflets to the Japanese people. The papers said that something terrible would happen if the Japanese did not surrender right away. But they refused.

On August 6, 1945, the first atomic bomb was dropped on **Hiroshima** (HIR uh SHEE muh), Japan. The bomb killed an estimated 70,000 people. Still the Japanese would not give up. Three days later, a second bomb was dropped on **Nagasaki** (NAH guh SAH kee). This city was a major industrial center and had an important seaport. The next day, Japan asked for peace.

The Japanese and the Allies signed the surrender document aboard the USS *Missouri* in Tokyo Bay. Truman declared **September 2, 1945, V-J Day**, "Victory in Japan Day." World War II was over.

The city of Nagasaki after the atomic bomb

223

Germany After WW II

Great Britain
Soviet Union
United States
France

Aftermath

After World War II, Germany had to pay damages to the Allies. The country of Germany was divided into four parts. The Soviet Union, the United States, Great Britain, and France each occupied a part. When a country is **occupied**, it is controlled by a foreign military force. The Soviet Union also officially controlled much of Eastern Europe.

The United States occupied Japan. Korea was split into North Korea and South Korea. The Soviet Union occupied North Korea. The United States occupied South Korea. Japan had to pay damages to the countries whose land it had taken over during the war.

Casualties and Cost

World War II proved to be the most costly war to that point in history. The cost of the war reached about $1.5 trillion. But many people lost more than money. They lost their farms, homes, and businesses. Many lost family members. More than forty million military personnel and civilians died in World War II. Many others lost everything they owned.

Shift in Power

The world was divided into two groups. Each group was led by a "superpower." In the West, the United States became the leading nation. It was dedicated to preserving peace and freedom. In the East, the Soviet Union became the leader. It sought to expand its dictatorship influence and stir up revolution.

Comparing WW I to WW II		
	World War I	**World War II**
Duration	4 years	6 years
Casualties	Over 30 million	Over 40 million
Financial cost	$351 billion	$1.5 trillion
Countries involved	28	Over 60

Note: Figures are approximate.

Chapter 11

Recovery and the Cold War

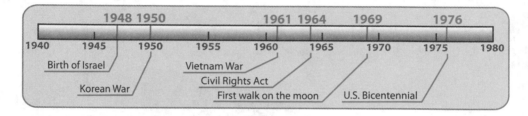
After the War

World War II was over! The United States was at peace. However, it faced new challenges. The world after the war was not the same as the one that had existed before. New problems, new threats, and new fears emerged.

A new enemy, communism, threatened democracy worldwide. Communism spread through Asia, Eastern Europe, and Africa. Meanwhile, in the United States, black Americans struggled to achieve equal rights. The country would also have new opportunities and new technology that would bring new prosperity.

The Forties—A Time of War and Recovery

The 1940s began with the bombing of Pearl Harbor and *Franklin D. Roosevelt* as president. Roosevelt worked to end World War II. He died less than a month before victory was reached in Europe. *Harry Truman* became president in 1945.

Keeping the Peace

In April of 1945, President Truman welcomed delegates from fifty nations. They met in San Francisco, California, for two months. Their meeting resulted in the forming of the **United Nations** (UN). The UN was designed to listen to international problems and to try to find peaceful solutions.

Today, the United Nations headquarters is in New York City. On the building, where all who enter can see it, are the words from Isaiah 2:4:

UN Headquarters

"They shall beat their swords into plowshares, and their spears into pruninghooks: nation shall not lift up sword against nation, neither shall they learn war any more."

226

President Truman had a sign on his desk that read: "The buck stops here." It meant he was responsible for all decisions.

An organization to keep peace seemed to be a good idea. The UN has helped keep peace in many countries. However, it has not been able to stop countries from going to war against each other. Until Christ brings peace to men, there will be no lasting peace.

Cold War and Changes in Life

When World War II was over, the United States soon learned that the Soviets were trying to take over all the nations they could. The United States and the Soviet Union did not go into direct military battle with each other. But the tensions between them resulted in many disputes between their governments.

This type of conflict between nations is called a **cold war.**

The Soviet Union continued to work to make other countries Communist. The United States sent help and money to many nations trying to stay free. The Soviets tried to spread their influence to Greece and Turkey. President Truman wanted to help Greece and Turkey. In May of 1947, Truman asked the United States Congress to give these countries economic aid. The money was necessary to stop the Soviets from overtaking governments. This policy of aiding countries fighting Communist takeovers became known as the **Truman Doctrine**.

Many Americans feared another "Depression" after World War II. But they found plenty of jobs. Industries began producing peacetime goods instead of guns and tanks. Many Americans wanted new comforts such as televisions. They wanted labor-saving devices such as dish-washers and power lawn mowers. In the cities, the cost of land was high and there were housing shortages. As a result, more Americans moved to the suburbs.

"Peace I leave with you, my peace I give unto you: not as the world giveth, give I unto you. Let not your heart be troubled, neither let it be afraid."
John 14:27

227

Israel—God's Chosen People

From the days of Joshua through the time of Daniel, the children of Israel struggled to possess the land God had promised to them. By AD 70, many Jews were living in the land of Palestine. Israel's capital city of Jerusalem was attacked by the Romans. The temple and the entire city were destroyed. Many Jews were taken from their land.

> "I will multiply your seed as the stars of heaven, and all this land that I have spoken of will I give unto your seed, and they shall inherit it for ever."
>
> **Exodus 32:13**

By the mid 1800s small numbers of Jews living in Europe began to move back into Palestine. Theodor Herzl, a German Jew, wanted the Jews to have their own homeland. In 1896, Herzl began a movement to obtain a homeland. The movement became known as **Zionism**. The word *Zion* is often used to refer to Jerusalem or to the whole Jewish nation.

Theodor Herzl

Israel 1948–49

Legend:
- United Nations Israel in 1948
- Post Arab-Israeli War 1949

During World War I, Great Britain issued the **Balfour Declaration**. The British promised the Jews that they could settle in Palestine. The Arabs already living in Palestine did not want the Jews living in the same land. Great Britain wanted to please the Arabs and sent the Jews back to Europe.

The Zionist Jews did not give up. The Holocaust had swayed the world's sympathy toward the Jews. Zionist groups in Palestine began working toward establishing a Jewish nation. The United Nations attempted to divide Palestine peacefully between the Arabs and the Jews. Finally, the Israelis declared their independence in **1948**. After that, the Arabs attacked the Jews and sought to drive them out of Palestine. Against great odds, the Jews were victorious. The modern state of Israel was born.

The Fifties—A Time of Optimism and Struggle

The Korean War

After World War II, Korea was divided along the 38th parallel. In June of 1950, Communist North Korea invaded non-Communist South Korea. This sparked the Korean War. The United Nations sent soldiers, and President Truman chose General Douglas MacArthur to lead them. By October, the United Nations forces appeared close to victory. Then thousands of soldiers from Communist China poured over the border into North Korea. They pushed MacArthur's forces back into South Korea.

General MacArthur thought that, to win the war, the bases and supply lines in China should be bombed. President Truman was worried that expanding the war into China might lead to World War III. Truman wanted to keep the war in Korea. MacArthur disagreed with the president's policy. President Truman then called MacArthur home.

Neither North Korea nor South Korea could gain an advantage in the fighting. Talks to end the war began. But the fighting continued for two more years. In July of 1953, a cease-fire agreement was signed. The boundary between North and South Korea remained about where it was before the war started. But the United States had succeeded in saving South Korea from communism.

The Korean War Memorial honors veterans of this war with nineteen statues on patrol.

The Korean War 1950–53

Russia
China
Tumen River
Yalu River
North Korea
Sea of Japan (East Sea)
Korea Bay
Pyongyang
Cease-fire line July 27, 1953
38th parallel
0   50 mi
0   50 km
Seoul
Yellow Sea
South Korea
Japan

Just before the Korean War was over, *Dwight D. Eisenhower* became president. This World War II hero ran against Adlai E. Stevenson. The people decided that they "liked Ike."

Communism

The United States government found out about a British-American spy ring. It had been operating during World War II. Julius and Ethel Rosenberg were convicted of betraying the United States by passing secrets about atomic weapons to the Soviet Union. They were executed in 1953 for treason.

The Soviets continued to work to bring communism to other countries. In 1954, Communist North Vietnam decided to take over non-Communist South Vietnam. The United States offered to help South Vietnam by sending military advisors.

Many Americans were afraid of communism. Senator Joseph McCarthy began to investigate people of whom he was suspicious. Some of the people he accused lost friends and jobs. By 1954, the Senate determined that McCarthy had been accusing people without enough evidence.

Civil Rights Movement

In America, both the northern and southern parts of the country practiced segregation. This type of **segregation**, or separation of races, was more noticeable in the South. There black citizens struggled to live under **Jim Crow laws**. These laws segregated blacks from whites in public places such as schools, theaters, restaurants, and buses. Blacks and whites even had separate restrooms and drinking fountains. The struggle of black Americans to gain equality was called the **civil rights movement**. Civil rights are those rights guaranteed by the Constitution to every American citizen.

This railway depot in Florida had segregated waiting rooms.

Rosa Parks is fingerprinted at her arrest.

her seat so he could sit. She refused to stand. For this, Mrs. Parks was arrested and fined.

A Baptist minister named Martin Luther King Jr. protested the arrest of Mrs. Parks. He urged all black citizens to **boycott,** or stay away from, the Montgomery bus system. Over ninety percent of the city's blacks joined the bus boycott. They refused to ride city buses for over a year. This caused the Montgomery bus system to lose money. The fight did not end until the United States Supreme Court prohibited the segregation of public transportation.

The first victory for the civil rights movement was a United States Supreme Court decision in 1954. The court ordered schools to desegregate "with all deliberate speed." Every school was to be open to children of all races. President Eisenhower hoped that all the states would follow the court's instructions. But many local governments refused to obey.

Just before Christmas in 1955, Rosa Parks, a black seamstress, boarded a bus in Montgomery, Alabama. The law had divided the bus into two sections, with blacks sitting in the back. Mrs. Parks chose to sit in the white section, in one of the few empty seats on the bus. Soon a white passenger boarded the bus. He asked Mrs. Parks to give up

Martin Luther King Jr., civil rights leader

231

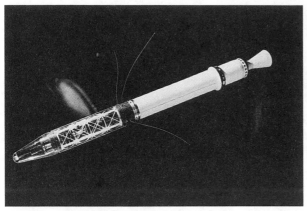

Explorer I was launched from Cape Canaveral, Florida, on January 31, 1958.

Space Race

During the Cold War, the United States was the world's technological leader. However, in 1957, the Soviet Union announced the successful launch of *Sputnik I.* This was the world's first satellite to orbit the earth. A month later the Soviets launched *Sputnik II* with the dog Laika on board.

The **"space race"** between the United States and the Soviet Union had begun. The Americans were embarrassed to be behind the Soviets. Congress approved the **National Aeronautics and Space Administration** (NASA) to direct America's space program. In 1958, the United States launched the satellite *Explorer I.*

Technology continued to advance. In schools everywhere, teachers emphasized science and mathematics. Engineers designed smaller equipment to use on space missions. At that time a single computer would take up a whole room. Computer scientists began the quest to make computers smaller.

Imagine using a computer that fills an entire room! This type of computer was used by the U.S. government and large businesses during the 1950s.

In the News

There were other events that made national headlines during the Eisenhower presidency. In 1954, the United States and Canada worked together on a project called the **St. Lawrence Seaway**. The St. Lawrence River was deepened. This allowed big ocean ships to sail from the Atlantic Ocean through the river to the Great Lakes. The project helped the economies of both countries. The moving water through the river was also used to provide electrical power.

In 1956, the Federal-Aid Highway Act was passed. The United States government paid for ninety percent of an **interstate highway system**. These roads are now the main highways in the United States.

Two territories joined the United States in 1959. **Alaska** and **Hawaii** became the forty-ninth and fiftieth states. They are different from the other states. They are not attached to the mainland. These states are also unique because of their populations. About one-fifth of Alaskan citizens are Eskimo, Aleut, or other Indian tribes. Half of Hawaii's citizens descend from Japanese, Chinese, Filipino, or Korean immigrants.

This lock is part of the St. Lawrence Seaway.

John and Jacqueline Kennedy on the night of the presidential election

The Sixties—A Time of Progress and Uncertainty

Continued Communism Threat

In 1961, *John F. Kennedy* became president. He represented bright hope for America. At age forty-three, Kennedy was the youngest man ever elected president. In America, he was the first Catholic president, and he was the first president to be born in the 1900s.

Communism continued to be a menace in Europe. In Germany, East Berlin was Communist. West Berlin was non-Communist. Thousands of Germans in East Berlin escaped into the free city of West Berlin. In 1961, the Soviet dictator ordered the construction of a concrete wall around West Berlin. Armed guards stood waiting to shoot anyone who tried to cross the **Berlin Wall**.

Communism also threatened the safety of the United States. Cuba, a Communist country, is very close to the coast of Florida. Fidel Castro was the Communist dictator of Cuba. Castro's economy caused hardships for the Cuban people. Many Cubans fled to the United States. The United States military trained some of these Cubans. In 1961, these Cuban troops returned to Cuba. They tried to take the Cuban government from the Communists, but the invasion failed.

Fidel Castro (front)

The Cuban Missile Crisis

Cuba is located about one hundred miles off the coast of Florida. In October of 1962, President Kennedy learned that the Soviet Union had placed missiles in Cuba. Nuclear bombs could be loaded on the missiles. If launched, the missiles could strike and destroy many American cities. This could start a nuclear war. President Kennedy demanded that the Soviets remove the missiles. To enforce his demands, Kennedy ordered a blockade of Cuba. He declared that any Soviet ship that was carrying weapons would be turned back before reaching Cuba.

Missile site in Cuba

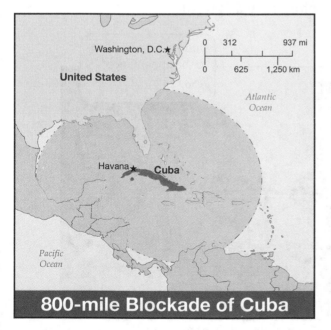

800-mile Blockade of Cuba

The situation was tense. President Kennedy urged President Khrushchev of the Soviet Union to turn his ships around. Khrushchev told Kennedy to lift the blockade. Kennedy refused and declared that the blockade would not be lifted until the missile sites in Cuba were removed.

No one knew what would happen. Many people expected war. Many Americans began building bomb shelters in their yards or basements. At last, President Khrushchev ordered his troops in Cuba to take down the missile launching pads. They were to dismantle them, and return them to the Soviet Union. The **Cuban Missile Crisis** was over.

John Glenn enters the *Friendship 7*. The spacecraft circled the earth three times.

Space Race Speeds Up

In May of 1961, Alan Shepard became the first American astronaut to go into outer space. Twenty days later, President Kennedy announced his goal for the country. He said, "I believe that this nation should commit itself to achieving the goal, before this decade is out, of landing a man on the moon and returning him safely to earth." In early 1962, John Glenn Jr. became the first American to orbit the earth. Glenn received a ticker-tape parade and was celebrated as a national hero.

Civil Rights Movement Continues

After the bus boycott in Alabama, there were other civil rights protests. In August of 1963, **Martin Luther King Jr.** organized a demonstration. Its purpose was to gather support for proposed civil rights laws. Over 200,000 people joined the **march on Washington**. The crowd included both blacks and whites.

King delivered his famous "I have a dream" speech in front of the Lincoln Memorial. The speech was about brotherly unity and freedom from racial injustice. Later, President Kennedy publicly supported a civil rights bill. But the laws did not pass while he was president.

"Judge not according to the appearance."
John 7:24

The march on Washington

The Kennedys in Dallas

Johnson took his oath of office on board the plane that had brought Kennedy to Dallas.

A Change in Presidents

Then came November 22, **1963**. President and Mrs. Kennedy were riding in their convertible limousine. They waved to crowds that lined the streets of Dallas, Texas. Suddenly, three shots rang out. The president slumped over in his seat. The limousine raced to the hospital where President Kennedy died. The death of the young president was a great blow to the country.

On the afternoon of Kennedy's death, Vice President Johnson was on the presidential airplane, Air Force One. There on board the plane, *Lyndon Johnson* was sworn in as president. He called Kennedy's death "a loss that cannot be weighed."

The Vietnam War

Under President Johnson, more American troops were sent to help the South Vietnamese in their fight against Communism. Most of the soldiers had been drafted into the military service. Brave Americans gave their lives for the freedom of South Vietnam. Many people wondered whether the United States should even have been involved in the war. Some men who were drafted burned their draft cards and refused to go to war. Some went to Canada to avoid going into military service.

The Vietnam War 1961–1973

Taiwan

China

North Vietnam
★ Hanoi

Hong Kong

Gulf of Tonkin

South China Sea

Hainan

Vientiane

DMZ (Demilitarized Zone)

Thailand

Republic of the Philippines

Bangkok

Cambodia

Phnom Penh

South Vietnam

Maylay Peninsula

Saigon

Gulf of Siam

Mekong Delta

Allied with U.S.

Communist countries

Neutral countries

Front row: Martin Luther King Jr., Robert Kennedy, Roy Wilkins, and Lyndon Johnson.

Laws Passed

Some progress was made in civil rights during Johnson's presidency. The **Civil Rights Act of 1964** opened all hotels, restaurants, and other businesses to people of all races. The Twenty-fourth Amendment was ratified in 1964. It prohibited states from charging poll taxes. A **poll tax** required people to pay money in order to vote. Poll taxes were popular in the South because they kept both poor blacks and poor whites from voting. The Voting Rights Act of 1965 ended unfairness in voting.

President Johnson also persuaded Congress to create programs to help the poor. There was a program to help children with their education.

There was also a program to help some Americans with medical care. All these programs were expensive. This overspending put the nation in more debt.

Death of Two Leaders

The government could change the laws. But the government could not erase hatred from the hearts of some people. In April of 1968, Martin Luther King Jr. was shot to death. After King's death, riots broke out across the country.

Senator Robert Kennedy was the brother of the late president, John F. Kennedy. Robert Kennedy had joined the race to be president. He was campaigning in California. While he was in a Los Angles hotel, he was shot and killed. Two American leaders had been **assassinated,** or murdered, within two months.

Robert Kennedy greets supporters in Detroit (May 1968).

238

Comparing and Contrasting Civil Rights

Writers sometimes use clue words to compare things or events. Some examples of clue words that compare are *similar to*, *like*, or *resembling*. Writers also use clue words to contrast things or events. Examples of clue words that contrast are *different from*, *but*, *unlike*, or *however*.

You can use these clue words as you compare and contrast information. The information you will be comparing and contrasting is about the treatment of blacks before the 1950s and 1960s.

As you work, ask yourself questions using the clue words to compare and contrast. Ask, "How are these events or things similar?" and "How are these events or things different?"

1. Get your Activity Manual and a Bible.

2. Use your Student Text to complete the chart. Look for the things or events that compare and contrast the treatment of black people in the different time periods.

3. Use your Bible to answer some of the questions.

Close Election

In 1969, *Richard Nixon* became president. At the time, the country was in turmoil because of the racial riots and the Vietnam War. Nixon believed that most of the people were quiet, decent, hard-working citizens. He desired to give these citizens the peace and order they wanted.

A Walk on the Moon

On **July 16, 1969**, many people around the world watched their televisions in fascination. They gazed on as three astronauts got into the spacecraft. *Apollo 11* lifted off from Florida's Cape Kennedy. The astronauts fired the engines to escape Earth's gravity. *Apollo 11* was headed to the moon!

The three-stage rocket took three days to reach the moon. Commander Neil Armstrong looked for a safe landing spot. He finally found a spot when the lunar module was almost out of fuel.

Americans were thrilled to hear Mission Control in Texas speak to the astronauts. "We copy you down, *Eagle*," Mission Control said. The answer came through as "Tranquility Base here. The *Eagle* has landed." Americans were on the moon! Six hours after landing, Armstrong stepped onto the moon and said, "That's one small step for a man, one giant leap for mankind."

The *Saturn V* rocket was the launch vehicle for the *Apollo* flights to the moon. (*Apollo 11* crew: Neil Armstrong, Michael Collins, and Edwin "Buzz" Aldrin)

With television cameras in place, the world was able to watch as Armstrong and Aldrin planted the American flag on the moon and as Aldrin set up equipment for studying the moon's surface.

The astronauts left an American flag and a plaque on the moon. Inscribed on the plaque were the names of the *Apollo 11* astronauts and President Nixon. There was also the statement, "We came in peace for all mankind."

The Seventies—A Time of Unrest and Change

Visit to Communist China

Americans feared that someday China might join forces with the Soviet Union. In 1972, President Nixon was the first American president to visit Communist China. Camera crews and reporters went with him. Nixon toured the Great Wall and other scenic sites that had been closed to foreigners for years. The President attended banquets and met with Chinese leader Chairman Mao Zedong (MOW ZUH-DONG). Nixon was proud of the improved relations between the United States and China. He laid the groundwork for resuming trade with this huge country.

President Nixon stands on the Great Wall during his visit to China.

People who opposed the Vietnam War often held peace demonstrations in the 1960s.

The End of the Vietnam War

With Nixon as president, the soldiers in Vietnam began returning home. In 1973, the United States and North Vietnamese reached an agreement to end the war. The United States brought all its troops home. Prisoners of war were exchanged. Men who had been in prison camps returned as heroes. Some soldiers were also met by angry people who felt America's part in the war had been unjust.

The Fall of a President

President Nixon won re-election in 1972. During the campaign five men were arrested for breaking into the Democratic Party's national headquarters. The break-in took place in the **Watergate** office building in Washington, D.C. The men were part of Nixon's re-election committee. There was no evidence that Nixon knew about the break-in.

At the same time, Vice President Spiro Agnew was accused of accepting bribes and not paying taxes. He had to resign. The Twenty-fifth Amendment was used to pick a new vice president. Gerald Ford took the oath of office in December of 1973.

The Watergate investigation dragged on. The American people were angry about the Watergate break-in. It became clear that Nixon was trying to **cover up** or hide the break-in. Congress intended to **impeach** the president, or accuse him of crimes. President Nixon resigned on August 9, 1974.

President Nixon bids farewell as he leaves office.

Gerald Ford

The Unelected President

When President Nixon resigned, *Gerald Ford* became president. He was the only president who was not elected by the American people. After only a month, Ford granted a **pardon** to Richard Nixon. Ford forgave Nixon for any crimes he might have committed while in office. Ford said that trying the former president in court would cause the country more agony. The other five men were not pardoned for their crimes. Many Americans were dismayed that Nixon could go free while the others stayed in jail.

The End of South Vietnam

The North Vietnamese Communists attacked the city of Saigon in South Vietnam. President Ford asked Congress to give aid to South Vietnam. Congress refused. In 1975, the last American troops left South Vietnam. The country quickly fell to the North Vietnamese. The Vietnam War was the longest war America ever fought. It was also the only war it lost. More than 58,000 Americans died trying to keep the South Vietnamese free. Vietnam united under a Communist government.

President Ford meets with the National Security Council near the end of the Vietnam War.

Boat People

In the late 1970s, the North Vietnamese controlled the city of Saigon. Thousands of South Vietnamese fled from the country. They wanted to escape the Communist government. People from Cambodia and Laos also fled. They went to other Southeast Asian countries, the United States, and Canada. A person who flees for refuge, or safety, is called a **refugee**. Many refugees crowded onto rafts or into other small boats. These boats were not designed for ocean travel. Many refugees suffered dehydration, starvation, or death by drowning. Some became victims of pirates.

Vietnamese refugees who attempted to flee their native country to other countries by boat were called "**boat people**." Vietnamese refugees settled in cities all over America, many of them on the West Coast. Later, the term *boat people* was used to describe refugees from other areas who fled their homelands by boat. Boat people have fled Cuba and Haiti to the United States. Today, those seeking refuge from the conditions in their native country are still "echoing" in the world.

Bicentennial Celebration

After Watergate and the Vietnam War, Americans needed something to celebrate. In 1976, they celebrated the **Bicentennial**, or the two hundredth anniversary of the founding of the United States of America. All over America, people celebrated the Bicentennial. Many cities had parades and fireworks displays. On July 4, there was even a parade of sailing ships!

The Peanut Farmer

For years, James (Jimmy) Carter Jr. had stood for equal rights for blacks. He ran his father's peanut warehouse in Georgia. When his church voted to stop blacks from attending, only the Carters and one other family voted against it. Later, Jimmy Carter became a Georgia state senator and then the governor of Georgia.

Tall ships in New York Harbor were part of the Bicentennial celebration.

In 1977, *Jimmy Carter* became president. He wanted to end racial **discrimination,** or the unfair treatment of ethnic groups. An **ethnic group** is a group of people who share the same customs, racial background, or language. Carter appointed many qualified women and people of minority ethnic groups to government positions.

Domestic Affairs

President Carter wanted to heal the feelings left by the Vietnam War. In January of 1977, he offered **amnesty**, or a group pardon by the government, to all those who had dodged the draft to avoid fighting in Vietnam. Many veterans who had loyally fought in the war were angry with the amnesty.

Declaration of Independence

By the mid-1770s, conflict was growing between the American colonists and Great Britain. Both sides had different political, religious, and economic ideas. These differences triggered the Revolutionary War (War for Independence) in America.

In 1776, the Second Continental Congress met. It was made up of men who represented the thirteen colonies in America. Richard Henry Lee made a motion to the Congress "that these United Colonies are, and of right ought to be, free and independent States."

The Congress asked a group of men to write a document declaring freedom from Britain. The members of the group were John Adams, Benjamin Franklin, Roger Sherman, Robert Livingstone, and Thomas Jefferson. The declaration was approved by Congress on July 2. The Declaration of Independence was finished July 4, 1776. John Hancock was the first to sign the document. Signing it took courage. The British could consider those who signed as traitors.

Declaration of Independence, by John Trumbull

National Archives

The Declaration of Independence is one of three documents known as the Charters of Freedom. The other two documents are the United States Constitution and the Bill of Rights. Today, these documents are kept in the National Archives Building in Washington, D.C. The Declaration of Independence is treasured as a symbol of liberty.

Americans celebrate July 4 as Independence Day. This is America's birthday and a national holiday. France gave the Statue of Liberty to America in honor of America's 100th birthday. The Declaration of Independence continues to echo the independence of the United States of America.

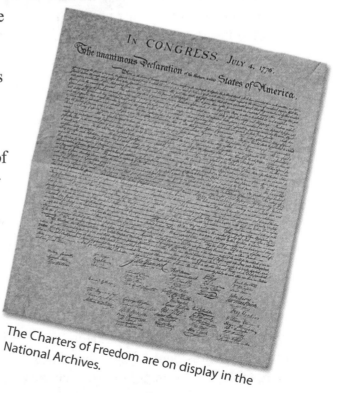

The Charters of Freedom are on display in the National Archives.

247

President Carter hosted peace talks with President Sadat (left) of Egypt and Prime Minister Begin (right) of Israel.

Foreign Affairs

In the early 1900s, the United States helped construct the Panama Canal in Central America. At that time, the United States government signed a treaty to use and protect the canal zone. By 1971, Panama wanted more control. The two countries negotiated a new treaty. Carter signed the **Panama Canal Treaty** in 1977. The new treaty allowed the United States and Panama to operate the canal together until 2000. Then Panama would take over. The treaty also said the canal was to remain open to all countries. It was hoped this would improve relations in Latin America.

President Carter also held peace talks between the Israelis and the Arabs. Since Israel had become a nation, it had been in constant conflict with its Arab neighbors. Carter invited the president of Egypt and the prime minister of Israel to meet with

him at Camp David. This was the presidential retreat in Maryland. In 1978, the three leaders signed an agreement known as the **Camp David Accords**. Israel agreed to return the Sinai Peninsula to Egypt. Egypt agreed to become the first Arab nation to recognize Israel as a nation and to give a guarantee of peace.

Looking to the Eighties

After World War II, the United States was the successful leader of the non-Communist world. The Cold War began because of tensions between the United States and the Soviet Union. The new United Nations could not keep world peace and stop conflicts between nations. It could not control the spread of communism. The United States continued to provide protection for the non-Communist world.

In America, the people's differing opinions on civil rights and the Vietnam War created problems. The government tried to improve American life. But the nation fell into more debt. The assassinations and resignations in the 1960s and 1970s made people wonder whether America's moral values were changing for the worse.

But the Bicentennial gave the people a reason to celebrate. They continued to search for better times as the next decade approached.

Chapter 12

To a New Millennium

	1981		1991		2001		2009	
1975	1980	1985	1990	1995	2000	2005	2010

Iran hostage crisis ends — Cold War ends — War on Terror begins — First black U.S. president takes office

Entering the Eighties

Relations between the United States and the Soviet Union were improving. In 1979, the Americans and Soviets signed a treaty. The treaty would reduce nuclear weapons in both countries. President *Jimmy Carter* gave the treaty to the Senate for approval. But before the treaty was approved, the Soviet army invaded Afghanistan. The tension between the United States and the Soviet Union increased. President Carter withdrew the treaty from the Senate.

U.S. President Carter and Leonid Brezhnev of the Soviet Union sign the nuclear weapons treaty known as SALT II.

The Eighties— A Time of Strength and Challenge

Invasion of Afghanistan

The Soviet invasion of Afghanistan angered Americans. President Carter said that no grain would be sold to the Soviets. He also announced a **boycott**. The boycott protested the invasion of Afghanistan. No American athletes would compete in the 1980 Olympic Games held in Moscow, the capital

Representatives from the U.S. military greet the shah (right) during one of his visits to the United States.

mission for the remaining hostages. The mission failed.

The **Iran hostage crisis** was in the news every day. Carter hoped the hostages would be released before his presidency ended. He even worked for their release through his last night in office. The word of their release came on January 20, 1981, just minutes after Ronald Reagan took office. The hostages had been in captivity for 444 days.

of the Soviet Union. Other nations also decided to join the boycott of the Olympic Games.

Iran Hostage Crisis

The Middle Eastern country of Iran was ruled by a shah. When the Iranian people revolted in 1979, the shah was forced to flee the country. He eventually came to the United States for medical treatment.

Some Iranians were angry with the United States for allowing the shah to enter the country. An angry group of Iranian student radicals stormed the American embassy in Tehran, Iran. They took sixty-one Americans hostage. Some of the hostages were soon released. President Carter approved a rescue

Carter welcomes a released hostage.

Swearing-in ceremony of Sandra Day O'Connor

A New Direction

The presidency of *Ronald Reagan* began in 1981. Many Americans welcomed the new president's strong authority and inspiring public speaking. His presidency brought many changes.

One thing President Reagan did was replace liberal judges with more conservative ones. One of his appointments to the Supreme Court of the United States was **Sandra Day O'Connor**. In 1981, she became the first woman to serve as a Supreme Court justice.

War Memorial

In Washington, D.C., the **Vietnam War Memorial** was dedicated in 1982. The names of thousands of Americans killed during the war are engraved on the granite wall. Veterans, family members, and friends visit "The Wall" and statues at the memorial each year. They come to remember their experiences. They also come to honor the memory of those who gave their lives for their country.

Medicine and Technology Progress

During President Reagan's years in office, great progress was made in medicine and technology. In 1982, Barney Clark, a retired dentist, received the world's first artificial heart. The heart kept him alive for 112 days. Also during the eighties, many homes and schools obtained personal computers.

Vietnam War Memorial

President and Mrs. Reagan pay their respects to the victims of the Beirut attack.

Defense Against Communism

President Reagan took a strong stand against Communism. The United States sent aid to countries fighting against Soviet takeover. Reagan oversaw a huge increase in America's military power. In 1983, Reagan proposed a defense system to destroy enemy missiles. The Strategic Defense Initiative was commonly known as "Star Wars."

American marines were in Lebanon as part of a United Nations peace-keeping effort. In 1983, a truck with explosives drove into the marine headquarters in Beirut. Two hundred forty-one American marines were killed.

President Reagan ordered the American troops to move from Beirut. The troops were assigned to warships off the coast of Lebanon.

Also in 1983, Communist rebels overthrew the government of Grenada, a small island in the Caribbean Sea. The rebels killed Grenada's president. They threatened the lives of about seven hundred American students in a medical school there. Several Caribbean nations asked the United States for help. The Americans made a surprise attack. American troops and forces from the Caribbean nations restored peace to Grenada. The United States oversaw a free election there in 1984.

Re-election by a Landslide

Former Vice President Walter Mondale faced President Reagan in the 1984 elections. Mondale chose Geraldine Ferraro as his running mate. She was the first female vice-presidential candidate for a major party. On election night, Reagan won every state but Mondale's home state of Minnesota. It was one of the biggest *landslides*, or overwhelming victories, in American history.

Space Shuttle Tragedy

On January 28, 1986, seven astronauts boarded the space shuttle *Challenger*. One of the astronauts was Christa McAuliffe. She was to be the first schoolteacher to ride a shuttle. Then, just seventy-three seconds after liftoff, the shuttle exploded and disintegrated. All seven astronauts were killed. Many people

Crew of the space shuttle *Challenger*

thought this tragedy would end the American space program. But almost three years later, the shuttle *Discovery* had a successful mission.

The Berlin Wall

Since the Berlin Wall was built in 1961, it had been a symbol of Communism. In 1987, President Reagan visited West Germany. He spoke to several thousand people gathered at the Brandenburg Gate of the wall. People in East Berlin could hear the speech too. Reagan said, "Mr. Gorbachev, tear down this wall." He was directing a strong statement to Mikhail Gorbachev (GOHR buh chahf), the president of the Soviet Union.

President Reagan speaking in front of the Brandenburg Gate in West Berlin

President Reagan gives his support to George H. W. Bush for president.

Election of 1988

George H. W. Bush was elected president in 1988. He had served as President Reagan's vice president for eight years. Under Reagan, the military strength of the United States had increased. America's military power was an advantage. However, a huge cost had resulted. President Bush inherited a national debt of over three trillion dollars. Just as people must pay banks for the use of borrowed money, the government must pay those from whom it has borrowed.

Destruction of the Berlin Wall

For many years countries surrounding the Soviet Union were ruled by Communist governments. Many citizens of these countries wanted to be free. In 1989, many of these Communist governments fell.

One of the most dramatic moments in the fall of Communism was the destruction of the Berlin Wall. In October of **1989**, East German protesters began hammering away at the concrete structure. People from East Germany poured into West Berlin. Family members were reunited and were experiencing freedom for the first time. East Germany's government collapsed. In 1990, East Germany reunited with West Germany to become one nation.

Lamplight shines through holes in the Berlin Wall as it is being torn down.

Former President Reagan awards Mikhail Gorbachev the first Ronald Reagan Freedom Award at the Reagan Library in 1992.

The Nineties—A Time of Power and Hope

The End of the Cold War

The citizens of the Soviet Union were unhappy with Communism. In December of **1991**, eleven of the fifteen Soviet republics declared their independence from the Soviet Union. They established the Commonwealth of Independent States. Then on Christmas Day in 1991, the Soviet president, Mikhail Gorbachev, re-signed. The Soviet Union separated into different countries. President Bush announced to the American people, "Our adversary of forty-five years, the one nation that posed a worldwide threat to freedom and peace, is now seeking to join the community of democratic nations."

The most important of the new republics was **Russia**. It had more than half of the population and more than three-fourths of the landmass of the former Soviet Union. Russia was a world power on its own. The United Nations granted Russia the Soviet Union's seat on the UN Security Council. Russians enjoyed greater freedom than they had at any other time in their history. However, shortages of food and supplies, as well as political unrest, marked the country's difficult change from tyranny to freedom.

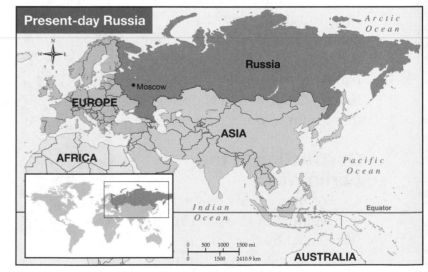

National Debt

America became a nation in 1775, but it did not have enough money to run its own government. At the time, America was at war with England. War was expensive. America had to borrow money from banks and other sources. This borrowing caused the United States to have a national debt. **National debt** is the amount of money that a government has borrowed from banks and other countries. This debt in America has not been paid back.

An elected president *inherits the debt*, or has the responsibility of the debt. Some presidents have been able to reduce the national debt during their presidencies. But since 1961, America's national debt has continued to increase. The debt increases when the government spends more than it collects. The government collects money through taxes, tariffs, and other sources. **Tariffs** are taxes placed on imported and exported goods. America's debt "echoes" from the beginning of the nation and into the future.

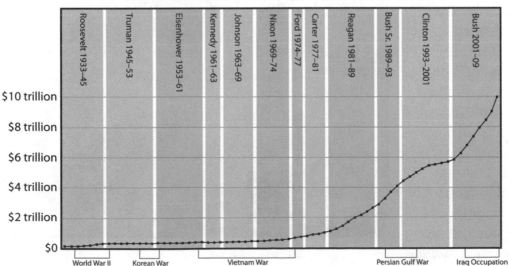

257

Civil Rights for the Disabled

President Bush signed the **Americans with Disabilities Act of 1990**. This civil rights law banned job discrimination against the disabled. It required public places to

provide better conditions for the disabled. Businesses now provide special parking places for the disabled and install ramps and wider doors for wheelchairs.

The Persian Gulf War

Much of the world's oil supply is in the Middle East. Saudi Arabia and Kuwait (koo WAYT) are two countries that produce oil. Under the dictator Saddam Hussein, Iraq invaded Kuwait in the summer of 1990. Hussein wanted the wealth from Kuwait's oil for his nation. He announced that Kuwait was part of Iraq. Iraqi troops also gathered along the Saudi Arabian border. Many people were afraid Iraq would attack Saudi Arabia. Iraq threatened to take control of the oil there too.

The United Nations told Hussein to remove his troops from Kuwait by January 15, 1991. Thirty-eight United Nations leaders launched a war to free Kuwait. The United States Congress also approved the war. It was America's first official declaration of war since World War II. The **Persian Gulf War** began on January 16 with five weeks of around-the-clock bombing. This attack was code-named *Operation Desert Storm*. Some computer-guided missiles were fired from ships in the Persian Gulf.

Patriot missiles were used in the Persian Gulf War.

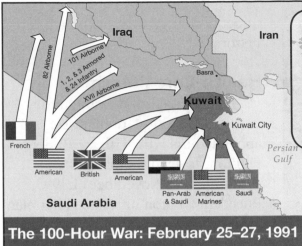

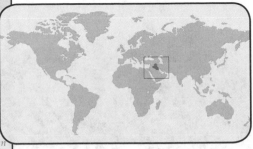

The 100-Hour War: February 25–27, 1991

A surprise ground attack in the desert came next. American General H. Norman Schwarzkopf (SHWORTS kof) ordered soldiers and tanks into the desert west of Kuwait. This force circled around the Iraqi army and trapped it. The ground fighting was over within one hundred hours. The war ended on February 27, 1991, when Iraq pulled out of Kuwait. President Bush addressed a television audience:

> Kuwait is liberated. Iraqi's army is defeated. Our military objectives are met.... No one country can claim this victory as its own. It was not only a victory for Kuwait but a victory for all the coalition partners. This is a victory for the United Nations, for all mankind, for the rule of law, and for what is right.

Government Posts

The chairman of the Joint Chiefs of Staff is the highest military post, or position. Americans were proud of General Colin Powell. He was the first black American to hold this post. Together with General Schwarzkopf, he led the United Nations forces during the Persian Gulf War. Other black Americans held important government posts. They held the positions of cabinet secretary, Supreme Court justice, and congressman. These men and their positions showed progress for civil rights.

President Bush (center) and General Powell (right) at a briefing before Operation Desert Storm

259

President Clinton (front right) and Vice President Al Gore (front left) seated with the Clinton Cabinet. The cabinet is a group of advisers the president chooses to help him lead the nation.

The 1992 Election

The Cold War was over between the United States and the Soviet Union. Americans were now concerned about affairs at home. In 1992, *William (Bill) Clinton* was elected president. President Clinton hoped to improve the nation's economy. He wanted to provide health insurance for all Americans. During his presidency, the United States had one of the greatest periods of economic growth in the nation's history.

Health-Care Reform

President Clinton wanted to develop a health-care plan. He appointed his wife, Hillary Rodham Clinton, to lead the planning committee. In November of 1993, President Clinton introduced her plan to Congress. At first, Americans were attracted to the promises of everyone having insurance at low costs. But by January of 1994, the national mood had shifted. The economy was booming. Medical costs had not risen. Support faded as taxpayers began to see how much Clinton's plan was going to cost. In the end, the plan did not come up in Congress for a vote.

The First Lady promoting the National Health Care Reform.

Increasing World Trade

We live in a **global economy**. This is the world market in which companies in different countries buy and sell goods. That is why you have items that were made in other countries. Global trade offers many opportunities but also causes some problems. Some industries shut down because of the increased competition. Some businesses move their factories to other countries where the labor costs are lower.

President Clinton proposed the **North American Free Trade Agreement** (NAFTA) to open new markets for businesses. This agreement was between the United States, Canada, and Mexico. **Free trade** means that countries agree not to put tariffs on each other. Congress approved NAFTA in 1993. There is still controversy about the success of this agreement.

President Bill Clinton signs NAFTA into law.

Newt Gingrich talks about the Contract with America.

1994 Midterm Election

President Clinton faced many problems in his first two years in office. Voters were most upset by his failure to meet his goals. A Republican in the House of Representatives named Newt Gingrich came up with a plan. His plan would increase the number of Republicans in the House during the 1994 midterm election. Republicans in the House signed a "**Contract with America**." The contract promised that Republicans would submit ten popular bills for a vote in the first one hundred days of the next session of Congress. The election was a success. Republicans now controlled both the House and the Senate. In the first hundred days, all ten bills were submitted. Some of the bills passed House approval but failed in the Senate.

Presidents

George Washington, Abraham Lincoln, and Ronald Reagan are a few of the well-known presidents of the United States. Others such as Martin Van Buren, Millard Fillmore, and William McKinley are not as well-known. Each president belongs to a political party. A **political party** is a group of people who share similar views about the government. During the mid-1800s, the two main parties became known as Republican and Democrat.

Each party has its own beliefs about the government. There are also differences within each party. People holding different views are often described as being *conservative* or *liberal*. A **conservative** is a person who has traditional views and values. A **liberal** is a person who does not support traditional views and values.

Generally, conservatives want reduced government control of the economy. They support lowering taxes on businesses and on the income of the people. They support the right for people to have guns and are strong supporters of national defense.

Liberals generally believe that government programs and regulations are ideal and better for the country. Liberals press for social programs such as government-sponsored welfare and health-care coverage for all people. Liberals usually support higher taxes. They also oppose gun ownership and disapprove of military action in foreign countries.

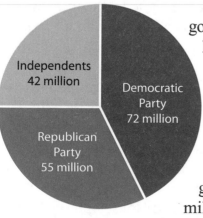

Independents 42 million

Democratic Party 72 million

Republican Party 55 million

Political parties, 2008

Do you recognize each president?

Civil War in Bosnia

In 1992, civil war broke out in Bosnia. One group, the Serbs, wanted to clear the country of the other two groups, the Croats (KRO ahts) and the Muslims. Thousands of refugees were forced out of Bosnia. In 1995, President Clinton invited representatives from the three groups to a meeting in Dayton, Ohio. The leaders of the warring groups signed the **Dayton Accords**. This agreement ended the war in Bosnia.

Refugees flee Kosovo.

The 1996 Campaign

President Clinton won re-election in 1996. During his campaign he stayed focused on several important ideas and avoided any controversies. Clinton declared, "The era of big government is over."

The Balkan Peninsula

Kosovo (KOH suh VOH) was a small region in Yugoslavia. Most of the people there were Albanian Muslims. The people in Kosovo wanted independence from Yugoslavia. But the Yugoslav leader, Slobodan (SLOH BUH dayn) Milosevic (muh LOH suh VITCH), refused. He sent troops into Kosovo. The conflict forced thousands to flee from Kosovo.

President Clinton sent American forces to join the United Nations and NATO to stop the conflict. In July of 1999, peace was restored in Kosovo.

The Balkan Peninsula

Austria
Hungary
Slovenia
Croatia
Vojvodina
Romania
Bosnia
Sarajevo
Yugoslavia
Serbia
Adriatic Sea
Italy
Montenegro
Kosovo
Bulgaria
Macedonia
Albania
Greece

--- Dayton Accords line
Muslims and Croats
Serbs

The impeachment trial of President Clinton in the Senate

Impeachment of a President

In 1998, a vote was taken in the House of Representatives to impeach President Clinton. **Impeach** means to put the president on trial before the Senate. For only the second time in American history, the president would be tried. If convicted, he would be removed from office. Chief Justice William Rehnquist presided over the trial. President Clinton was charged with both obstruction of justice and **perjury**, or lying under oath. In the end, the Senate declared him not guilty of either charge.

Technology During the 1990s

Computer technology progressed as the nation moved toward the twenty-first century. Fax machines were used to transmit copies of documents. Electronic mail, or e-mail, also became a new way to communicate. Students used the Internet to do research right from their homes. Filmmakers, artists, and musicians used computer technology as well.

As the year 2000 approached, people had a new concern. Computers were not programmed to change from the year 1999 to the year 2000. People feared a world-wide computer crash. Computer professionals worked on the problem through most of 1999. They adjusted computer programs to avoid disaster. Worldwide celebrations took place with little notice of computers.

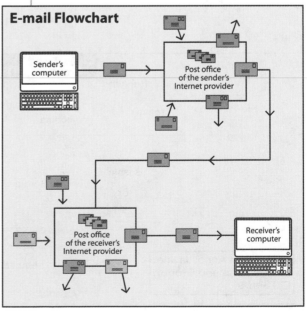

E-mail Flowchart

Sender's computer

Post office of the sender's Internet provider

Post office of the receiver's Internet provider

Receiver's computer

The 21st Century— A New Millennium

First President of the Century

George W. Bush was chosen by the Republicans to run for president in 2001. Vice President Al Gore ran as the Democratic candidate. Gore won the popular vote of the election. However, a presidential election is won by a system called the Electoral College. *George W. Bush* had more electoral votes than Gore and became the forty-third president.

President Bush introduced his philosophy in a speech. He said, "I call my philosophy and approach **compassionate conservatism**. It is

President Bush pleased conservatives when he chose Condoleezza Rice as Secretary of State. She was the first black woman to hold the office.

compassionate to actively help our fellow citizens in need. It is conservative to insist on responsibility and results." Bush reduced the growth of spending on welfare but did not forget the poor. He made federal funds available to faith-based and other volunteer programs. Faith-based programs are programs set up by church groups and other religious organizations. The money supported social programs such as restoring housing for the poor and homeless. Many of Bush's other achievements also made conservatives happy.

President Bush signs the No Child Left Behind Act in 2001. The act was to try to improve education in America.

Becoming President

Most states hold a *primary*, or an election, for each political party. The primary decides whom a state wants as that party's candidate. Some states hold a *caucus,* or a meeting of party leaders, to select a candidate. At the end, one candidate will emerge as the winner for each party. Each candidate chooses a vice president. Then both parties hold a convention to officially nominate the candidates.

The candidates hold rallies to express their views. Persuasive political speeches are made. Nationally televised debates help the people form opinions.

Each state is assigned a number of electoral votes. One candidate wins all the electoral votes in a state. On Election Day, citizens cast their votes for president. Election Day is the Tuesday after the first Monday in November. The popular vote determines which candidate receives the state's electoral votes. This process is called the **Electoral College**. A candidate must win at least 270 electoral votes to become the president of the United States.

Qualifications for President
1. At least 35 years old
2. Natural-born U.S. citizen
3. Has lived in the U.S. for 14 years

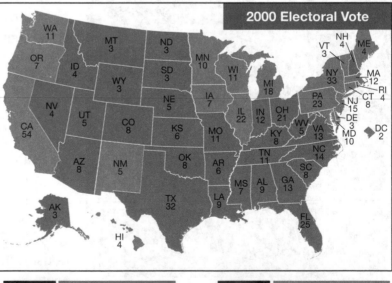

2000 Electoral Vote

George W. Bush (R)
Electoral 271
Popular 50,456,062

Albert Gore, Jr. (D)
Electoral 266
Popular 50,996,582

Determining a President

The number of electors for the Electoral College of each state varies. The amount is based on the number of members the state has in the House of Representatives and the Senate. An Electoral College Map shows the total number of electors for each state.

On Election Day night, the election results are counted. When a state's results are determined, that state is colored on an Electoral College Map. Usually, red indicates the state has chosen the Republican candidate. Blue indicates the Democratic candidate.

1. Get your Activity Manual page, a red crayon, and a blue crayon.

2. Color the *Electoral College* map according to the state list that your teacher gives you.

3. Use a calculator to see which candidates received at least 270 electoral votes and will become the next president and vice president.

War on Terror

September 11, 2001, is often referred to as "nine-eleven" or "9/11." On that day, the United States and much of the world were shocked. Terrorists *hijacked*, or took control, of four commercial airliners. A **terrorist** is a person who uses violence to promote a cause. The terrorists flew two of the planes into the Twin Towers of the World Trade Center in New York City. These tall buildings collapsed, causing many deaths. Another hijacked plane crashed into the side of the Pentagon. The Pentagon is the headquarters of the United States Department of Defense located in Arlington County, Virginia. The crew and passengers of the fourth plane learned of the fate of the other hijacked planes through phone calls. They attempted to seize control of their plane. It crashed into a field near Shanksville in rural Somerset County, Pennsylvania. There were no survivors on any of the flights.

On the day after the attacks, Congress declared a **war on terror**. A war on terror is not like other wars. It does not fight military armed forces. Instead, it fights terrorists who hide and blend in with civilians. President Bush announced the creation of the Office of Homeland Security. This office was formed to coordinate a national security strategy. After the 9/11 destruction and senseless loss of life, the people of the United States turned to their faith and patriotism for comfort. The tragedy helped pull the nation together.

"Ground Zero" was used to describe the World Trade Center site.

Demonstrating Patriotism

National holidays are set aside each year to express citizens' pride and love for their country. People display flags, watch fireworks, and listen to patriotic music. Bands play. Parades of soldiers march down the street.

A sailor returns from war.

What does American **patriotism** mean? For Americans, patriotism is a sense of noble pride. It is a connection with previous generations who made our country great. As patriotic Americans, we stand and quote the Pledge of Allegiance. We sing the national anthem. We recognize that the flag stands for truth, honor, and justice.

Look for ways patriotism is expressed in your town or neighborhood. Do you see American flags displayed? Patriotism is also seen through attitudes and actions of the people. Our response to government officials should be respectful and supportive. Honor should be given to former and current members of the military. Adults can show patriotism by voting.

Patriotic Americans need to be ready to stand for what is right. Patriotism is important to the survival of our country. Without patriotism, soldiers would be unwilling to fight on the battlefield. Patriotism unites our country in times of crisis as it did on 9/11.

President Ronald Reagan's casket is loaded into a hearse on June 11, 2004. The pallbearers represent the military services.

Afghanistan War

In Afghanistan, Osama bin Laden founded **al-Qaeda**, a network of terrorists. The Taliban, or Afghani fighters, allowed bin Laden into Afghanistan. There, he trained terrorists. In 2001, the United States led a coalition against Afghanistan.

A wanted poster of Osama bin Laden on the Internet

A **coalition** is a group of nations that work together to achieve a goal. The coalition destroyed training camps and toppled the Taliban government. Later, the Afghanistan government was rebuilt. The nation had its first free elections. By the end of 2004, many of the al-Qaeda leaders had been captured or killed. However, Osama bin Laden was not captured.

Iraq War

President Bush had what were considered to be reliable reports. The reports said that Saddam Hussein had weapons of mass destruction in Iraq. A **weapon of mass destruction** (WMD) is a weapon which can kill large numbers of people. It may also cause great damage to buildings. The reports also said Iraq was cooperating with terrorist organizations. President Bush tried unsuccessfully to get the United Nations to force Iraq to remove the weapons.

In 2003, President Bush led a coalition against Iraq. The coalition wanted to remove Hussein from power. It wanted to prevent any WMDs from falling into the hands of terrorists. It wanted to make the Middle East and the rest of the world safer. The coalition quickly crushed the Iraqi military and captured Hussein and his major lieutenants.

Saddam Hussein after his arrest

General Colin Powell holds up a vial of anthrax, one kind of WMD.

The Iraqi people elected their own government officials. Iraq became a democracy. Religious groups opposed the new government. They used terrorist violence. This gave al-Qaeda forces an opportunity for their terror operations. They wanted to drive the United States out of Iraq. It was necessary for the United States to continue to stay in Iraq. The coalition helped Iraq rebuild the country and enforce peace.

Supreme Court Justices

In November of 2004, President Bush was re-elected as president of the United States. The theme of the election had been foreign policy, particularly the war on terror and the war in Iraq.

One of the most important decisions Bush made was to appoint justices to the Supreme Court. When there is a vacancy on the Court, a president appoints a justice. This enables the president to affect the direction of the court and the decisions the justices make. The Senate can also affect the direction by rejecting an appointment made by the president. President Bush nominated two conservative judges. In 2005, John Roberts became chief justice of the Supreme Court. And in 2006, Samuel Alito Jr. became an associate justice of the Supreme Court.

John Roberts is sworn in as chief justice in the East Room of the White House in 2005.

The Supreme Court justices in 2008

Energy Independence

The two largest sources of energy in the United States are oil and coal. America's dependence on these two sources is debated among conservationists, companies, and other groups. In 2008, President Bush signed a bill that increased conservation of energy sources. The bill also expanded the use of clean **renewable energy**. Renewable sources of energy can be replaced naturally. Solar or wind energy are examples of renewable energy.

Fences between Mexico and the United States try to help keep illegal immigrants out.

Immigration Decisions

The United States is a nation of immigrants. An **immigrant** is a person who comes to live in a new country. At first, most immigrants came from countries of northern Europe. Over the years more and more immigrants poured into the United States from many other countries.

A large number of immigrants live in the United States illegally. The majority of these people come from Mexico or Central America. They come in search of higher wages. Illegal immigration has created problems with employment laws. It has also caused stress on America's education and public health systems.

In some areas, dependence on oil has been replaced with energy from wind turbines.

A passport is needed to travel between countries.

Election of 2008

For the 2008 election, Democrats nominated Senator

Barack Obama

Barack Obama as their presidential candidate. Obama chose Senator Joseph Biden as his vice-presidential running mate. Republicans nominated Senator John McCain as their candidate. McCain's running mate was Alaska governor Sarah Palin. She was the first female vice-presidential Republican nominee.

After the national conventions, most campaign polls showed the two presidential candidates essentially even. About six weeks before

the election, the United States and many other nations faced a serious economic crisis. This affected the outcome of the election.

Barack Obama was the first black president to be elected in America. In his victory speech, Obama proclaimed that "change has come to America." He became the forty-fourth president of the United States on January 20, 2009.

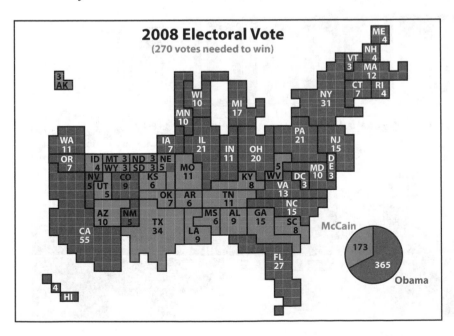

2008 Electoral Vote
(270 votes needed to win)

ME 4
NH 4
VT 3
MA 12
CT 7
RI 4
NY 31
AK 3
WI 10
MI 17
MN 10
PA 21
NJ 15
WA 11
IA 7
IL 21
IN 11
OH 20
OR 7
ID 4
MT 3
ND 3
NE 5
WY 3
SD 3
MO 11
DE 3
MD 10
NV 5
UT 5
CO 9
KS 6
KY 8
WV 5
DC 3
VA 13
OK 7
AR 6
TN 11
NC 15
AZ 10
NM 5
TX 34
MS 6
AL 9
GA 15
SC 8
CA 55
LA 9
FL 27
HI 4

McCain 173
Obama 365

The Future of America

Americans look forward to the future and changes to come. The decisions of America's leaders will affect every citizen, even you. Whether the United States declines or prospers, the Christian's hope remains in God. Christians know that their leader's heart "is in the hand of the Lord." The Lord "turneth it whithersoever he will," as Proverbs 21:1 says. Pray for your country's leaders.

"Some trust in chariots, and some in horses: but we will remember the name of the Lord our God."
Psalm 20:7

RESOURCE TREASURY

Contents

USS *Arizona* Memorial

On December 7, 1941, Japanese military attacked the United States Pacific fleet at Pearl Harbor, Hawaii. The surprise attack caused the United States to enter World War II. In 1962, the USS *Arizona* Memorial was dedicated. The USS *Arizona* still remains underwater where over 1,000 soldiers are entombed. A white concrete and steel structure has been built above the sunken ship.

The sunken USS *Arizona* can be seen below the water.

Normandy American Cemetery and Memorial

The Normandy American Cemetery and Memorial is located in Colleville-sur-Mer, Normandy, France. This cemetery has been given to the United States for the 9,387 American soldiers who died during the D-day invasion during World War II. The graves face westward toward the United States and overlook Omaha Beach and the English Channel.

A chapel is in the middle of the cemetery. Each grave is marked with a white cross. Jewish American graves are marked with a Star of David emblem instead of a cross.

The chapel

Korean War Veterans Memorial

The Korean War Veterans Memorial was authorized in 1986. The memorial honors the soldiers who served, those who died, those who are missing in action, and those who were prisoners of war during the Korean War. The memorial is located near the Vietnam Veterans Memorial in Washington, D.C.

The nineteen statues stand about seven feet tall. They represent soldiers from the Army, Marines, Navy, and Air Force. The statues are made from a reflective material so that in the bright sunlight they seem to come to life. White lights illuminate the statues at night. Faces of unidentified Americans are carved into a reflective wall near the statues. Another wall has the words "Freedom Is Not Free" engraved into it.

The Moving Wall

The Three Soldiers

Vietnam Veterans Memorial

Located in Washington, D.C., this memorial honors those who fought, those who died, and those who were missing in action during the Vietnam War. The memorial includes the Vietnam Veterans Memorial Wall, *The Three Soldiers* statue, and the Vietnam Women's Memorial. As of May of 2007, there were 58,256 names engraved on the Wall.

The Three Soldiers statue consists of young men dressed and armed for the American service. They are a Hispanic, a Caucasian, and an African American. The Vietnam Women's Memorial is dedicated to the women who served as nurses. The nurses in the memorial are named Faith, Hope, and Charity.

A half-scale replica of the Vietnam Veterans Memorial Wall was constructed in 1984. This mobile memorial is called "The Moving Wall." The memorial is transported across America, allowing thousands of people to see it each year.

Vietnam Women's Memorial

279

National September 11 Memorial

On September 11, 2001, al-Qaeda crashed two airplanes into the Twin Towers in New York City and crashed another airplane into the Pentagon. The National September 11 Memorial will be on the site of the two towers in New York. It has been dedicated to the 2,749 victims and first responders in the towers, those who died at the Pentagon, those who died near Shanksville, Pennsylvania, from Flight 93, and the victims from the February 26, 1993, World Trade Center bombing.

Plans for the memorial include two large pools surrounded with thirty-foot waterfalls. The pools and waterfalls will be located exactly where the two towers had been. The names of the victims will be inscribed on the walls around both pools. Visitors will be able to go below the waterfalls and view the pools from a lower level. Hundreds of trees will fill the area around the pools and a museum.

Design plan for the memorial

New office buildings are planned near the memorial.

Tomb of the Unknown Soldier

In Arlington National Cemetery, the Tomb of the Unknown Soldier stands as a special tribute to all soldiers whose remains were not able to be identified. This monument was established in 1921 for the burial of an unknown soldier from World War I. In 1932, a marble memorial was placed above the tomb. In 1958, an unknown soldier from World War II and another from the Korean War were buried beside the memorial. An unknown soldier from the Vietnam War was buried between their graves in 1984. However, in 1998, the Vietnam soldier was identified through DNA testing. His

remains were returned to his family. This grave remains empty.

The tomb has been guarded by specially trained members of the Third U.S. Infantry twenty-four hours a day, 365 days a year since July 2, 1937. The words "Here Rests In Honored Glory An American Soldier Known But To God" are engraved on the memorial.

Veterans Day

First celebrated in 1919, Veterans Day was originally a holiday known as Armistice Day—the anniversary of the ending of World War I. In 1954, President Dwight D. Eisenhower changed the name of the holiday to Veterans Day when he signed an act of Congress "to honor veterans on the eleventh day of November of each year . . . a day dedicated to world peace."

An armistice celebration in Paris

Eisenhower (left) was himself a veteran.

Armed Forces Day

In 1949, Armed Forces Day was created to replace three separate days: Army Day, Navy Day, and Air Force Day. It was aimed at promoting unity in the honoring of the Armed Forces. Armed Forces Day is observed on the third Saturday in May. Each year, a special prayer is prepared by the Armed Forces Chaplains Board to be used by all the military chaplains on this day.

President George Bush and his wife, Barbara, visit with General Schwarzkopf and troops during the Gulf War.

Presidents' Day

Presidents' Day, also referred to as Washington-Lincoln Day, is celebrated on the third Monday in February. In 1968, a law went into effect which provided workers with a three-day holiday for several federal holidays. This "Monday holiday law" provided for a day to honor George Washington and Abraham Lincoln, both of whom were born in February. Today, most states recognize this holiday and extend it to honoring other presidents.

Abraham Lincoln
The Granger Collection, New York

Painting portraying the surrender of Cornwallis to George Washington

Martin Luther King Jr. Day

Dr. Martin Luther King Jr. was a Baptist minister and an African American civil rights leader. He led the Bus Boycott in Montgomery, Alabama, to protest against segregation. King also organized the march on Washington where he delivered a moving speech, "I have a dream," in front of the Lincoln Memorial. In 1964, King was awarded the Nobel Peace Prize. King was assassinated in 1968.

In 1983, legislation was passed making the third Monday in January a federal holiday to honor King's birthday. In 1986, Americans observed the day for the first time. The day is celebrated with parades and speeches given by civil rights and political leaders.

Martin Luther King Jr. receiving the Nobel Peace Prize

French Style

The land around Louisiana was settled primarily by French colonists. If you go to New Orleans today, you will hear many people still speaking French. You will see homes built in the colonial French style. A house with a sloping tile roof and sturdy posts along the outside points to a French influence.

Spanish Style

The Southwest and Florida were home to many of the first colonists from Spain. If you visit any of the large cities in these regions, you may hear Spanish being spoken. The homes have painted stucco or adobe walls, tiled roofs, wide verandas, and small court-yards. These features are clues that the homes were built like those in Spain.

Georgian Style

In the eighteenth century, the Georgian house became a symbol of a wealthy family. These fine two-story houses were large and square with a symmetrical appearance. The style was named after the kings of England who ruled between 1714 and 1830. Georgian homes were popular in the Northeast and Southeast regions.

Roman Style

Thomas Jefferson, the third president of the United States, was an accomplished architect. He designed his famous home, Monticello. Jefferson chose the Roman style he had often seen during his travels to Europe. The house has a central dome and a wide front porch with six Roman-style columns. Above the columns is a triangular section called a pediment. The pediment has a small window in the shape of a semicircle.

Greek Style

In the early 1800s, people built mansions and public buildings that resembled Greek temples. Tall white columns graced front porches and often surrounded the building as well. Some columns were even built inside homes, along the sides of rooms. The bases and tops of the columns were ornately carved in classic Greek patterns.

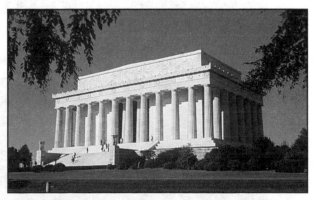

The Lincoln Memorial is based on Greek architecture.

Victorian Style

After the American Civil War, people were ready for a new style of home. In the 1860s, the Victorian house became popular in America. The home was named for the era in which Queen Victoria ruled England.

Victorian homes are often called "gingerbread houses." They usually have many fancy details on the outside, like intricately carved wooden posts or decorative trim under the eaves. Many houses also have balconies, gables, towers, and turrets. Some look almost like castles.

The people of the Victorian age liked to decorate the insides of their houses too. Victorians were sentimental—they saved things that held a special meaning for them. They liked to display souvenirs, photographs, and dried flowers everywhere. Victorians also liked rich-looking things like dark wood furniture, heavy curtains, oriental rugs, and statues.

George Washington *(1732–1799)* 1

Years in Office: 1789–1797
Vice President: John Adams
Home State: Virginia
Political Party: None
Birthplace: Westmoreland County, Virginia
First Lady: Martha Dandridge Custis Washington

John Adams *(1735–1826)* 2

Years in Office: 1797–1801
Vice President: Thomas Jefferson
Home State: Massachusetts
Political Party: Federalist
Birthplace: Braintree, Massachusetts
First Lady: Abigail Smith Adams

Thomas Jefferson *(1743–1826)* 3

Years in Office: 1801–1809
Vice Presidents: Aaron Burr and George Clinton
Home State: Virginia
Political Party: Democratic-Republican
Birthplace: Shadwell, Virginia
First Lady: Martha Jefferson Randolph (daughter)

James Madison *(1751–1836)* 4

Years in Office: 1809–1817
Vice Presidents: George Clinton and Elbridge Gerry
Home State: Virginia
Political Party: Democratic-Republican
Birthplace: Port Conway, Virginia
First Lady: Dolley Payne Todd Madison

James Monroe *(1758–1831)* 5

Years in Office: 1817–1825
Vice President: Daniel Tompkins
Home State: Virginia
Political Party: Democratic-Republican
Birthplace: Westmoreland County, Virginia
First Lady: Elizabeth Kortright Monroe

John Quincy Adams *(1767–1848)* 6

Years in Office: 1825–1829
Vice President: John C. Calhoun
Home State: Massachusetts
Political Party: Democratic-Republican
Birthplace: Braintree, Massachusetts
First Lady: Louisa Catherine Johnson Adams

Andrew Jackson *(1767–1845)* 7

Years in Office: 1829–1837
Vice Presidents: John C. Calhoun and Martin Van Buren
Home State: Tennessee
Political Party: Democratic
Birthplace: Waxhaw, South Carolina
First Lady: Emily Donelson (late wife's niece)

Martin Van Buren *(1782–1862)* 8

Years in Office: 1837–1841
Vice President: Richard M. Johnson
Home State: New York
Political Party: Democratic
Birthplace: Kinderhook, New York
First Lady: Angelica Singleton Van Buren (daughter-in-law)

William Henry Harrison *(1773–1841)* 9

Years in Office: 1841
Vice President: John Tyler
Home State: Ohio
Political Party: Whig
Birthplace: Berkeley, Virginia
First Lady: Anna Tuthill Symmes Harrison

John Tyler *(1790–1862)* 10

Years in Office: 1841–1845
Vice President: none
Home State: Virginia
Political Party: Whig
Birthplace: Greenway, Virginia
First Lady: Letitia Christian Tyler

James Knox Polk *(1795–1849)* 11

Years in Office: 1845–1849
Vice President: George M. Dallas
Home State: Tennessee
Political Party: Democrat
Birthplace: Mecklenburg County, North Carolina
First Lady: Sarah Childress Polk

Zachary Taylor *(1784–1850)* 12

Years in Office: 1849–1850
Vice President: Millard Fillmore
Home State: Kentucky
Political Party: Whig
Birthplace: Orange County, Virginia
First Lady: Margaret Mackall Smith Taylor

Millard Fillmore *(1800–1874)* 13

Years in Office: 1850–1853
Vice President: none
Home State: New York
Political Party: Whig
Birthplace: Locke, New York
First Lady: Abigail Powers Fillmore

Franklin Pierce *(1804–1869)* 14

Years in Office: 1853–1857
Vice President: William R. King
Home State: New Hampshire
Political Party: Democratic
Birthplace: Hillsborough, New Hampshire
First Lady: Jane Means Appleton Pierce

James Buchanan *(1791–1868)* 15

Years in Office: 1857–1861
Vice President: John C. Breckinridge
Home State: Pennsylvania
Political Party: Democratic
Birthplace: Cove Gap, Pennsylvania
First Lady: Harriet Lane (niece)

Abraham Lincoln (1809–1865)   16

Years in Office: 1861–1865
Vice Presidents: Hannibal Hamlin and Andrew Johnson
Home State: Illinois
Political Party: Republican
Birthplace: Hardin County, Kentucky
First Lady: Mary Todd Lincoln

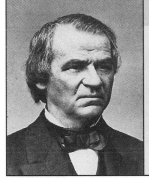

Andrew Johnson (1808–1875)   17

Years in Office: 1865–1869
Vice President: none
Home State: Tennessee
Political Party: Democratic
Birthplace: Raleigh, North Carolina
First Lady: Eliza McCardle Johnson

Ulysses Simpson Grant (1822–1885)   18

Years in Office: 1869–1877
Vice Presidents: Schuyler Colfax and Henry Wilson
Home State: Illinois
Political Party: Republican
Birthplace: Point Pleasant, Ohio
First Lady: Julia Dent Grant

Rutherford Birchard Hayes (1822–1893)   19

Years in Office: 1877–1881
Vice President: William A. Wheeler
Home State: Ohio
Political Party: Republican
Birthplace: Delaware, Ohio
First Lady: Lucy Ware Webb Hayes

James Abram Garfield *(1831–1881)* 20

Years in Office: 1881
Vice President: Chester A. Arthur
Home State: Ohio
Political Party: Republican
Birthplace: Orange, Ohio
First Lady: Lucretia Rudolph Garfield

Chester Alan Arthur *(1829–1886)* 21

Years in Office: 1881–1885
Vice President: none
Home State: New York
Political Party: Republican
Birthplace: Fairfield, Vermont
First Lady: Mary Arthur McElroy (sister)

Grover Cleveland *(1837–1908)* 22

Years in Office: 1885–1889
Vice President: Thomas A. Hendricks
Home State: New York
Political Party: Democratic
Birthplace: Caldwell, New Jersey
First Lady: Frances Folsom Cleveland

Benjamin Harrison *(1833–1901)* 23

Years in Office: 1889–1893
Vice President: Levi P. Morton
Home State: Indiana
Political Party: Republican
Birthplace: North Bend, Ohio
First Lady: Caroline Scott Harrison

Grover Cleveland *(1837–1908)* 24

Years in Office: 1893–1897
Vice President: Adlai E. Stevenson
Home State: New York
Political Party: Democratic
Birthplace: Caldwell, New Jersey
First Lady: Frances Folsom Cleveland

William McKinley *(1843–1901)* 25

Years in Office: 1897–1901
Vice Presidents: Garret A. Hobart and Theodore Roosevelt
Home State: Ohio
Political Party: Republican
Birthplace: Niles, Ohio
First Lady: Ida Saxton McKinley

Theodore Roosevelt *(1858–1919)* 26

Years in Office: 1901–1909
Vice President: Charles W. Fairbanks
Home State: New York
Political Party: Republican
Birthplace: New York, New York
First Lady: Edith Kermit Carow Roosevelt

William Howard Taft *(1857–1930)* 27

Years in Office: 1909–1913
Vice President: James S. Sherman
Home State: Ohio
Political Party: Republican
Birthplace: Cincinnati, Ohio
First Lady: Helen Herron Taft

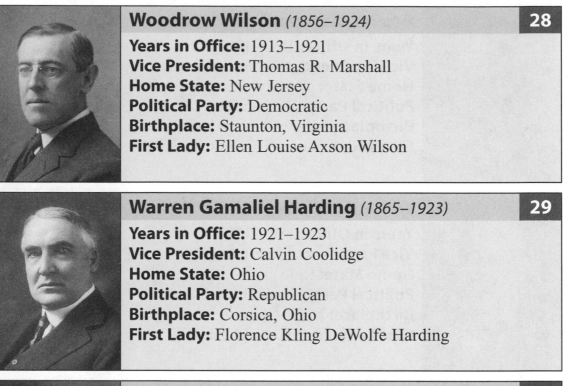

Woodrow Wilson *(1856–1924)*   28

Years in Office: 1913–1921
Vice President: Thomas R. Marshall
Home State: New Jersey
Political Party: Democratic
Birthplace: Staunton, Virginia
First Lady: Ellen Louise Axson Wilson

Warren Gamaliel Harding *(1865–1923)*   29

Years in Office: 1921–1923
Vice President: Calvin Coolidge
Home State: Ohio
Political Party: Republican
Birthplace: Corsica, Ohio
First Lady: Florence Kling DeWolfe Harding

Calvin Coolidge *(1872–1933)*   30

Years in Office: 1923–1929
Vice President: Charles G. Dawes
Home State: Massachusetts
Political Party: Republican
Birthplace: Plymouth, Vermont
First Lady: Grace Anna Goodhue Coolidge

Herbert Clark Hoover *(1874–1964)*   31

Years in Office: 1929–1933
Vice President: Charles Curtis
Home State: California
Political Party: Republican
Birthplace: West Branch, Iowa
First Lady: Lou Henry Hoover

Franklin Delano Roosevelt *(1882–1945)* | 32

Years in Office: 1933–1945
Vice Presidents: John N. Garner, Henry A. Wallace,
    and Harry S. Truman
Home State: New York
Political Party: Democratic
Birthplace: Hyde Park, New York
First Lady: Anna Eleanor Roosevelt

Harry S. Truman *(1884–1972)* | 33

Years in Office: 1945–1953
Vice President: Alben W. Barkley
Home State: Missouri
Political Party: Democratic
Birthplace: Lamar, Missouri
First Lady: Elizabeth Virginia Wallace Truman

Dwight David Eisenhower *(1890–1969)* | 34

Years in Office: 1953–1961
Vice President: Richard M. Nixon
Home State: New York
Political Party: Republican
Birthplace: Denison, Texas
First Lady: Marie Geneva Doud Eisenhower

John Fitzgerald Kennedy *(1917–1963)* | 35

Years in Office: 1961–1963
Vice President: Lyndon B. Johnson
Home State: Massachusetts
Political Party: Democratic
Birthplace: Brookline, Massachusetts
First Lady: Jacqueline Lee Bouvier Kennedy

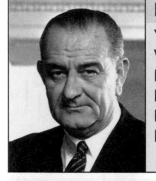

Lyndon Baines Johnson *(1908–1973)*   36

Years in Office: 1963–1969
Vice President: Hubert H. Humphrey
Home State: Texas
Political Party: Democratic
Birthplace: Stonewall, Texas
First Lady: Claudia Taylor Johnson

Richard Milhous Nixon *(1913–1994)*   37

Years in Office: 1969–1974
Vice Presidents: Spiro Agnew and Gerald Ford
Home State: New York
Political Party: Republican
Birthplace: Yorba Linda, California
First Lady: Thelma Catharine Ryan ("Pat") Nixon

Gerald Rudolph Ford *(1913–2006)*   38

Years in Office: 1974–1977
Vice President: Nelson Rockefeller
Home State: Michigan
Political Party: Republican
Birthplace: Omaha, Nebraska
First Lady: Elizabeth Bloomer Ford

James Earl Carter *(1924–)*   39

Years in Office: 1977–1981
Vice President: Walter Mondale
Home State: Georgia
Political Party: Democratic
Birthplace: Plains, Georgia
First Lady: Rosalynn Smith Carter

Ronald Wilson Reagan *(1911–2004)*   40

Years in Office: 1981–1989
Vice President: George Bush
Home State: California
Political Party: Republican
Birthplace: Tampico, Illinois
First Lady: Nancy Davis Reagan

George Herbert Walker Bush *(1924–)*   41

Years in Office: 1989–1993
Vice President: Dan Quayle
Home State: Texas
Political Party: Republican
Birthplace: Milton, Massachusetts
First Lady: Barbara Pierce Bush

William Jefferson Clinton *(1946–)*   42

Years in Office: 1993–2001
Vice President: Al Gore
Home State: Arkansas
Political Party: Democratic
Birthplace: Hope, Arkansas
First Lady: Hillary Rodham Clinton

George Walker Bush *(1946–)*   43

Years in Office: 2001–2009
Vice President: Dick Cheney
Home State: Texas
Political Party: Republican
Birthplace: New Haven, Connecticut
First Lady: Laura Welch Bush

Barack Obama *(1961–)* 44

Years in Office: 2009–
Vice President: Joseph Biden
Home State: Illinois
Political Party: Democratic
Birthplace: Honolulu, Hawaii
First Lady: Michelle Robinson Obama

The population and area data were collected from the 2007 United States Census information.

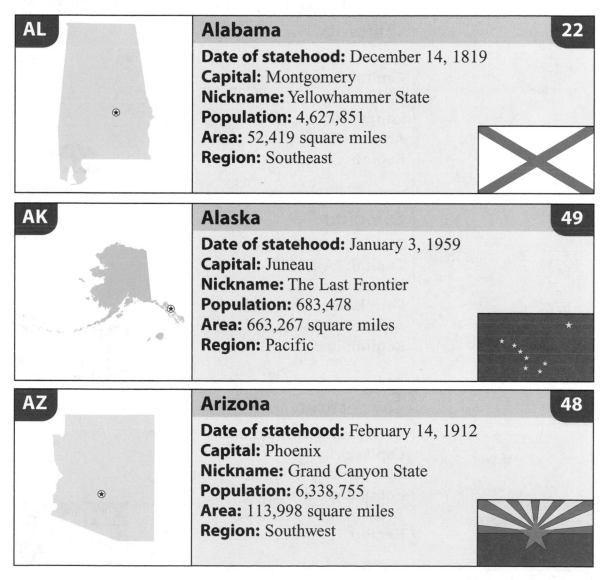

AL	**Alabama**	22

Date of statehood: December 14, 1819
Capital: Montgomery
Nickname: Yellowhammer State
Population: 4,627,851
Area: 52,419 square miles
Region: Southeast

AK	**Alaska**	49

Date of statehood: January 3, 1959
Capital: Juneau
Nickname: The Last Frontier
Population: 683,478
Area: 663,267 square miles
Region: Pacific

AZ	**Arizona**	48

Date of statehood: February 14, 1912
Capital: Phoenix
Nickname: Grand Canyon State
Population: 6,338,755
Area: 113,998 square miles
Region: Southwest

AR | Arkansas | 25

Date of statehood: June 15, 1836
Capital: Little Rock
Nickname: The Natural State
Population: 2,834,797
Area: 53,179 square miles
Region: Southeast

CA | California | 31

Date of statehood: September 9, 1850
Capital: Sacramento
Nickname: Golden State
Population: 36,553,215
Area: 163,696 square miles
Region: Pacific

CO | Colorado | 38

Date of statehood: August 1, 1876
Capital: Denver
Nickname: Centennial State
Population: 4,861,515
Area: 104,094 square miles
Region: Rocky Mountain

CT | Connecticut | 5

Date of statehood: January 9, 1788
Capital: Hartford
Nickname: Constitution State
Population: 3,502,309
Area: 5,543 square miles
Region: Northeast

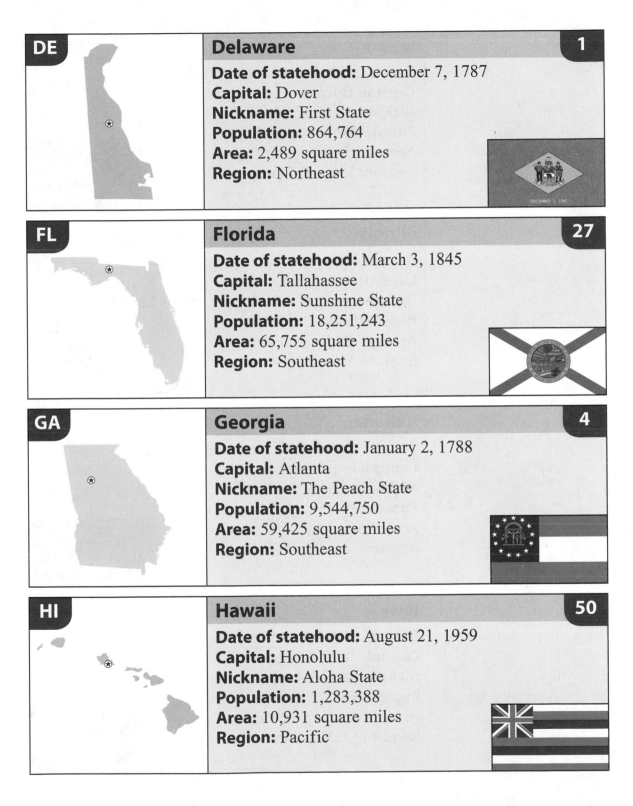

DE · Delaware · 1

Date of statehood: December 7, 1787
Capital: Dover
Nickname: First State
Population: 864,764
Area: 2,489 square miles
Region: Northeast

FL · Florida · 27

Date of statehood: March 3, 1845
Capital: Tallahassee
Nickname: Sunshine State
Population: 18,251,243
Area: 65,755 square miles
Region: Southeast

GA · Georgia · 4

Date of statehood: January 2, 1788
Capital: Atlanta
Nickname: The Peach State
Population: 9,544,750
Area: 59,425 square miles
Region: Southeast

HI · Hawaii · 50

Date of statehood: August 21, 1959
Capital: Honolulu
Nickname: Aloha State
Population: 1,283,388
Area: 10,931 square miles
Region: Pacific

ID

Idaho 43

Date of statehood: July 3, 1890
Capital: Boise
Nickname: Gem State
Population: 1,499,402
Area: 83,570 square miles
Region: Rocky Mountain

IL

Illinois 21

Date of statehood: December 3, 1818
Capital: Springfield
Nickname: Prairie State (or Land of Lincoln)
Population: 12,852,548
Area: 57,914 square miles
Region: Middle West

IN

Indiana 19

Date of statehood: December 11, 1816
Capital: Indianapolis
Nickname: Hoosier State
Population: 6,345,289
Area: 36,418 square miles
Region: Middle West

IA

Iowa 29

Date of statehood: December 28, 1846
Capital: Des Moines
Nickname: Hawkeye State
Population: 2,988,046
Area: 56,272 square miles
Region: Middle West

KS

Kansas 34

Date of statehood: January 29, 1861
Capital: Topeka
Nickname: Sunflower State
Population: 2,775,997
Area: 82,277 square miles
Region: Middle West

KY

Kentucky 15

Date of statehood: June 1, 1792
Capital: Frankfort
Nickname: Bluegrass State
Population: 4,241,474
Area: 40,409 square miles
Region: Southeast

LA

Louisiana 18

Date of statehood: April 30, 1812
Capital: Baton Rouge
Nickname: Pelican State (or Sportsman's Paradise)
Population: 4,293,204
Area: 51,840 square miles
Region: Southeast

ME

Maine 23

Date of statehood: March 15, 1820
Capital: Augusta
Nickname: Pine Tree State
Population: 1,317,207
Area: 35,385 square miles
Region: Northeast

MD | Maryland | 7

Date of statehood: April 28, 1788
Capital: Annapolis
Nickname: Old Line State
Population: 5,618,344
Area: 12,407 square miles
Region: Northeast

MA | Massachusetts | 6

Date of statehood: February 6, 1788
Capital: Boston
Nickname: Bay State
Population: 6,449,755
Area: 10,555 square miles
Region: Northeast

MI | Michigan | 26

Date of statehood: January 26, 1837
Capital: Lansing
Nickname: Wolverine State
Population: 10,071,822
Area: 96,716 square miles
Region: Middle West

MN | Minnesota | 32

Date of statehood: May 11, 1858
Capital: St. Paul
Nickname: Gopher State
Population: 5,197,621
Area: 86,939 square miles
Region: Middle West

MS

Mississippi 20

Date of statehood: December 10, 1817
Capital: Jackson
Nickname: Magnolia State
Population: 2,918,785
Area: 48,430 square miles
Region: Southeast

MO

Missouri 24

Date of statehood: August 10, 1821
Capital: Jefferson City
Nickname: Show-Me State
Population: 5,878,415
Area: 69,704 square miles
Region: Middle West

MT

Montana 41

Date of statehood: November 8, 1889
Capital: Helena
Nickname: Treasure State
Population: 957,861
Area: 147,042 square miles
Region: Rocky Mountain

NE

Nebraska 37

Date of statehood: March 1, 1867
Capital: Lincoln
Nickname: Cornhusker State
Population: 1,774,571
Area: 77,354 square miles
Region: Middle West

NV

Nevada — 36

Date of statehood: October 31, 1864
Capital: Carson City
Nickname: Silver State
Population: 2,565,382
Area: 110,561 square miles
Region: Rocky Mountain

NH

New Hampshire — 9

Date of statehood: June 21, 1788
Capital: Concord
Nickname: Granite State
Population: 1,315,828
Area: 9,350 square miles
Region: Northeast

NJ

New Jersey — 3

Date of statehood: December 18, 1787
Capital: Trenton
Nickname: Garden State
Population: 8,685,920
Area: 8,721 square miles
Region: Northeast

NM

New Mexico — 47

Date of statehood: January 6, 1912
Capital: Santa Fe
Nickname: Land of Enchantment
Population: 1,969,915
Area: 121,589 square miles
Region: Southwest

NY

New York 11

Date of statehood: July 26, 1788
Capital: Albany
Nickname: Empire State
Population: 19,297,729
Area: 54,556 square miles
Region: Northeast

NC

North Carolina 12

Date of statehood: November 21, 1789
Capital: Raleigh
Nickname: Tar Heel State
Population: 9,061,032
Area: 53,819 square miles
Region: Southeast

ND

North Dakota 39

Date of statehood: November 2, 1889
Capital: Bismarck
Nickname: Flickertail State (or Sioux State)
Population: 639,715
Area: 70,700 square miles
Region: Middle West

OH

Ohio 17

Date of statehood: March 1, 1803
Capital: Columbus
Nickname: Buckeye State
Population: 11,466,917
Area: 44,825 square miles
Region: Middle West

OK | Oklahoma | 46

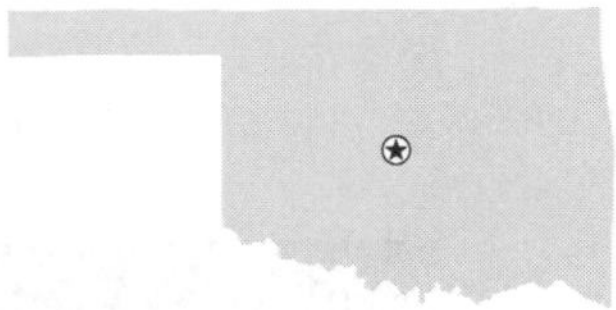

Date of statehood: November 16, 1907
Capital: Oklahoma City
Nickname: Sooner State
Population: 3,617,316
Area: 69,898 square miles
Region: Southwest

OKLAHOMA

OR | Oregon | 33

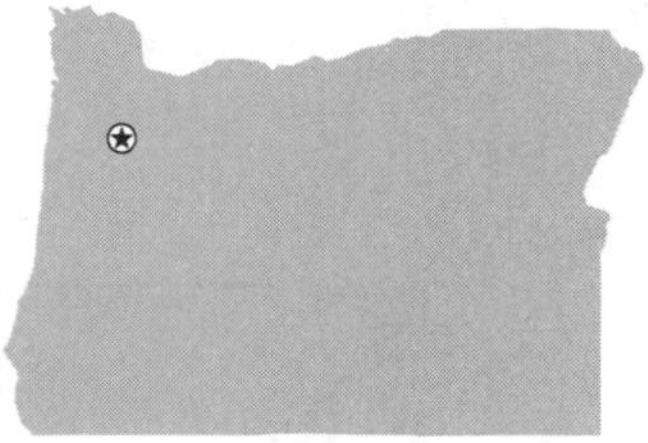

Date of statehood: February 14, 1859
Capital: Salem
Nickname: Beaver State
Population: 3,747,455
Area: 98,381 square miles
Region: Pacific

STATE OF OREGON
1859

PA | Pennsylvania | 2

Date of statehood: December 12, 1787
Capital: Harrisburg
Nickname: Keystone State
Population: 12,432,792
Area: 46,055 square miles
Region: Northeast

RI | Rhode Island | 13

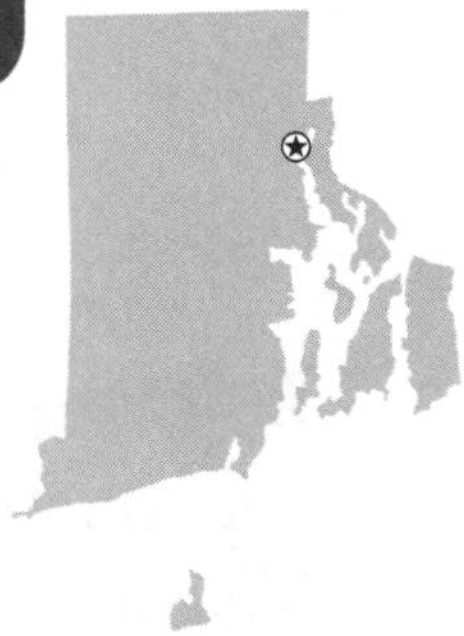

Date of statehood: May 29, 1790
Capital: Providence
Nickname: The Ocean State
Population: 1,057,832
Area: 1,545 square miles
Region: Northeast

SC | South Carolina | 8

Date of statehood: May 23, 1788
Capital: Columbia
Nickname: Palmetto State
Population: 4,407,709
Area: 32,020 square miles
Region: Southeast

SD | South Dakota | 40

Date of statehood: November 2, 1889
Capital: Pierre
Nickname: Coyote State (or Mount Rushmore State)
Population: 796,214
Area: 77,116 square miles
Region: Middle West

TN | Tennessee | 16

Date of statehood: June 1, 1796
Capital: Nashville
Nickname: Volunteer State
Population: 6,156,719
Area: 42,143 square miles
Region: Southeast

TX | Texas | 28

Date of statehood: December 29, 1845
Capital: Austin
Nickname: Lone Star State
Population: 23,904,380
Area: 268,581 square miles
Region: Southwest

UT | Utah | 45

Date of statehood: January 4, 1896
Capital: Salt Lake City
Nickname: Beehive State
Population: 2,645,330
Area: 84,899 square miles
Region: Rocky Mountain

VT | Vermont | 14

Date of statehood: March 4, 1791
Capital: Montpelier
Nickname: Green Mountain State
Population: 621,254
Area: 9,614 square miles
Region: Northeast

VA | Virginia | 10

Date of statehood: June 25, 1788
Capital: Richmond
Nickname: Old Dominion
Population: 7,712,091
Area: 42,774 square miles
Region: Southeast

WA | Washington | 42

Date of statehood: November 11, 1889
Capital: Olympia
Nickname: Evergreen State
Population: 6,468,424
Area: 71,300 square miles
Region: Pacific

WV | West Virginia | 35

Date of statehood: June 20, 1863
Capital: Charleston
Nickname: Mountain State
Population: 1,812,035
Area: 24,230 square miles
Region: Southeast

WI | Wisconsin | 30

Date of statehood: May 29, 1848
Capital: Madison
Nickname: Badger State
Population: 5,601,640
Area: 65,498 square miles
Region: Middle West

WY | Wyoming | 44

Date of statehood: July 10, 1890
Capital: Cheyenne
Nickname: Equality State
Population: 522,830
Area: 97,814 square miles
Region: Rocky Mountain

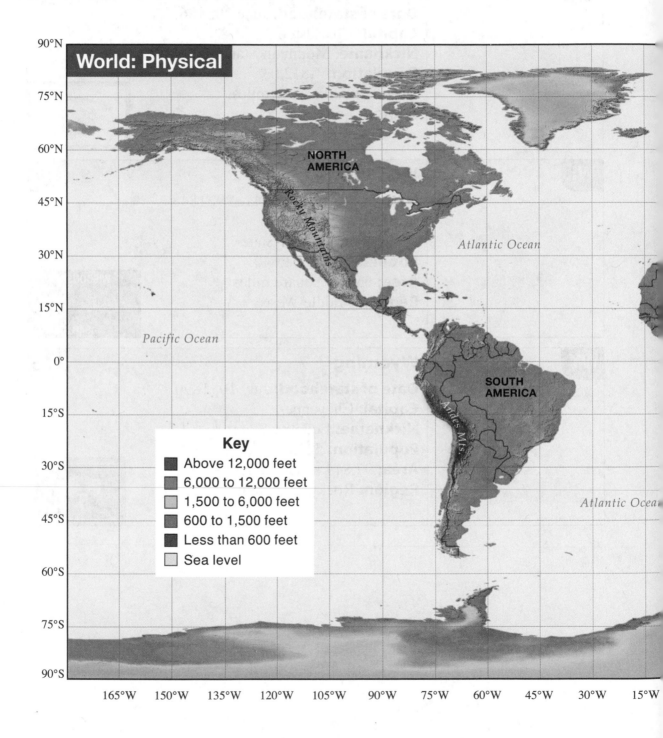

World: Physical

NORTH
AMERICA

Rocky Mountains

Atlantic Ocean

Pacific Ocean

SOUTH
AMERICA

Andes Mts.

Atlantic Ocean

Key
- Above 12,000 feet
- 6,000 to 12,000 feet
- 1,500 to 6,000 feet
- 600 to 1,500 feet
- Less than 600 feet
- Sea level

90°N
75°N
60°N
45°N
30°N
15°N
0°
15°S
30°S
45°S
60°S
75°S
90°S

165°W 150°W 135°W 120°W 105°W 90°W 75°W 60°W 45°W 30°W 15°W

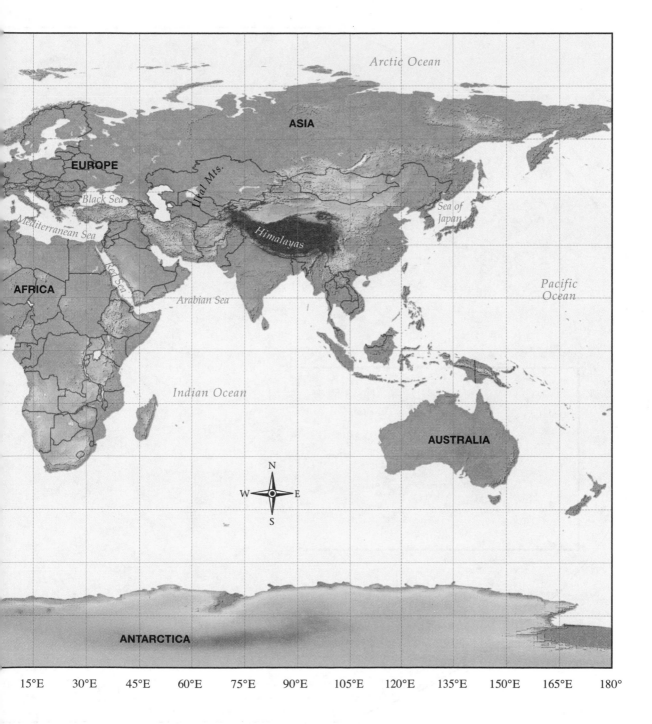

Arctic Ocean

ASIA

EUROPE

Ural Mts.

Black Sea

Mediterranean Sea

Himalayas

Sea of
Japan

AFRICA

Red Sea

Arabian Sea

Pacific
Ocean

Indian Ocean

AUSTRALIA

N
W   E
S

ANTARCTICA

15°E   30°E   45°E   60°E   75°E   90°E   105°E   120°E   135°E   150°E   165°E   180°

World: Political

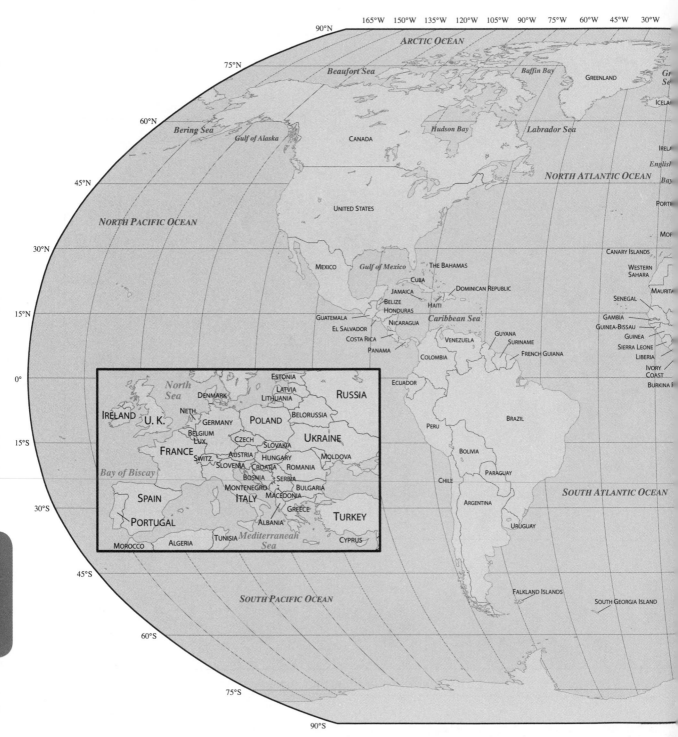

ARCTIC OCEAN

Beaufort Sea

Baffin Bay

GREENLAND

Bering Sea

Gulf of Alaska

CANADA

Hudson Bay

Labrador Sea

ICELA

IRELA

Englis!

Bay

PORT

NORTH ATLANTIC OCEAN

NORTH PACIFIC OCEAN

UNITED STATES

MOF

CANARY ISLANDS

WESTERN SAHARA

MEXICO

Gulf of Mexico

THE BAHAMAS

MAURITA

CUBA

SENEGAL

JAMAICA

DOMINICAN REPUBLIC

BELIZE

HAITI

GAMBIA

GUINEA-BISSAU

HONDURAS

GUATEMALA

NICARAGUA

Caribbean Sea

GUINEA

EL SALVADOR

SIERRA LEONE

COSTA RICA

VENEZUELA

GUYANA

LIBERIA

PANAMA

SURINAME

IVORY COAST

COLOMBIA

FRENCH GUIANA

BURKINA F

ECUADOR

BRAZIL

PERU

BOLIVIA

CHILE

PARAGUAY

SOUTH ATLANTIC OCEAN

ARGENTINA

URUGUAY

FALKLAND ISLANDS

SOUTH GEORGIA ISLAND

SOUTH PACIFIC OCEAN

Europe inset:

ESTONIA

LATVIA

North Sea

DENMARK

LITHUANIA

RUSSIA

IRELAND

U.K.

NETH.

GERMANY

POLAND

BELORUSSIA

BELGIUM

LUX.

CZECH

UKRAINE

FRANCE

SWITZ.

AUSTRIA

SLOVAKIA

HUNGARY

MOLDOVA

SLOVENIA

CROATIA

ROMANIA

Bay of Biscay

BOSNIA

SERBIA

MONTENEGRO

BULGARIA

SPAIN

ITALY

MACEDONIA

TURKEY

PORTUGAL

GREECE

ALBANIA

MOROCCO

ALGERIA

TUNISIA

Mediterranean Sea

CYPRUS

Norwegian Sea

RWAY

SWEDEN

FINLAND

RUSSIA

Sea of Okhotsk

ESTONIA

LATVIA

NMARK

LITHUANIA

BELORUSSIA

GERMANY

POLAND

IUM

CZECH   SLOVAKIA

UKRAINE

KAZAKHSTAN

MONGOLIA

AUSTRIA   HUNGARY

TZ

SLOVENIA   CROATIA   ROMANIA

MOLDOVA

Caspian Sea

Aral Sea

Sea of Japan

BOSNIA   SERBIA   BULGARIA

UZBEKISTAN

KYRGYZSTAN

NORTH KOREA

MONTENEGRO   MACEDONIA

GEORGIA

ITALY   GREECE

ALBANIA

Black Sea

ARMENIA   AZERBAIJAN

TURKMENISTAN

TAJIKISTAN

SOUTH KOREA   JAPAN

TURKEY

CYPRUS   SYRIA

East China Sea

NORTH PACIFIC OCEAN

TUNISIA

LEBANON

IRAQ

IRAN

AFGHANISTAN

Mediterranean Sea

ISRAEL

JORDAN

PAKISTAN

NEPAL   BHUTAN

CHINA

IA

LIBYA

EGYPT

KUWAIT

TAIWAN

QATAR

U.A.E.

Gulf of Oman

INDIA

NIGER

CHAD

SAUDI ARABIA

OMAN

MYANMAR

LAOS

South China Sea

Philippine Sea

NIGERIA

Red Sea

YEMEN

Arabian Sea

BANGLADESH

THAILAND

PHILIPPINES

Gulf of Aden

Bay of Bengal

KAMPUCHEA

CENTRAL AFRICAN

SUDAN

DJIBOUTI

Andaman Sea

VIETNAM

CAMEROON

REPUBLIC

SOMALIA

Gulf of Thailand

SRI LANKA

ETHIOPIA

BRUNEI

GABON

UGANDA

KENYA

MALAYSIA

CONGO

RWANDA

BURUNDI

SINGAPORE

DEMOCRATIC

Java Sea

INDONESIA

PAPUA

REPUBLIC OF CONGO

TANZANIA

NEW GUINEA

ANGOLA

INDIAN OCEAN

Arafura Sea

ZAMBIA

Timor Sea

Gulf of Carpentaria

ZIMBABWE

Coral Sea

NAMIBIA

MALAWI

FIJI

BOTSWANA

MOZAMBIQUE

MADAGASCAR

NEW CALEDONIA

AUSTRALIA

SWAZILAND

LESOTHO

SOUTH AFRICA

Great Australian Bight

Tasman Sea

N

W   E

S

NEW ZEALAND

ANTARCTICA

317

United States: Physical

Washington
Olympia ★
▲ Mt. Rainier
▲ Mt. St. Helens
Salem ★
Oregon

Montana
Helena ★

North Dakota
Bad
Lands
Bismarck ★

Boise ★
Idaho

South Dakota
Pierre ★

Wyoming
Black
Hills

Nevada
Great
Salt Lake
Salt Lake City ★

Cheyenne ★
Platte R.
Nebraska

Sacramento ★
Carson City ★
Utah

Denver ★
Pikes
▲ Peak
Colorado
Rocky Mountains

Kansas

Arkansas R.

Sierra Nevada

Grand
Canyon

Oklahoma

Pacific
Ocean

California
Arizona

Santa Fe ★
New Mexico

Oklahoma City ★

Phoenix ★

Texas

Austin ★

Rio Grande

Alaska
Yukon River

Juneau ★

Honolulu ★

Hawaii

0   200 Miles
0   200 KM

0   100 Miles
0   100 KM

Minnesota

Lake Superior

Wisconsin
Saint Paul ★

Michigan

Lake Huron

Lake Michigan

Madison ★
Lansing ★

Iowa
Des Moines ★

Indiana

Indianapolis ★

Ohio
Columbus ★

Lake Ontario

Lake Erie

Green Mountains

Maine
Augusta ★

Vermont
Montpelier ★
Concord ★

New Hampshire

Albany ★
Boston ★
Massachusetts

New York
Hartford ★
Providence ★
Rhode Island
Connecticut

Pennsylvania
Harrisburg ★
Trenton ★
New Jersey

Dover ★
Delaware

Missouri R.

Springfield ★

Illinois

Jefferson City ★

Missouri

West Virginia
Charleston ★

Washington D.C.

Annapolis ★
Maryland

Ohio R.

Frankfort ★

Kentucky

Richmond ★
Virginia

Appalachian Mountains

Nashville ★

Tennessee

North Carolina
Raleigh ★

Little Rock ★

Arkansas

Columbia ★

South Carolina

Alabama
Montgomery ★

Atlanta ★

Georgia

Atlantic Ocean

Louisiana
Jackson ★

Baton Rouge ★

Mississippi

Tallahassee ★

Florida

Gulf of Mexico

N
W E
S

| 0 | | 250 miles | | 500 miles |

| 0 | | 250 km | 500 km |

Key
- Above 12,000 feet
- 6,000 to 12,000 feet
- 1,500 to 6,000 feet
- 600 to 1,500 feet
- Less than 600 feet
- Sea level

United States: Political

NEW HAMPSHIRE

MAINE

Augusta

VERMONT

MASSACHUSETTS

Montpelier

Concord

Boston

Albany

Providence

RHODE ISLAND

NEW YORK

Hartford

CONNECTICUT

MINNESOTA

MICHIGAN

WISCONSIN

Lansing

PENNSYLVANIA

Madison

Harrisburg

Trenton

NEW JERSEY

OHIO

IOWA

INDIANA

Columbus

Washington,

Dover

DELAWARE

Des Moines

D.C.

Annapolis

ILLINOIS

Indianapolis

W.

VIRGINIA

MARYLAND

Springfield

Richmond

Charleston

VIRGINIA

Jefferson City

Frankfort

MISSOURI

KENTUCKY

Raleigh

Nashville

N. CAROLINA

ARKANSAS

TENNESSEE

Columbia

Little Rock

ALABAMA

Atlanta

S. CAROLINA

Jackson

GEORGIA

Montgomery

LOUISIANA

Tallahassee

Baton Rouge

MISSISSIPPI

FLORIDA

N

W   E

S

Honolulu

HAWAII

Geogloss

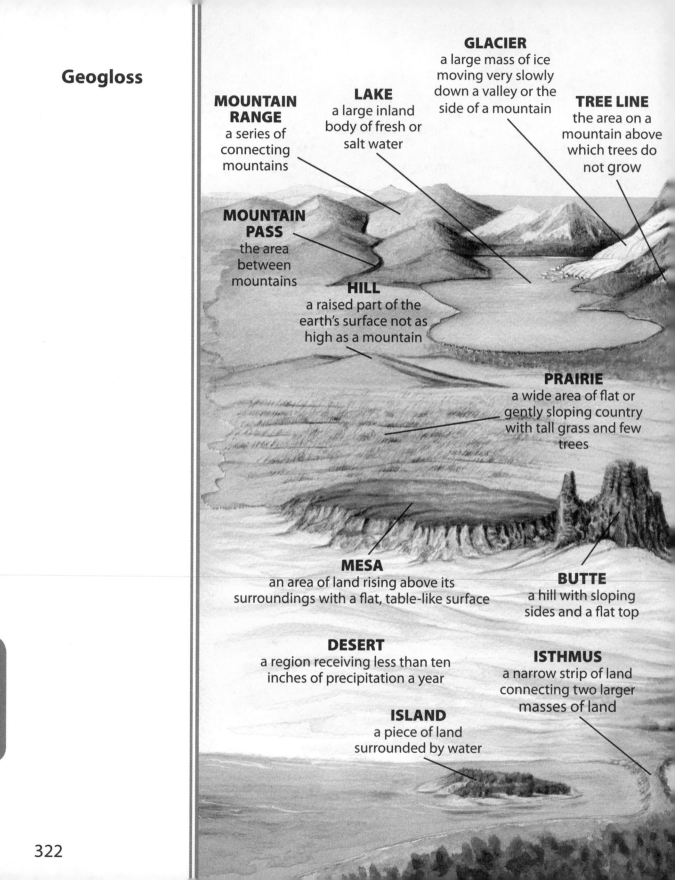

GLACIER
a large mass of ice moving very slowly down a valley or the side of a mountain

MOUNTAIN RANGE
a series of connecting mountains

LAKE
a large inland body of fresh or salt water

TREE LINE
the area on a mountain above which trees do not grow

MOUNTAIN PASS
the area between mountains

HILL
a raised part of the earth's surface not as high as a mountain

PRAIRIE
a wide area of flat or gently sloping country with tall grass and few trees

MESA
an area of land rising above its surroundings with a flat, table-like surface

BUTTE
a hill with sloping sides and a flat top

DESERT
a region receiving less than ten inches of precipitation a year

ISTHMUS
a narrow strip of land connecting two larger masses of land

ISLAND
a piece of land surrounded by water

MOUNTAIN
an area of land rising high above its surroundings

SEA LEVEL
the level of the ocean's surface often used to determine elevation of land

VOLCANO
an opening in the crust of the earth through which molten rock, dust, ash, and hot gases are thrown out

RIVER
a natural stream of water flowing into another larger body of water

VALLEY
a long, narrow area of low land between mountains

BASIN
a natural or man-made hollow filled with water

HARBOR
a sheltered area of water along a coast serving as a port for ships

BAY
a broad part of a sea or lake partly surrounded by land

PLAIN
a large, flat area of land without any trees

STRAIT
a narrow channel connecting two bodies of water

PENINSULA
a piece of land almost surrounded by water and connected to a larger body of land

COAST
the edge of land touching the sea

CLIFF
a high or steep overhanging edge of rock or earth

OCEAN or SEA
the large body of salt water covering over three-fourths of the earth

Biographical Dictionary

Carter, Jimmy (1924–) The thirty-ninth president of the United States. He wanted to end the unfair treatment of ethnic groups.

Chanute, Octave (1832–1910) An American inventor who made an improved glider with rubber joints so the wings could move with the wind.

Churchill, Winston (1874–1965) The prime minister of Great Britain during World War II.

Clark, William (1770–1838) The explorer, along with Meriwether Lewis, to travel the route that became the Oregon Trail.

Daimler, Gottlieb (1834–1900) A German inventor who improved the gasoline engine that is the basis for most car engines that are used today.

Eisenhower, Dwight (1890–1969) The supreme Allied commander during World War II. He became the thirty-fourth president of the United States.

Ferdinand, Archduke Francis (1863–1914) The heir to the throne of Austria-Hungary whose assassination caused the start of World War I.

Ford, Henry (1863–1947) An American inventor who designed and produced an automobile that the average person could afford—the Model T. He pioneered the use of the assembly line.

Grey, Sir Edward (1862–1933) The British secretary for foreign affairs at the beginning of World War I.

Harding, Warren G. (1865–1923) The first American president to be voted for by women. He became the twenty-ninth president in 1920 and promised a "return to normalcy."

Hirohito (1901–1989) The emperor of Japan during World War II.

Hitler, Adolf (1889–1945) The leader of the German Nazi Party and the dictator of Germany during World War II. He passed the Nuremberg Laws that took away Jews' freedoms.

Hoover, Herbert (1874–1964) The thirty-first president of the United States. He took most of the blame for the Great Depression.

King, Dr. Martin Luther Jr. (1929–1968) A civil rights leader and black American who organized protests in the 1950s and 1960s.

Langley, Samuel (1834–1906) An American inventor who was the head of the Smithsonian Institution at the time he built the *Great Aerodrome.*

Lenin, Vladimir (1870–1924) A Communist revolutionary who became the leader of Russia during World War I.

Lenoir, Jean Joseph (1822–1900) A French inventor who patented the first gasoline engine in the 1860s.

Lewis, Meriwether (1774–1809) The explorer, along with William Clark, to travel the route that became the Oregon Trail.

MacArthur, Douglas (1880–1964) The American commander who led an attack against Japan during World War II.

Mussolini, Benito (1883–1945) The leader of the Italian Socialist Party and the dictator of Italy during World War II.

O'Connor, Sandra Day (1930–) The first woman to serve as a Supreme Court justice. She was appointed by President Reagan.

Pike, Zebulon (1779–1813) An American who explored the Rocky Mountains. One mountain, Pikes Peak, is named for him.

Roosevelt, Franklin Delano (1882–1945) The thirty-second president of the United States. He was the only president elected to four terms. He was president during the Great Depression and World War II.

Sitting Bull (1831–1890) The Sioux leader.

Stalin, Joseph (1878–1953) The Communist leader of the Soviet Union during World War II.

Taylor, Hudson (1832-1905) An English missionary to China.

Wilson, Woodrow (1856–1924) The twenty-eighth president of the United States. He was president during World War I when America joined the Allies.

Wright, Orville (1871–1948) **and Wilbur** (1867–1912) The American brothers who worked together to design and build airplanes. Orville made the first successful flight in 1903.

Glossary

A

alliance An agreement between two or more parties to help each other.

Allies The alliance that included Great Britain, France, the United States, and other countries during World War I and World War II.

alphabet agencies The name given to the new programs that President Franklin D. Roosevelt tried to implement.

al-Qaeda A network of terrorists started by Osama bin Laden.

Americans with Disabilities Act The civil rights law that banned job discrimination and required better conditions for the disabled.

amnesty A pardon for offences against the government. President Carter offered amnesty to all those who had dodged the draft during the Vietnam War.

Anasazi Native Americans who lived primarily in the Southwest United States. They were farmers and built their homes in the walls of cliffs.

antique Something made long ago.

archaeologist A person who excavates and studies ancient sites.

armistice An agreement to stop fighting.

artifact An object made by people, such as a piece of pottery, clothing, or a building.

assassinate To murder, especially someone of political importance.

assembly line Several workers doing one part of a total job.

atheist A person who does not believe in God.

atomic bomb A weapon invented by American scientists that was dropped on Hiroshima and Nagasaki.

Axis powers The alliance of Italy, Germany, and Japan formed during World War II.

B

Balfour Declaration A statement issued by Great Britain in 1917 promising the Jews that they could settle in Palestine.

bank holiday The holiday when leaders of the Treasury Department closed the banks after the stock market crash.

bankrupt Out of money and unable to meet one's financial obligations.

bartering Trading goods for other goods.

Battle of Jutland The battle in which the British fought the Germans in the North Sea during World War I.

Battle of the Marne The battle in which French soldiers fought German soldiers at the Marne River during World War I and caused the Germans to retreat.

Battle of the Somme The battle that occurred when the British attacked the Germans at a point along the Somme River during World War I.

Battle of Verdun The longest and bloodiest battle of World War I when the French and Germans fought at Verdun, France.

bear market A market when stock prices are falling or expected to fall.

Berlin Wall The guarded concrete wall that separated East and West Berlin from 1961 to 1989. The wall was put up by East Germany to keep the people in Communist East Berlin from crossing over to non-Communist West Berlin.

Bicentennial The two hundredth anniversary of the founding of the United States of America.

"Big Three" The World War II Allied leaders Winston Churchill of England, Joseph Stalin of the Soviet Union, and Franklin Roosevelt of the United States.

Black Thursday A panic on October 24, 1929, to sell stocks that caused the stock market to crash.

Black Tuesday A stock market crash on October 29, 1929, when stocks quickly lost more than half their value.

blitzkrieg The fast-moving German attack during World War II called the "lightning war."

blockade The closing off of an area, a city, or a harbor to keep people and supplies from going in or out.

"boat people" Vietnamese refugees who attempted to flee their native country by boat.

boycott The act of refusing to use, buy, or deal with a store or company or organization in order to express a protest.

budget A plan that determines how money will be spent.

bull market A market when stock prices are rising or expected to rise.

C

capital The chief city of a nation; where a nation's or a state's government headquarters is located.

capitalist economy An economy in which individual people and corporations own the businesses and decide what to produce based on consumer demands.

cardinal directions North, east, south, west.

cartographer A person who makes maps.

cartography The art of making maps.

censor To examine material before it is published so that the government can remove ideas it does not approve of.

Central Powers The alliance of Germany and Austria-Hungary during World War I.

Challenger The space shuttle that disintegrated shortly after liftoff, killing seven astronauts.

circulation The movement of money from person to person or from place to place.

Civil Rights Act of 1964 Legislation that outlawed racial segregation, opening public places, schools, and employment to all races.

civil rights movement Black Americans' struggle to gain equality.

coalition A group of nations that work together to achieve a goal.

cold war A political war with no direct military conflict, such as the one between the United States and the Soviet Union.

collective farm A large farm formed by combining individual smaller farms.

Columbia River A river flowing along the boundary between Washington and Oregon into the Pacific Ocean. The mouth of the Columbia River was discovered by Captain Robert Gray.

communism A system in which the government owns all the businesses and property.

communist economy An economy in which the government controls the supply, decides what items to produce, and determines the prices for those items.

compassionate conservatism The term President George W. Bush used when describing his "philosophy and approach."

compass rose A small design on a map that shows the directions.

competition Businesses of the same product working against each other to get the consumers' business by producing and selling quality products at a lower price.

concentration camp A place where people were kept as prisoners and forced to do heavy labor.

Confederate States of America The nation formed by the eleven states that seceded from the Union at the start of the Civil War.

conservation The protection and wise use of natural resources.

conservative A person who has traditional views and values; a supporter of conservative political policies.

consumer A person who purchases or uses any product.

consumer-driven product A product whose success depends on its ability to adapt or change to meet consumer preferences.

continent A large land mass on the earth. There are seven: Asia, Europe, North America, South America, Africa, Australia, and Antarctica.

cover up To hide the truth.

credit 1. To make a purchase by paying a small part of the price at first, and then continuing to make payments until the debt is paid. **2.** A bank loaning a person money to buy an item, with the agreement that the person will gradually pay the bank back.

Cuban Missile Crisis The incident when the Soviet Union placed missiles that could carry nuclear bombs in Cuba. President John Kennedy ordered a blockade of Cuba until the Soviet Union dismantled the missiles.

cultural map A map that shows the main cultural regions; the people in each region have the same basic customs, beliefs, and languages.

culture 1. A people's way of life. **2.** A way of living that includes the language, religion, government, economy, customs, and arts of a group of people.

"Custer's Last Stand" A battle in which two Indian tribes defeated General George Custer and his men.

custom A practice that makes one group of people different from other people.

D

D-day (June 6, 1944) The day in World War II when Allied forces commanded by Dwight Eisenhower carried out an attack on the beaches of Normandy.

deadlock The situation when neither side gains ground during a war.

demand What and how much the consumer wants to purchase.

democracy A government in which the people themselves or their representatives make all the important decisions for their country.

deposit To place money in a bank account for safekeeping.

der Führer A German phrase that means "the leader." This title was preferred by Adolf Hitler.

dictator A ruler who has absolute control in a government.

dictatorship A form of government that has total control over people's lives.

discrimination The unfair treatment of a group or individual.

distortion An inaccuracy that occurs when a flat map is used to show the earth's curved surface.

dividend Profit from stocks paid to stock-owners.

draft The system that chooses men to go to war.

Dust Bowl The name given to the central United States during the drought of 1930 when winds swept up the topsoil where farmers had plowed to plant wheat.

E

eastern front The line of trenches where fighting occurred between the Germans and the Allies in World War I.

Electoral College The body of electors who formally elect the president and vice-president of the United States.

emperor The male ruler of an empire.

empire A group of lands and countries under one government.

employer The boss who pays the employee for working.

equator The center line around the earth that divides the Northern Hemisphere from the Southern Hemisphere. The equator is a line of latitude.

ethnic group A group of people who share the same customs, racial background, or language.

exile Forced removal from one's native country without being allowed to return.

F

Fascists People who supported a dictatorship in which the government controlled the economy, kept opposition in check through terror and censorship, and had a policy of nationalism.

Federal Reserve System The central banking system of the United States. It controls the amount of bills and coins in circulation.

Fireside Chats President Franklin D. Roosevelt's radio talks in the 1930s in which he explained his plans and tried to calm fears about the Great Depression.

flapper A woman in the 1920s who dressed in a nontraditional way, such as wearing lipstick, "bobbed" hair cuts, and knee-length skirts.

Flyer The name of the Wright brothers' flying machine that made the first flight. It flew for twelve seconds and traveled 120 feet.

free trade Trade between countries without government restrictions and tariffs.

front A place where fighting is happening during a war.

G

gangster A member or leader of an organized group of criminals, such as Al Capone.

gas A kind of chemical weapon contained in shells; when the shell exploded, the poisonous gas spread through the air.

geographer A scientist who specializes in geography.

geography The study of the earth, its physical features, and the locations of human activities.

Gestapo Hitler's secret state police force used to find enemies of the government.

glider A machine that flies without engine power; Otto Lilienthal made one around 1890.

global economy The world market in which companies from different countries buy and sell goods.

Global Positioning System (GPS) A navigation system using satellites to provide latitude, longitude, altitude, and the accurate time.

Goode's Interrupted Projection A common map projection that cuts and flattens the earth like an orange peel.

Great Depression The economic crisis beginning with the stock market crash in 1929 and continuing through the 1930s when millions of people lost their jobs.

Great Salt Lake A large salt water lake located in Utah.

grid The pattern of longitude and latitude lines that intersect each other on a map; used to locate places on a map or globe.

H

harbor A sheltered place along a coast serving as a port for ships.

Hiroshima The city in Japan where the first atomic bomb was dropped during World War II.

historian A person who studies history.

history The record of activities and events in the lives of all the people who have ever lived; the study of the past.

Holocaust The slaughtering of six million Jews by the Nazis during World War II.

horsepower A measure of an engine's power based on how much weight a horse can pull.

I

immigrant A person who comes into a new country to live there permanently.

impeach To accuse a government official of a crime.

inflation An increase in prices when manufacturers cannot meet the demands of the consumers.

installments Payments that are made to a business when a consumer purchases a product on credit or to a bank in order to repay a loan.

interest A fee charged by the lender to borrow money.

intermediate directions Directions on a compass rose that are halfway between the cardinal directions; northeast, southeast, southwest, and northwest.

international Involving two or more nations.

International Date Line An imaginary line in the Pacific Ocean that marks where the date changes; it is at about 180 degrees longitude.

interstate highway system The network of roads connecting major cities in the United States.

invest To spend money in order to make a profit.

Iran hostage crisis The 1979 to 1981 incident when sixty-one American citizens were held by Iranian militants at the United States embassy in Tehran, Iran.

Iron Curtain The imaginary dividing line that separated Eastern Europe and the Soviet Union from Western Europe after World War II.

Iwo Jima A volcanic island in the Pacific Ocean less than 700 miles from Japan.

J–K

jazz An American style of music that became popular in the 1920s.

Jim Crow laws Laws that segregated blacks from whites in public places such as schools, theaters, restaurants, and on buses.

Kitty Hawk, North Carolina The place where the Wright brothers made their first flight.

L

labor union An organization of workers that can bargain with company owners for higher wages and better working conditions.

law of supply and demand The economic principle in which prices fall when goods are plentiful (manufacturers produce more than enough), but prices rise when goods are scarce (consumers want more than manufacturers produce).

liberal A person who does not have traditional views and values; a supporter of liberal political policies.

line of latitude A line parallel to the equator on a map.

lode A source of ore.

Lusitania A passenger ship that was sunk by a German U-boat during World War I; many people died, including Americans.

M

machine gun A gun introduced in World War I that could fire 450 shots a minute, which was much faster than a rifle.

"Mall, the" The open area in Washington, D.C., between the Capitol and the Lincoln Memorial.

manners Guidelines for behavior; ways to act or not to act.

manufacturer A business that makes the products that consumers purchase.

map key A list that tells what the symbols on a map represent.

map projection A method that cartographers use to show the earth's curved surface on a flat map.

map scale A line that compares distances on the map to distances in the real world (usually shows miles or kilometers as fractions of inches or centimeters).

march on Washington A civil rights protest organized by Martin Luther King Jr. in August 1963.

mass produce To make large quantities of products in factories, often with interchangeable parts.

Mercator Projection A common map projection that shows land correctly along the equator, but with the areas at the top and bottom of the map distorted or stretched.

Mexican War A war between the United States and Mexico lasting from 1846 to 1848. The United States defeated Mexico and gained territory in California, New Mexico, and Texas.

minting The process of making coins.

"miracle of deliverance" The name Winston Churchill gave to the rescue at Dunkirk during World War II.

mobility Ability to get from place to place.

Model T The name of Henry Ford's affordable, sturdy car introduced in 1908.

monopoly The control of making and selling of a product by one company.

N

Nagasaki The city in Japan where the second atomic bomb was dropped during World War II.

nation A large group of people with a common culture, history, and land.

National Aeronautics and Space Administration (NASA) A government agency established for research and development of space exploration.

national anthem The official song that represents a nation.

national debt The amount of money that a country has borrowed from banks and other countries and has not paid back.

national flag The official flag that represents a nation.

nationalism Strong patriotic feelings for one's own nation.

national symbol Something that represents a nation's identity.

natural resource A material in nature that God made for man's use.

Navajo code talkers Navajo radiomen who used their native language as a code during World War II.

Nazi The shortened term for National Socialist German Workers' Party, led by Adolf Hitler.

needs Things a person must have to live.

neutral country A country that does not take sides in a war between other countries.

New Deal President Franklin D. Roosevelt's idea for the government to plan projects that it would pay Americans to do.

no man's land The land between the trenches of opposing armies.

North American Free Trade Agreement (NAFTA) A law that went into effect in 1994 to open new markets for business between the United States, Canada, and Mexico.

Nuremberg Laws Laws that took away the Jews' freedoms as citizens of Germany.

O

occupied Controlled by a foreign military force.

ocean A large body of water; there are four: Atlantic, Arctic, Indian, and Pacific.

offensive An attack.

Okinawa An island in the Pacific Ocean near Japan; the scene of fierce fighting between the United States and the Japanese in the closing days of World War II.

Olympic Games International athletic competitions held every four years.

Operation Overlord The code name given to the Allied invasion of France during World War II.

Oregon Trail A route by which settlers traveled from Missouri to Oregon between the 1840s and 1870s. The route was first traveled by the explorers Meriwether Lewis and William Clark.

P

Panama Canal Treaty The 1977 treaty between the United States and Panama that allowed the canal to remain open and both countries to operate it until 2000.

parapet Walls made of dirt, sandbags, and barbed wire between the trenches of opposing sides during war.

pardon Forgiveness for a crime.

patent A governmental recognition given to the owner of an invention so that no one else can copy the idea.

patriotism National loyalty; love for and devotion to one's country.

Pearl Harbor The site of a U.S. naval base located on the island of Oahu in Hawaii; bombed by Japan on December 7, 1941.

peninsula A piece of land almost entirely surrounded by water.

perjury The telling of a lie when under oath.

Persian Gulf War The 1990 to 1991 war between a coalition of nations (by the United States) against Iraq, which had invaded Kuwait; code-named *Operation Desert Storm*.

petition A written request for a right or a benefit from someone in authority.

physical map A map that shows hills, mountains, rivers, valleys, plateaus, canyons, and other land features.

polio A disease that attacks the nervous system causing paralysis.

political boundary A line on a political map that shows the land belonging to the government of a country.

political map A map showing man-made boundaries around the countries.

political party A group of people who share similar views about the government.

poll tax A fee people were required to pay in order to vote.

primary source An original object or document from a particular time period.

prime meridian A line running north to south on a map that divides the Eastern Hemisphere and the Western Hemisphere.

profit The amount of money a company earns from selling its products that is more than the amount it costs to make the products.

Prohibition The ban on alcohol by the Eighteenth Amendment.

propaganda The use of words and pictures to portray news or individuals in a certain way to promote a cause.

propeller A device having a revolving hub with blades extending out to help move something forward; used by the Wright brothers on their flying machine.

R

Race to the Sea The period of World War I in which both the Germans and the Allies wanted to take control of the ports along the English Channel.

ratify To approve.

Red Flag Act An English law passed in 1865 that put limits on steam cars.

refugee A person who flees his country for refuge or safety in another country.

Reich The German empire, especially during the Nazi period.

renewable energy Usable energy obtained from sources that do not run out, such as the sun, wind, and water.

resources Valuable products that people must have in order to live.

revival A time of renewed interest in spiritual matters; meetings to encourage this, such as the meetings held in the 1920s by Billy Sunday, Bob Jones, and other evangelists.

revolution Rebellion against the government.

road map A map showing the cities and roads that connect one place to another.

S

Schlieffen Plan Germany's plan in the early 1900s to defeat France in the east and Russia in the west.

sea level The level of the surface of the ocean; shown as zero on the elevation key on some maps.

secondary source A new source created by a person who studies a primary source.

segregation Separation of races.

share Represents one portion of a company that can be bought and sold.

socialist economy An economy in which some businesses are owned by the government and some by the people. The government owns and controls one or more of the major resources and businesses.

soup kitchen A ministry or charity that offers free food to the poor and homeless.

Soviet Union Union of Soviet Socialist Republics (USSR).

space race An unofficial competition between the United States and the Soviet Union to see who could make the furthest advancements into space first.

speakeasies Places where alcohol was illegally sold in secret during the Prohibition era.

standard of living An economic measure of how well people in a country live.

St. Lawrence Seaway The inland waterway and canal system along the Saint Lawrence River connecting the Great Lakes to the Atlantic.

"Star-Spangled Banner, The" The national anthem of the United States.

stock Part of a company available to buy at a stock exchange; share.

stock exchange A place where people can buy and sell stocks.

stock market The business of buying and selling stocks at the stock exchange.

stock market crash A sudden dramatic decline in stock prices across the stock market.

suffrage The right to vote.

supply Items that a business or company produces.

swastika The black hooked cross emblem on the Nazi Party flag.

T

tank A large, armored weapon with guns that could be driven and could crush anything in its path.

tariff A tax that is placed on imported and exported goods.

terrorist A person who uses violence to promote a cause.

time zone A region of the earth that shares the same time.

topography The study of land features and their elevations.

Trail of Tears The name given to the forced march of the Creek, Choctaw, Chickasaw, Seminole, and Cherokee in which they had to leave their homes and travel a thousand miles to the new Indian Territory in Oklahoma. Many died on the journey.

trans-Alaska pipeline A pipeline that carries two million barrels of oil a day from Alaska's north coast to its south coast.

trench A long ditch used for protection and shelter during war.

truce A temporary halt to fighting.

Truman Doctrine A policy that committed the United States to helping countries fighting Communist takeovers.

U–V

U-boat A submarine used by the Germans to sink enemy ships.

United Nations (UN) The international organization created to listen to problems and try to find peaceful solutions under the terms signed by delegates from fifty nations in 1945. The UN headquarters is in New York City.

V-E Day "Victory in Europe Day" (May 8, 1945), which signaled the end of World War II in Europe. At that time the Allies still needed to defeat Japan.

V-J Day "Victory in Japan Day" (September 2, 1945), which marked the end of World War II.

Vietnam War Memorial A Washington, D.C., memorial dedicated to all those who fought, died, or were missing during the Vietnam War.

W–Z

wants Things a person would like to own but can do without.

war on terror The ongoing campaign by the United States and some of its allies to counter international terrorism.

war to end all wars A description given to World War I because some thought there could never be another war so severe.

Washington, D.C. The capital city of the United States.

Watergate Scandal A political scandal during the presidency of Richard Nixon that resulted in the conviction of several of Nixon's advisors and the resignation of Nixon.

weapon of mass destruction (WMD) A weapon that can kill large numbers of people and cause great damage to buildings.

western front The line of trenches between Belgium and Switzerland where fighting occurred between the Germans and the Allies during World War I.

wind tunnel A big box the Wright brothers built with a glass top and a fan at one end; it was used to help them accurately calculate the effects of air on different wing surfaces.

withdraw To remove or take money out of a bank account.

World War I (1914–1918) The war in which Great Britain, France, Russia, the United States, and other Allies defeated Germany, Austria-Hungary, and other Central powers.

World War II (1939–1945) The war in which Great Britain, France, the Soviet Union, the United States, China, and other Allies defeated Germany, Italy, and Japan (the Axis powers).

Zionism The movement to create a homeland for the Jews.

Index

Photo Credits

The following agencies and individuals have furnished materials to meet the photographic needs of this textbook. We wish to express our gratitude to them for their important contribution.

Alamy Images, Inc.
Alaska Division of Community and Business Development
American Automobile Manufacturers Association
Dr. Ward Andersen
AP/Wide World Photos
Appomattox Court House National Historical Park
Architect of the Capitol
Art Resource
Belgium Tourism
BigStockPhoto.com
BJU Press Files
Bob Jones University Museum & Gallery
George R. Collins
Consulate General of Japan
Corbis
COREL Corporation
DC Public Library
Terry Davenport
Defense Audiovisual Agency
Detroit Public Library
Dwight D. Eisenhower Library
Eastman Chemicals Division
Ewing Galloway, Inc.
Florida State Archives
Focal Point Publications
Fotolia
Franklin D. Roosevelt Library
General Douglas MacArthur Foundation
George Bush Presidential Library and Museum
George Bush Presidential Materials Project
Gerald R. Ford Library
German Information Center
Getty Images
The Granger Collection

Harry S. Truman Library & Museum
Henry Ford Museum
Illinois Historic Preservation Agency
Imperial War Museum
iStockphoto.com
Jimmy Carter Library National Archives
John F. Kennedy Presidential Library and Museum
Brian D. Johnson
JupiterImages Corporation
Kansas State Historical Society
Tim Keesee
Joyce Landis
Library of Congress
London Travel Museum
Louisiana Office of Tourism
NASA
National Archives
National Baseball Hall of Fame Library
National Baseball Library
National Gallery of Art
National Oceanic and Atmospheric Administration
National Park Service
Naval History and Heritage Command
Nebraska State Historical Society
Holly Nelson
New York Historical Society
The New York Public Library
NRCS Archives
Petro-Canada
Ed Richards
Ronald Reagan Library
Saint Lawrence Seaway Development Corporation

Saudi Aramco World
Dr. Ella Sekatau
The Senate Historical Office
Pete Souza
Gilbert Stuart
Thomas Sully
Supreme Court of the United States
Tennessee State Library and Archives
Texas State Library and Archives Commission
UN/DPI Photo
United States Department of Agriculture (USDA)
United States Mint
University of Washington Libraries
Unusual Films
U.S. Air Force
U.S. Department of Defense
U.S. Department of State
U.S. Energy Department and Resources Administration
U.S. Holocaust Memorial Museum
U.S. Marine Corps
U.S. Navy
Virginia War Museum
Dawn L. Watkins
The White House
White House Press Office
Wikimedia Commons
William J. Clinton Presidential Library
Woolaroc Museum
Wright State University
Young America's Foundation
Greg Zeman

Cover
Library of Congress (top); ©iStockphoto.com/ ranplett (bottom)

Chapter 1
©iStockphoto.com/jcarillet 1; PhotoDisc/Getty Images 2; © Andre Jenny / Alamy 5 (top); 2009 JupiterImages Corporation 5 (bottom); Unusual Films 7, 10, 20; US Department of Defense 18 (top right); © Bob Sexton. Image from BigStockPhoto.com 18 (bottom left); NASA 18 (bottom right)

Chapter 2
Library of Congress 21, 26 (top), 30, 33, 34 (top), 36 (bottom), 40 (bottom); From the Collections of the Henry Ford 23, 25 (bottom), 26 (bottom); American Automobile Manufacturers Association 24; Hulton Collection/Hulton Archive/Getty Images 25 (top); Courtesy of the National Automotive History Collection, Detroit Public Library 27 (top, bottom left), 28 (top, center); Shutterstock Images LLC/Margo Harrison 28 (bottom); ©Kevin Burke/Corbis 29; Terry Davenport 31 (all); © 2009 JupiterImages Corporation. All rights reserved. 34 (bottom); Courtesy of Special Collections and Archives, Wright State University 35 (bottom), 36 (top), 38, 39 (both); National Museum of the USAF 40 (top); ©iStockphoto.com/assalve 41

Chapter 3
© 2009 JupiterImages Corporation. All rights reserved. 43, 45; National Archives 46, 58, 61 (top), 65, 66; Imperial War Museum 47, 49, 50-51, 51 (inset), 54, 59, 61 (bottom), 67; Library of Congress 48 (both), 60 (both), 62 (bottom), 68; ©iStockphoto.com/igs942 53; Belgium Tourism 55; BJU Press Files 56; © 2009 JupiterImages Corporation. All rights reserved. 57 (left); Ed Richards 57 (right); Unusual Films 62 (top); Image copyright © The Metropolitan Museum of Art / Art Resource, NY 64

Chapter 4
Brynn Bruijn/Saudi Aramco World/SAWDIA 69; Dr. Ward Andersen 70, 74; Joyce Landis 71; © 2009 JupiterImages Corporation/AbleStock .com. All rights reserved. 72 (top); ©iStockphoto .com/Laraish 72 (bottom left); ©iStockphoto.com/ richcano 72 (bottom right); National Museum of the USAF 73 (top); Bob Jones University Museum & Gallery 73 (bottom); © Mardis /

Alamy Images 78 (top); Library of Congress 79 (top), 80 (both); ©iStockphoto.com/qingwa 79 (bottom); ©Vladislav Gurfinkel, Image from BigStockPhoto.com 83 (top); AP Photo/Vincent Thian 83; Unusual Films 84

Chapter 5
Unusual Films 85, 102, 103 (both), 108; National Park Service 88; Architect of the Capitol 89 (left); COREL Corporation 89 (center); photograph by Jack Szelka, courtesy of Dr. Ella Sekatau 89 (right); George R. Collins 91 (top); Dawn L. Watkins 91 (bottom); Appomattox Court House National Historical Park 92 (top); Brian D. Johnson 92 (bottom); Greg Zeman 93 (left); Louisiana Office of Tourism 93 (right); Tennessee State Library and Archives 94 (top left); © 2009 JupiterImages Corporation. All rights reserved. 94 (bottom); ©iStockphoto. com/chas53 96 (top); Photo Courtesy of Illinois Historic Preservation Agency 96 (bottom); NASA 97 (top); National Archives 97 (bottom); Kansas State Historical Society 98 (top); Nebraska State Historical Society 98 (bottom); National Baseball Hall of Fame Library 99 (top); © Bonnie Holm. Image from BigStockPhoto .com 99 (center); ©iStockphoto.com/stardeo 99 (bottom); Woolaroc Museum Bartlesville, Oklahoma 100; Courtesy Texas State Library and Archives Commission 101 (top); ©iStockphoto .com/CliffWalker 101 (center); PhotoDisc/Getty Images 101 (bottom); Library of Congress 106 (top right); © Alaska Division of Community and Business Development 106 (bottom left); U.S. Navy photo by Mass Communication Specialist Seaman Joe Painter 106 (bottom right)

Chapter 6
Library of Congress 109, 110, 112 (bottom), 114, 119, 121; National Archives 112 (top), 117 (bottom), 122; Unusual Films 113, 116 (bottom right), 124, 126 (bottom right); Ewing Galloway, Inc. 115 (top); National Portrait Gallery, Smithsonian Institution / Art Resource, NY 115, 116 (top); National Baseball Library 116 (bottom left); National Baseball Hall of Fame Library 117 (top); The New York Public Library 120; Florida State Archives 123

Chapter 7
Topone © Fotolia 127; National Archives 130-131 (background); © Robert Lutrick. Image from BigStockPhoto.com 130 (top); ©iStockphoto .com/Maher 130 (bottom); ©iStockphoto.com/

Chapter 12

Young America's Foundation 249; Jimmy Carter Library National Archives 250, 251 (both); Official White House Photograph 252 (top); ©iStockphoto.com/MarlaAzinger 252 (bottom); Courtesy Ronald Reagan Library 253, 254 (bottom), 256; NASA 254 (top); George Bush Presidential Library and Museum 255 (top); German Information Center 255 (bottom); ©iStockphoto.com/Cebolla4 258 (top); National Archives 258 (bottom), 270 (center); George Bush Presidential Materials Project 259; William J. Clinton Presidential Library 260 (top); AP/Wide World Photos 260 (bottom), 261 (bottom), 268 (top); AFP/Getty Images/ Richard Ellis 261 (top); AFP/Getty Images/Joel Robine 263; AFP/Getty Images/Paul J. Richards 264, 271 (top); U.S. Department of State/ Wikimedia.org 265 (top); AFP/Getty Images/ Tim Sloan 265 (bottom); Photo by Eric Draper, White House 266 (left); AFP/Getty Images/ Luke Frazza 266 (right); ©iStockphoto.com/ impactimage 268 (bottom); U.S. Navy photo by Mass Communication Specialist 2nd Class Joshua J. Wahl 269 (top); U. S. Navy photo by JO1(SW) M. J. Darby 269 (bottom); U.S. Navy photo 270 (left); Getty Images 270 (right); Photograph by Steve Petteway, Collection of the Supreme Court of the United States 271 (bottom); Douglas Knight © Fotolia 272 (top left); ©iStockphoto.com/paule858 272 top right; © 2009 JupiterImages Corporation/Stockxpert Images. All rights reserved. 272 (bottom left); PhotoDisc/Getty Images 272 (bottom right); Pete Souza 273 (left); Congressional Quarterly/Getty Images/Scott J. Ferrell 273 (right); U.S. Marine Corps 274

Resource Treasury

US Navy Photo by photographers Mate Airman Benjamin D. Glass 276 (top); © Douglas Peebles Photography / Alamy 276 (bottom); © 2009 JupiterImages Corporation/Stockxpert Images. All rights reserved. 277 (top); © Nicholas Pitt / Alamy 277 (bottom); Public Domain / Wikimedia Commons 278 (top); rb stevens © Fotolia 278 (bottom); U.S. Air Force photo/ Airman 1st Class Liliana Moreno 279 (top); Navy Photo/Chief Warrant Officer 4 Seth Rossman 279 (center); © Pierrette Guertin. Image from BigStockPhoto.com 279 (bottom); Getty Images 280 (left); AP Photo/WTC Memorial Foundation, LMDC 280 (right); Jane E. Rackley/Department of Defense 281 (top); ©iStockphoto.com/fintastique 281 (bottom); National Archives 282 (top); Dwight D. Eisenhower Library 282 (bottom); Defense Audiovisual Agency 283 (top); George R. Collins 283 (center), 287 (bottom left); David Valdez, The White House 283 (bottom); The Granger Collection, New York 284 (top); Architect of the Capitol 284 (bottom); AFP/Getty Images 285 (left); AP/Wide World Photos 285 (right); ©iStockphoto.com/johnston 286 (top); Unusual Films 286 (bottom); ©iStockphoto .com/Sisoje 287 (top); National Park Service/ Cecil W. Stoughton 287 (bottom right); © 2009 JupiterImages Corporation/Photos.com. All rights reserved. 288 (top); ©iStockphoto.com/cwinegarden 288 (bottom); Gilbert Stuart / Wikimedia Commons 289 (top); Public Domain 289 (center); New York Historical Society / Wikimedia Commons 289 (bottom); National Gallery of Art / Wikimedia Commons 290 (Madison); Library of Congress 290 (Monroe, John Quincy Adams), 291 (Van Buren, Tyler), 292-296 (all), 297 (Roosevelt, Truman, Eisenhower), 299 (Reagan, George H. W. Bush); Thomas Sully / Wikimedia Commons 290 (Jackson); Wikimedia Commons 291 (Harrison); National Archives 291 (Polk); John F. Kennedy Presidential Library and Museum 297 (Kennedy); Arnold Newman, White House Press Office (WHPO) 298 (Johnson); Department of Defense 298 (Nixon), 298 (Carter); Courtesy Gerald R. Ford Library 298 (Ford); © Bob McNeely, White House 299 (Clinton); © Eric Draper, White House 299 (Bush); © 2008 Pete Souza, White House 300 (Obama); All flags from page 301 to 313 came from Wikimedia Commons and COREL Corporation; Map Resources 1-5 (all maps), 8-300 (all maps), 301 (center map), 310 (Rhode Island map), 314-323 (all maps); Precision Graphics 6, 7 (all maps); Cartesia Maps 301 (top, bottom), 302-309 (all maps), 310 (Oklahoma, Oregon, Pennsylvania), 311-313 (all maps)